MW01625862

Frammenti della Vita

I gave my heart to nature and my soul to art.
I imagined myself as a prehistoric man, an Indian
and an Italian.... I carved the stone as if it were
fossilized semen ... the rhythm, the breath,
the metamorphosis of life. I carved by hand.
I was primitive. I loved art and lost myself in time.

Frammenti della Vita

The Art and Writings of

Jefferson D. Rubin

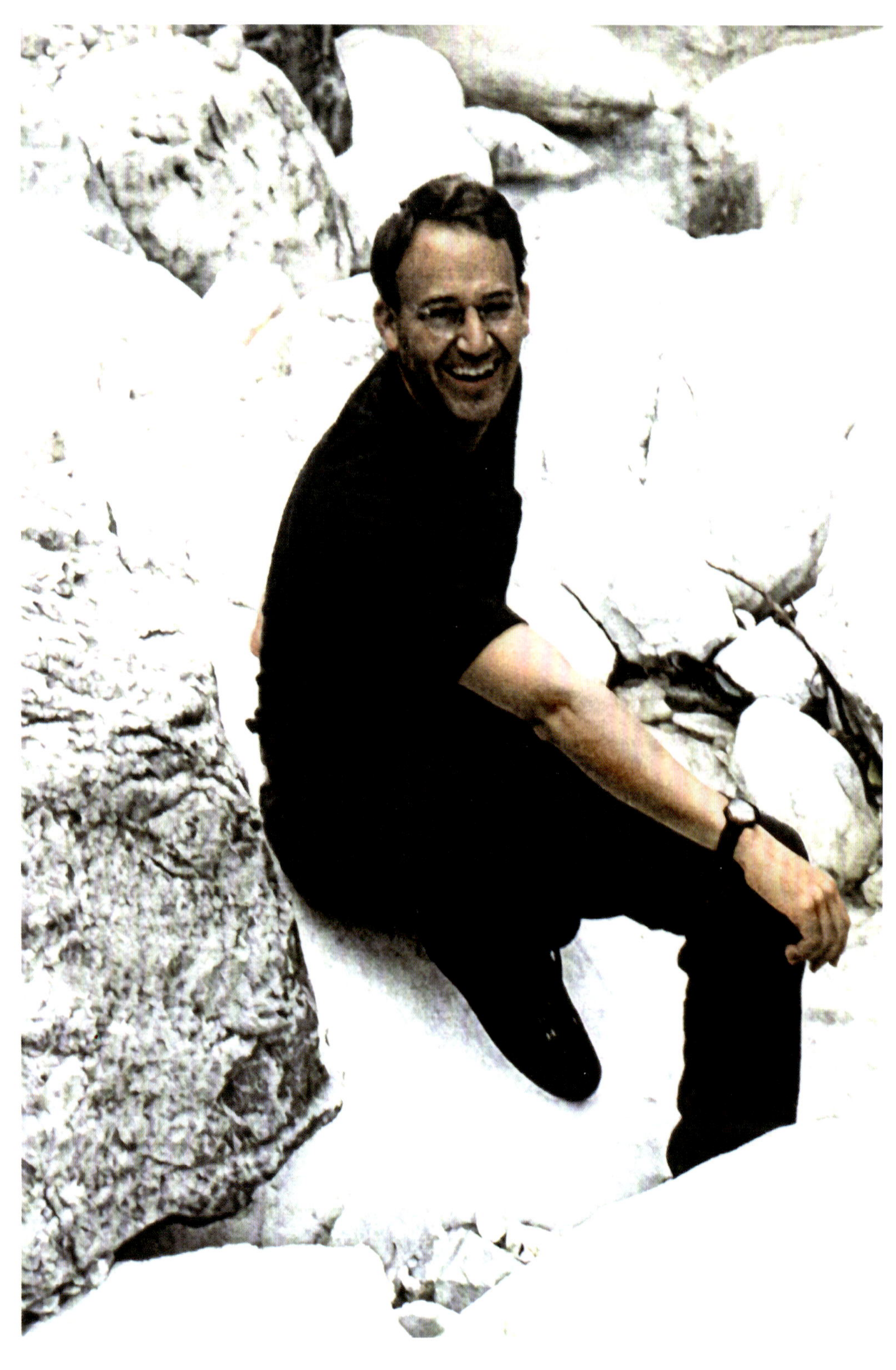

Jefferson at Monte Altissimo, the site where
Michelangelo quarried his marble near Pietrasanta, Italy.

MONTE ALTISSIMO

river runs white with marble
food spirit lives
energy reverberates,
marble to the sky,
clay below my feet.
Michelangelo walked this road
raised this hammer
breathed this breath
chiseled your features.
Monte Altissimo
what you provide
a magnet divine.

Today was a big day for me. I went to the quarry and gathered a good ton of *statuario*, white statuary marble. It is very difficult to find the pure white gold, but with the aid of an eighty-year old mountain goat *cavatore*, quarry worker, and a *Camioncino*, 1.5 ton truck, I was able to forage 12 small pieces and stake out the next "loot" for bigger blocks. You can imagine this man gracefully anteloping on the *tallace* slope of marble saying: "*Questo è bello, questo è statuario-puro, guarda com'è bello, bianco, transperente, portalo questo pezzo.*" [This is statuary, take it down! This is pure statuary, look how beautiful it is, white and transparent, take this piece.] I prefer to get marble directly from the mountain rather than buying it from a company or workshop, because the experience in getting it deepens my love and respect for the material and its maker.

MIO AMICO E FRATELLO

Marcello Giorgi, Pietrasanta, Italy

It was an afternoon in 1989 when I met Jefferson for the first time. I was working then as an assistant in the studio of a well-known sculptor when, one day, I heard the doorbell ring. I went to open the door and there in front of me I saw a *ragazzone*, a tall fellow with small glasses and an American accent. I thought, "Here's just another globetrotter who wants to meet the master."

For as it often happens in Pietrasanta, one comes to meet famous artists. Or there are young people looking for fame and fortune who come here attracted by their fascination with marble. Some stop only for a brief experience. Others, like Jefferson, fall in love with the city and may never leave again. Jefferson came often to visit me at the studio. He enjoyed watching while I worked. He was curious about everything I was doing. What struck me about him was his big open smile, true and sincere, and that great longing he had to learn and to know.

Before that particular job I had worked in an art foundry for many years, so I already had a good knowledge of both the process of lost wax fusion and of working in plaster and clay. Jefferson asked me a lot of questions, and I felt myself being enveloped in his enthusiasm. I was happy to be able to help him. We understood right from the beginning that there was something that magically connected us, our great passion for art, "*la bella arte*," as Jefferson would say. Often in the afternoon when I had finished working I would go to his house to help him prepare his molds for the foundry, or assist him with other technical matters. Jefferson, in exchange, would help me with my English. We spent a lot of time together. I was fascinated by his energy, by his desire to work, by that way he had of being free.

He would introduce himself as a *cicloartista*, a cycling artist, and naturally he always traveled by bike.... He told of how he came to Europe with a bicycle because he wanted to tour the world, but once he arrived in Italy, his heart told him to stay, to stop in the land of the Etruscans, in the land of the great masters and of beautiful sculptures. In the evenings spent at the coffee-bar he shared stories of his cycling travels. He would show us the watercolors he had painted while stopping in the places he loved, such as in the south of Italy where, while riding around the countryside, he had always managed to find someone who would

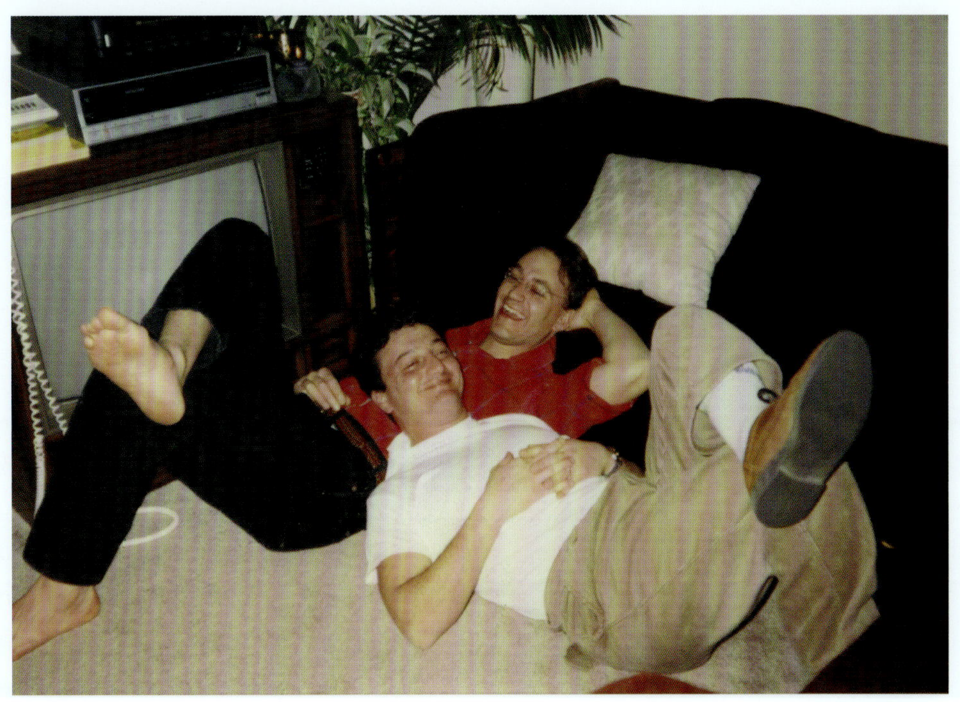

invite him to dinner. Sometimes he would tell me that he would stop in a city where he was moved by its art, spending the entire day drawing, and then, in his sleeping bag, spending the night at the feet of a large sculpture, looking at the stars, and writing poetry.

Jefferson and I soon became inseparable. These were the years in which I had begun my work as an independent craftsman. Difficult years, always without money, both Jefferson and I barely managing to get by, taking on any kind of job. Jefferson, while continuing with his own sculpting, would go to other artists' studios to rasp or polish marble "to bring them to life," as he would say. I worked for other artists or in some foundry, and every once in a while a good job would come along where we were able to work together and have great fun, but above all we gave to each other the courage to forge ahead.

Jefferson often came to my house for dinner, usually a simple dish of pasta, nothing fancy, but we always enjoyed ourselves. My wife, Santina, was always happy to put an extra plate on the table for Jefferson, and for me it was like having a brother.

We shared many moments together, difficult times and wonderful times. In those years, the art world was experiencing a period of great crisis, and in Pietrasanta it was becoming more and more difficult to find a job, even the odd job here and there. I was just barely able to provide for my family, and for Jefferson it was becoming more and more difficult to scrape by. So he left me some of his art work and departed for the United States.

In time we again began writing to each other and to reorganize our lives. He arranged to return to Italy for a short period of time in 1992 and participated with his works in an exhibition in Carrara I had organized, leaving again soon after the show ended.

Late in 1993, I remember, just a few days before Christmas, my telephone rang at seven in the morning. Even before answering I knew it was Jefferson, because only he called me at that hour. It was a very important telephone call for me. Jefferson knew of my economic situation, and he knew that it was just a matter of time before I would have to close my studio because I just couldn't make a living as things were. So, Jefferson invited me to come stay with him for a while, and as I could not afford it, he proposed an arrangement: the airline ticket to the United States in exchange for the making of the plaster mold of his life-size Adam which he had just finished. It was a great idea, and for me an immense joy. I said yes immediately.

So, on the 16th of January 1994, I left for Colorado. I can say without a doubt that it was the most fascinating experience of my life. Jefferson was fantastic. He organized my arrival as if I were a *gran maestro*. I still remember the posters and brochures he prepared, as well as the newspaper articles. We organized, in those three short weeks, several sculpture classes at La Scuola, his art school, and two unforgettable evenings where I lectured about Pietrasanta and he acted as interpreter. Jefferson connected me with numerous people, many his friends, all of whom were wonderful and whom I still carry in my heart. We went to visit foundries and art studios, we went skiing, and we saw many extraordinary things. As I write I can still see in my eyes those images that made me fall in love with Colorado and its people.

I returned to Italy with incredible energy. I had to succeed here and remain in Italy. Three months later fate decided to give me a hand. My big chance arrived. I succeeded in obtaining a large commission from the most important foundry of Pietrasanta. I risked everything, but in the end it was a great success. From that time on I have had no problem obtaining jobs. Indeed, it has been a continuous growth that carries on to this day.

For this I am also grateful to Jefferson. I learned from him never to give up, and to believe in what I do. Was it only by chance? Since returning from Colorado my life changed for the better. Jefferson has always stood close by me. He was the only person with whom I could confide and speak freely. He had a unique way of igniting me with his optimism. He thoroughly understood the nature of the problems that I lived. He was strong enough to bear my disappointments, sincere enough to help me confront reality, friend enough to allow me to face the world knowing that no one is alone.

With Jefferson gone, not only was it the farewell of a friend, of a brother. Jefferson was part of my family, part of my plans, part of my life's destiny, part of me. It is very difficult for me to speak of these things, because I keep them buried deep in my soul. While I write I see Jefferson again like in a superimposition, the same mouth, the same smile, that big smile that struck me so much when I met him the first time and that still today I feel its echo when I think of him, an image that distresses me, and at the same time makes me happy because I understand that Jefferson is with us and within us always.

Translation from Italian by Thea Tenenbaum,
Raffaele Malferrari, and Cinzia Waldrop-Sanniti.

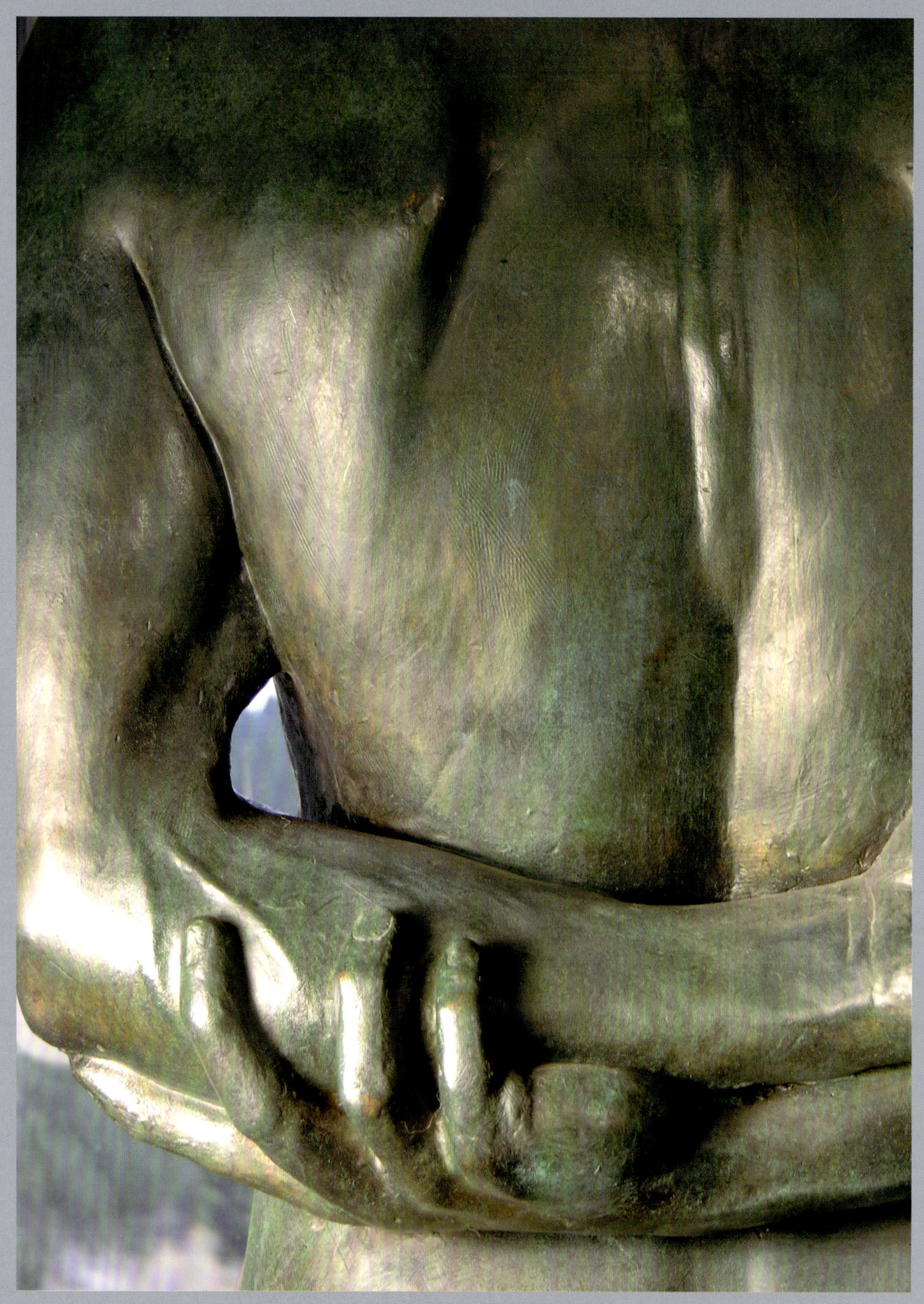

CONTENTS

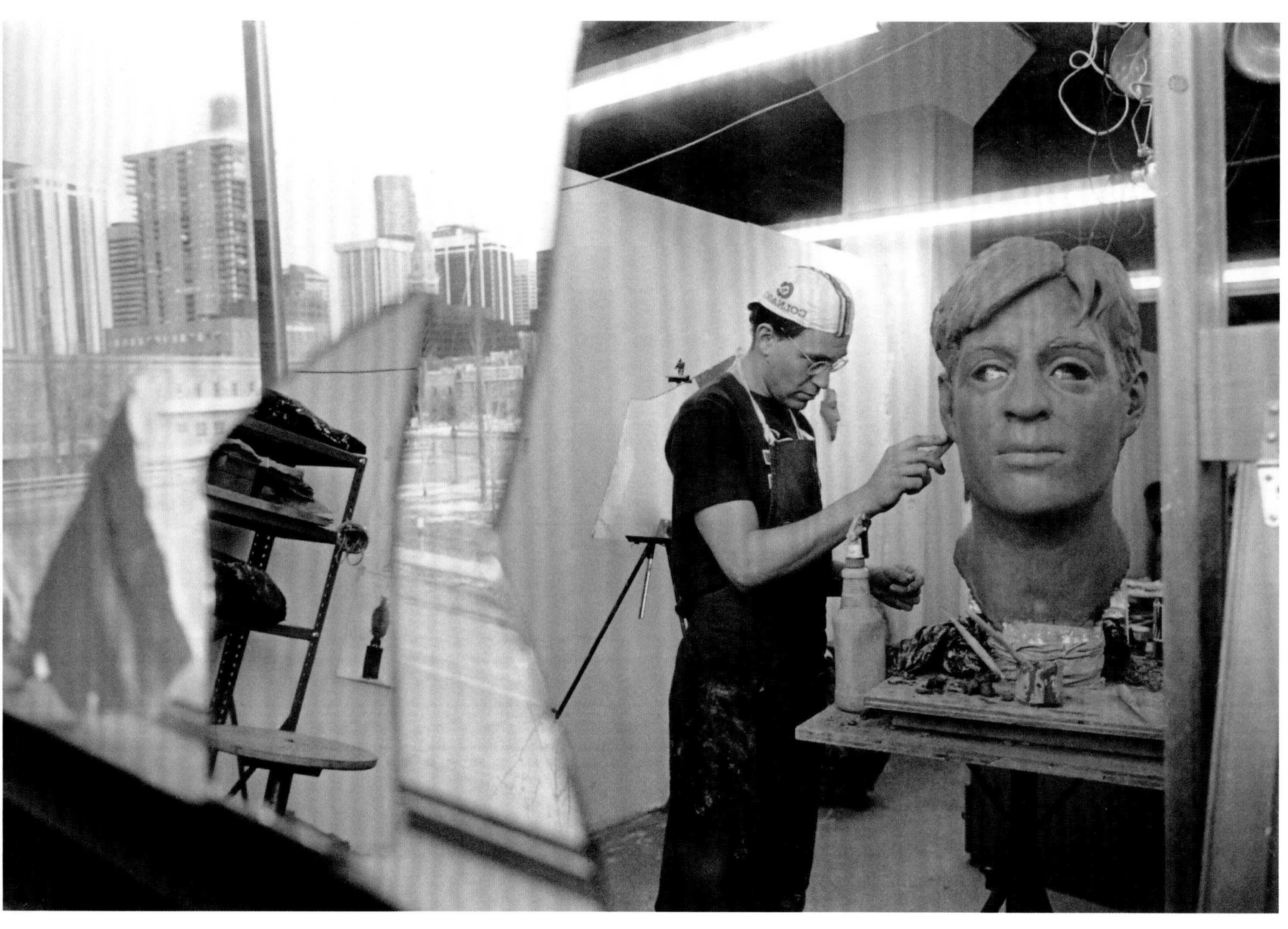

INTRODUCTION

Marian Granfield

The following collection of writings and artworks by Jefferson D. Rubin has a multiple purpose. It presents the artistic vision of a contemporary sculptor who championed the significance of a classical aesthetic in a world replete with modern tastes and sensibilities; it is the testament of a man who believed in the beauty and dignity of the human form; and it is a tribute to an artist by those of us who were charmed by his charismatic personality and moved by the force of his work. It is neither intended to be a chronological nor a complete presentation of this artist's work. Because it highlights fragments of his life, it is fitting to title the book *Frammenti della Vita (Fragments of a Life)* borrowing the term *frammenti* from Jefferson who used it in his art to symbolize, in his words, both antiquity "as the continual source of inspiration" and "the fragility of life itself." A large body of his work, which he characterized as *frammenti*, combined the lost elements of the ancient world with contemporary subjects. His conviction in the importance of classical art is resonated in his thoughtfully written and thought-provoking manuscripts, journal entries, letters and poetry from which numerous excerpts have been taken and presented in this book. Words like beauty, nobility, dignity, and humanism abound in his writings and find expression in his work. These quotations invite the reader to journey with Jefferson as he reveals some of his innermost thoughts about his life's work.

I was one of the fortunate ones immediately struck, or *colpito*, as Jefferson would say when describing his first encounter with Michelangelo's *David* at the young age of 11, by Jefferson and his art. Having just seen a film about the nineteenth-century French sculptor Camille Claudell, a student of Auguste Rodin, I knew I wanted to study figurative sculpture. I was reminded, however, that most contemporary university art programs and art schools engage in more experimental forms of expression where a chisel is often replaced with a welding torch. Although appreciative of conceptual and post-modern forms of expression, I recognize the unfortunate lack of seminal art courses that have become moribund from most art programs in institutions of higher learning.

The following day, my colleague and I were to interview an artist for a teaching post in a community art program. I'll never forget that day. A very serious-looking young man walked through the door with his portfolio. Neatly cropped hair, rimless glasses, very earnest and intellectual I thought. He opened his portfolio and revealed an exquisite presentation of sculpture including full figures, portraits, and bas-relief. As I watched him carefully turn each page I thought here is a sculptor in the tradition of Rodin! After the interview I insisted we hire him and I immediately registered as his first student.

That was my first encounter with Jefferson. What followed were several wonderful years during which we shared our thoughts and philosophies about art, our dreams and ambitions, and our friendship. Early on I learned of the challenges that Jefferson's chosen art form presented as he confronted the post-modern tastes of a contemporary, mainstream art world. The balance was tipped in his favor, however, by a growing number of supporters and patrons who chose words like "moving," "beautiful," and "inspirational" when encountering his work as well as by a number of galleries enthusiastic about showing his work.

From a very young age Jefferson knew that he would be an artist. This grew out of his love of classical sculpture that began with a family trip to Italy when he was just eleven, and his fascination with archaeology and ancient cultures that preceded it at the impressive young age of five. Jefferson's desire to create figurative art intensified in high school where he would often skip classes and hide in the school's art room to sculpt. What followed this clear, early artistic vision were years of study, apprenticeship and dedicated work that included residencies in Italy; various work positions over five years at the Metropolitan Museum of Art in New York surrounded by the work of his masters; ongoing studies in anatomy and sculpture; teaching and working in Denver, where he would later open his own school of classical sculpture, and a continuing creation of a body of impressive sculptural work. Influenced by his deep admiration for the art of the ancients, including Greek and Etruscan sculpture, and moved incessantly by the art of Michelangelo, Donatello, Rodin, Manzu, Messina and other great masters of sculpture, Jefferson's work became imbued with qualities of classical expression and humanism.

Jefferson always maintained the importance of studying the art of the past for direction and inspiration in refining his own personal style. The humanism expressed in the works of Michelangelo and Donatello resonated with his own love of the human form. Jefferson also believed that the nobility of the human spirit was best expressed in the art of the ancients—Greek and Roman statuary, revived and emulated during the Renaissance, and again during the eighteenth century when renowned archaeologist and art historian Johann Winckelmann correlated art with the culture that created it. In his treatise, *History of Ancient Art* (1764), Winckelmann wrote of the Golden Age in Greece and how its "noble simplicity and quiet grandeur" was expressed in the great art produced during that period. His theories greatly inspired Neoclassicism, an art style that prevailed in Europe during the latter part of the eighteenth century and continued well into the nineteenth century until the onset of Impressionism. Many artists during this period, especially during the French Revolution, embraced classical art as a means to emulate the ideals of this ancient culture and to inspire virtue in their own time. According to author Vernon Minor in his book *Art History's History* (1994), "Winckelmann was helping to establish the 'canon' of great works, those examples of art that express or somehow embody the highest values of our culture, are most worthy of emulation, and which should be studied through- out history. In these works we should find what it is that makes us human." As his many statements and sculptures in this collection reveal, Jefferson sought to do exactly that, to study and to embrace an art form that would perpetuate these very sentiments and find contemporary expression in his own work.

An artist and sculptor for more than twenty years, extending from his adolescence until his untimely death at the age of thirty-six, Jefferson was passionately engaged in a conversation with art history extending from antiquity to post modernism as he sought to breathe new life into the lost tradition of classical sculpture. Eventually this led to his founding of a Denver-based classical sculpture school, LaScuola Internazionale della Scultura, where he became its first director and teacher. After Jefferson's death, it became the vision of La Scuola's Board of Trustees to compile a book of his work and keep his passion alive.

Books and catalogues typically chronicle the lives and creative contributions of artists who have received widespread public acclaim. Their work is often closely analyzed by scholars, critics, and artists; viewed by the public; and thought to demonstrate artistic quality, appropriate subject matter, innovative style, and significant contributions. In a very real sense, these works educate the public about the essential question of "What is art?" The art that is preserved and reproduced in these books, however, does not adequately represent the larger body of artistic work that, for whatever reason, has gone relatively underrecognized. The loss of these cultural artifacts and creative expressions would be tragic were they not brought to the attention of a broader public with varying tastes.

During the early stages of this project I realized that the prodigious amount of illuminating autobiographical material available would enable Jefferson's art to be accompanied by inspirational thoughts, poetry and prose in his own voice. The art and texts that follow span a period from the early 1980s, beginning when Jefferson was only twenty-one and already "carving" out his place among artisans in Italy to his later years in Denver where he spent most of his time in his studio and sculpture school, producing an impressive body of work and training young artists.

Jefferson often stated that great art does not progress in a linear fashion, but rather exists in a spiral in which artists continually revisit universal themes and styles for inspiration. Likewise, this book is not a linear account but is intended to invite the reader into various periods in Jefferson's life presented through a juxtaposition of selected art and written passages that we believe the reader will also find to be inspirational. Its purpose is not to tell the story of his life, but rather, to present the richness of a life well lived in the pursuit of fulfilling one's goals and dreams. We pay homage to Jefferson.

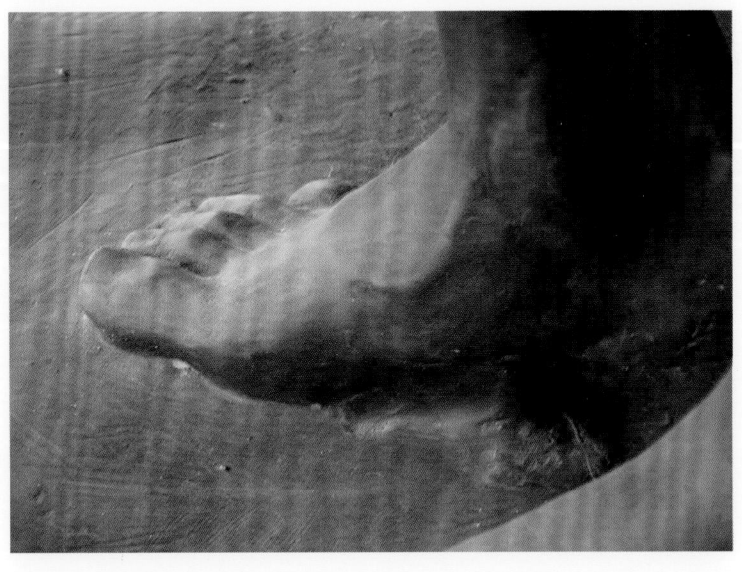

From antiquity I learned the ennoblement of the human form. Ennobling the human spirit is important in my work. I like to say my work has dignity.

This sculpture is a statement about man, both as a contemporary being who is responsible for his own actions and a historical figure tracing back to the concept of Man, as personified through Adam.

There are many dichotomies involved: strength and softness, pride and vulnerability, self-embrace and inevitable fall.... He's stepping forward though with reluctance.... Adam, taking responsibility for his own actions, is not blaming Eve. His hand holds an invisible apple, his face is a blank, virginal, classical stare. He's not yet weathered by the pain of living. Youthful, strong, athletic, beautiful. Even a side of feminine.

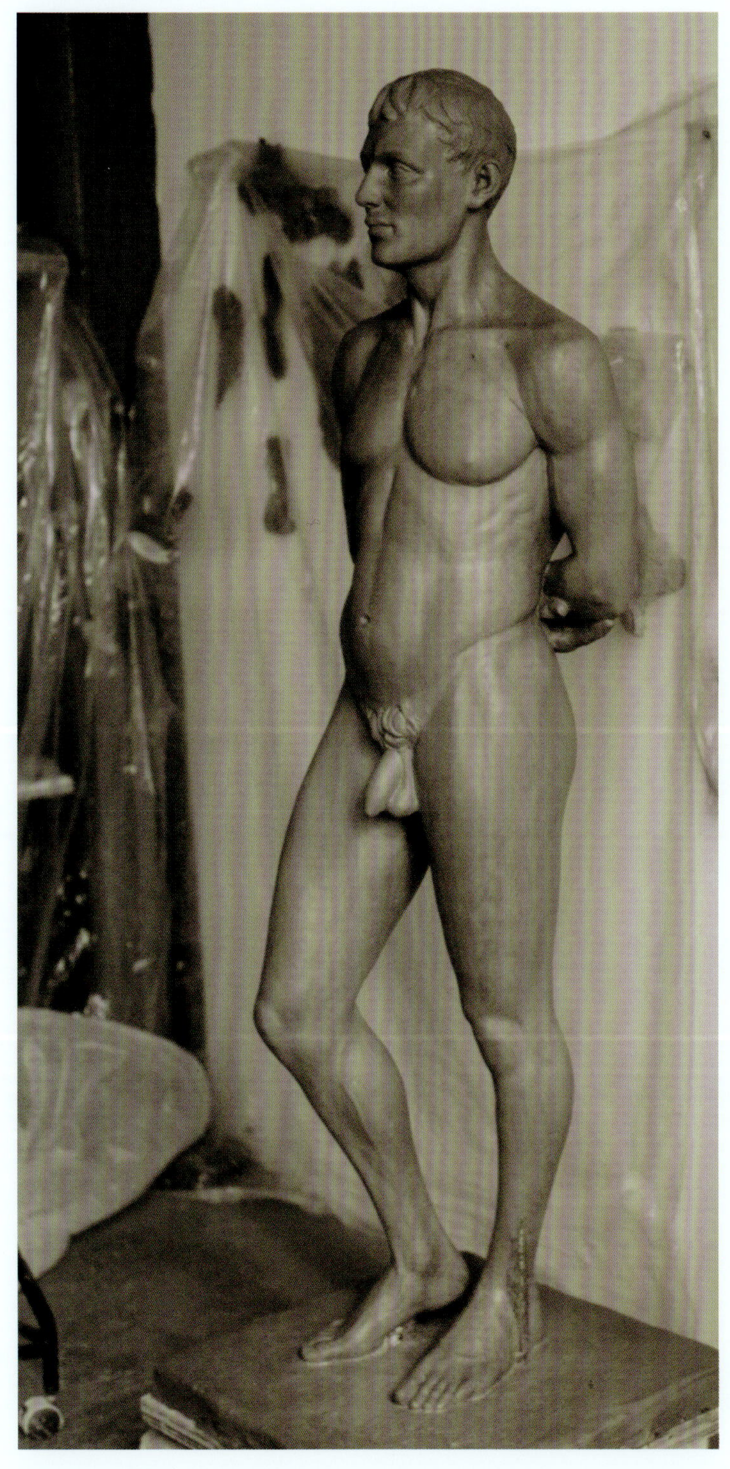

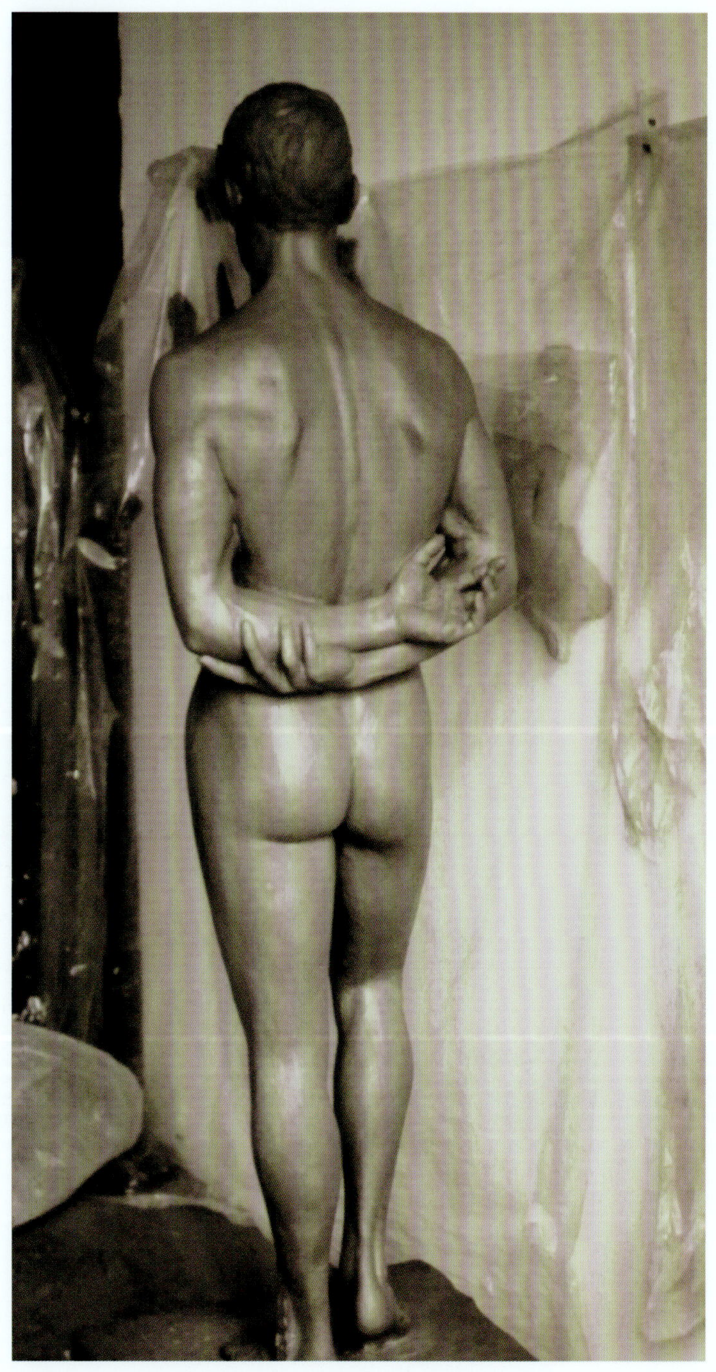

ADAM

There I stood, in that state
where no words can adequately
describe. Transfixed, focused,
immovable, blown away, unable
to speak—art had never done
this to me before. The hand ...
there was nothing more powerful.
I was standing in front of Michelangelo.
The *David*. I saw and I knew.
I wanted my family to leave me in Italy.
I wanted to apprentice to a master.
I was 11.

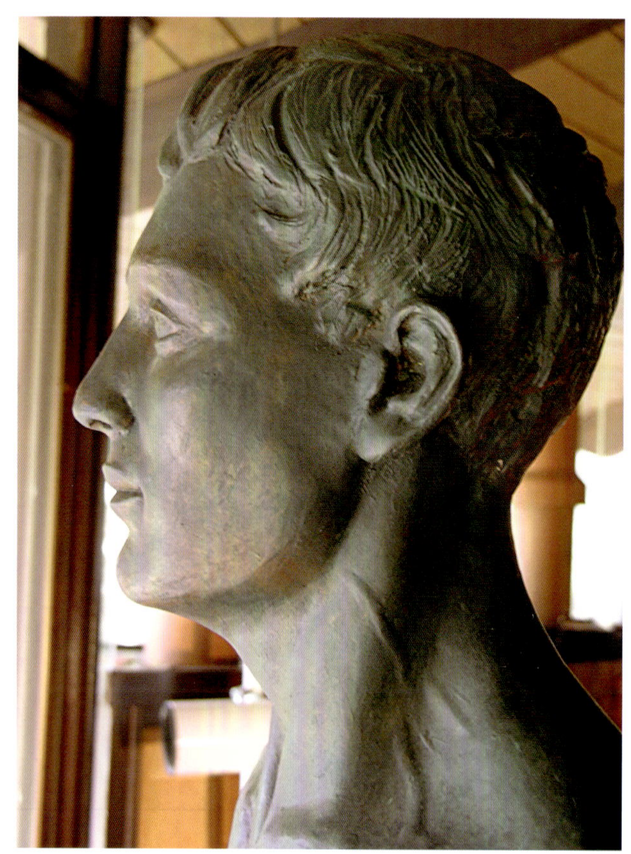

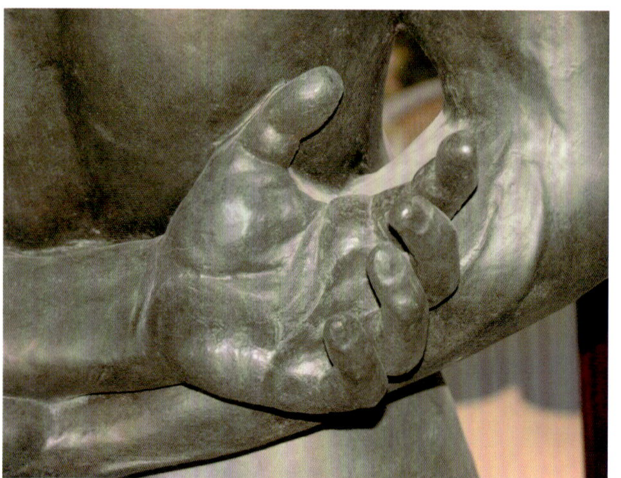

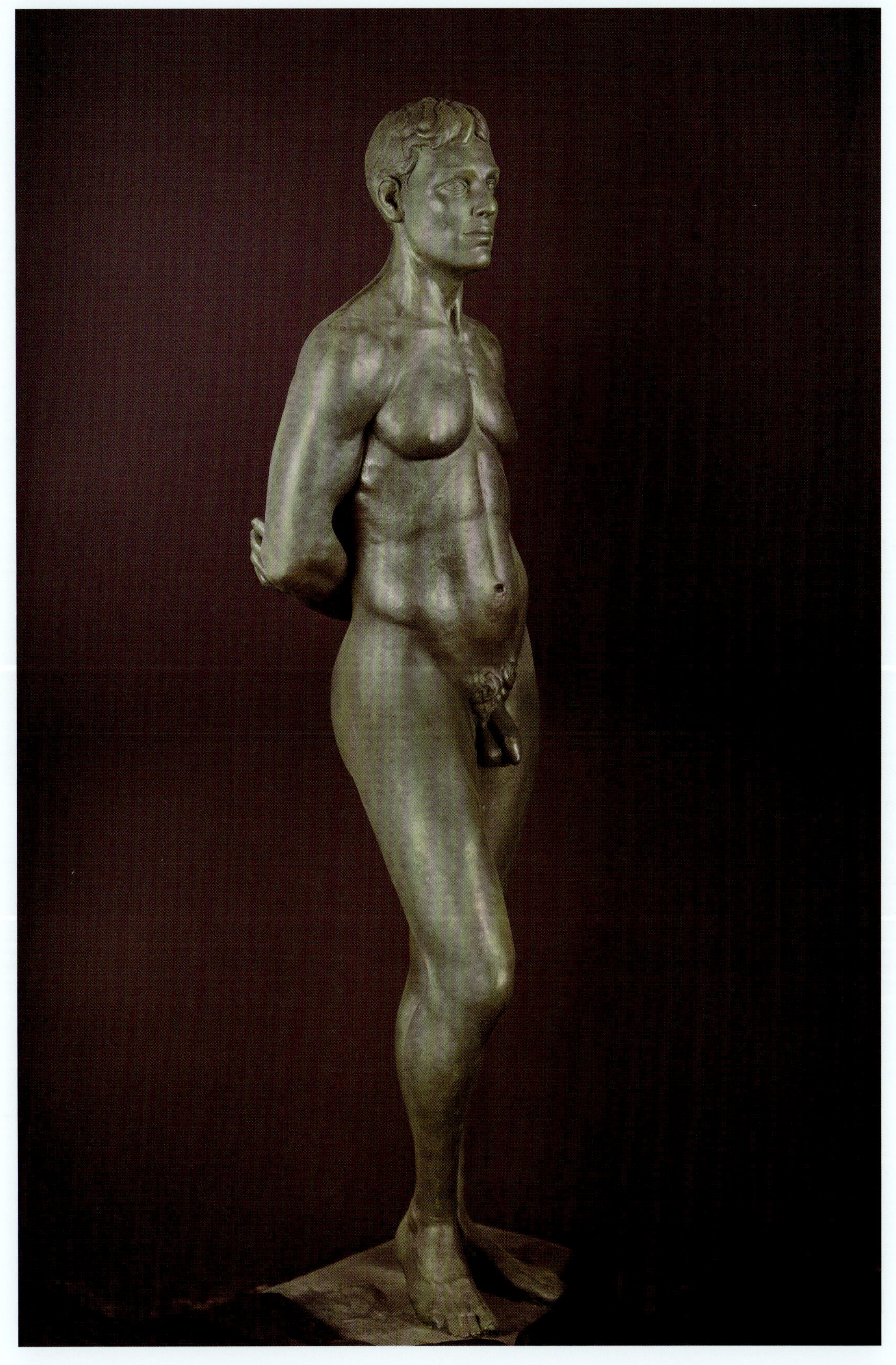

My work belongs to a tradition in present time and space which transcends the centuries. I share with Michelangelo the belief that the body is divine and, therefore, art which celebrates the intellect and spirituality of the body is divinely inspired.

Michelangelo was not the only one who spoke to me, yet I would forever be a stone captive of his genius. Works from antiquity, works by Donatello, works by Rodin, Manzu, Messina stirred deep love and reverence. It was the human figure I loved.

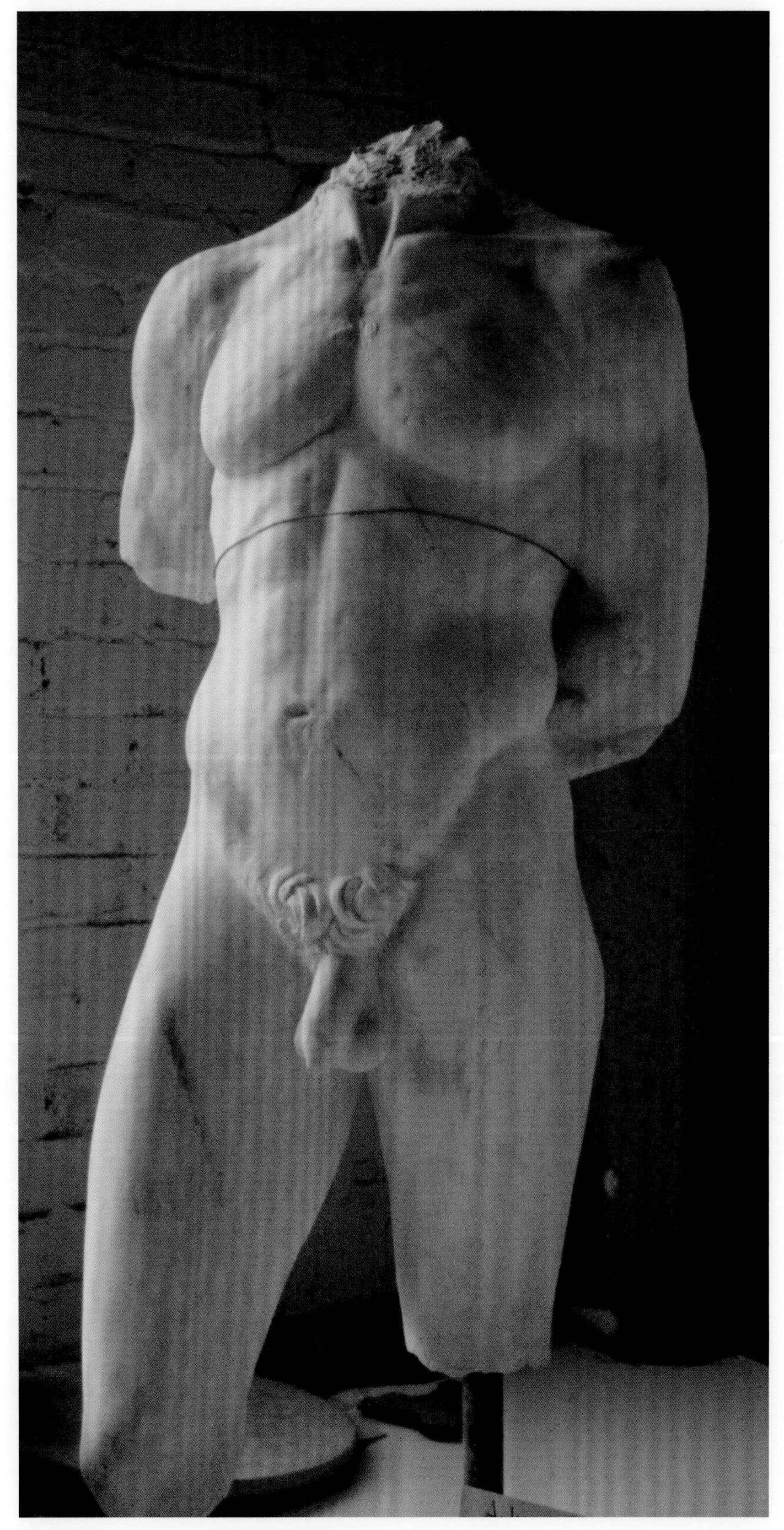

Michelangelo makes a distinction between *vista exteriore*, or external vision, and internal spiritual beauties, in his sonnet:

NON VIDER GLI OCCHI MIEI COSA MORTALE

"E se creata a Dio non fusse eguale,
Altro che 'l bel oli fuor ch'a fli ochi
piace Piu non vorria; ma perch'e si fallace,
Trascende ulla forma universale."

[If the soul were not created in God's image,
it would aspire only to external beauty,
gratifying to the senses. But since it knows
that beauty as false,
It ascends to the archetype of beauty.]

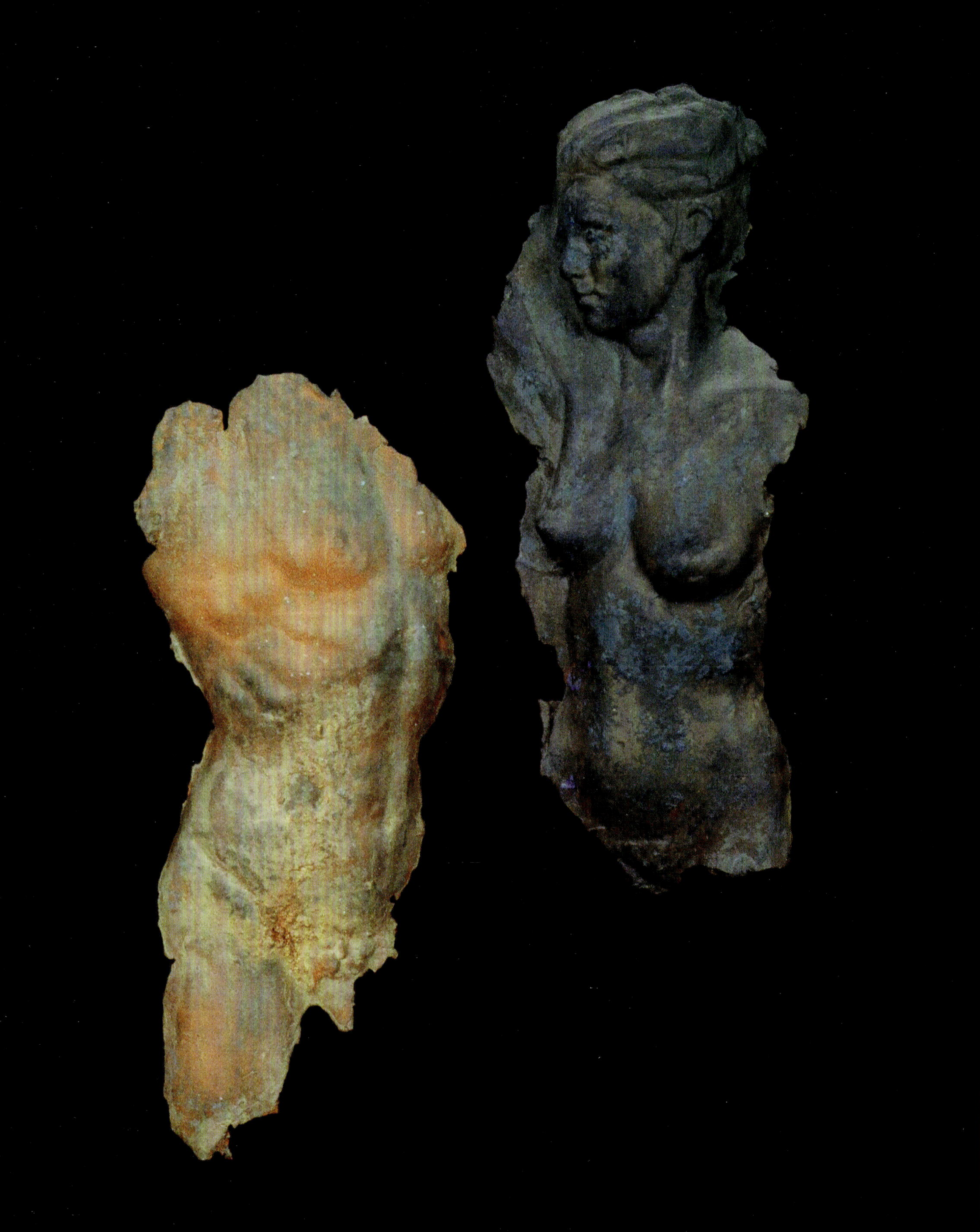

My work has a soul, an expression,
a beauty, it comes from the poetry
deep, deep, deep, down within me,
so deep that it is not me but a well in
which I take only a bucket full out at
a time. I have doubted it, denied it,
and feared it, but it exists and now
I want to drink long from it and live
in it. I am coming of age
but am far from mature.

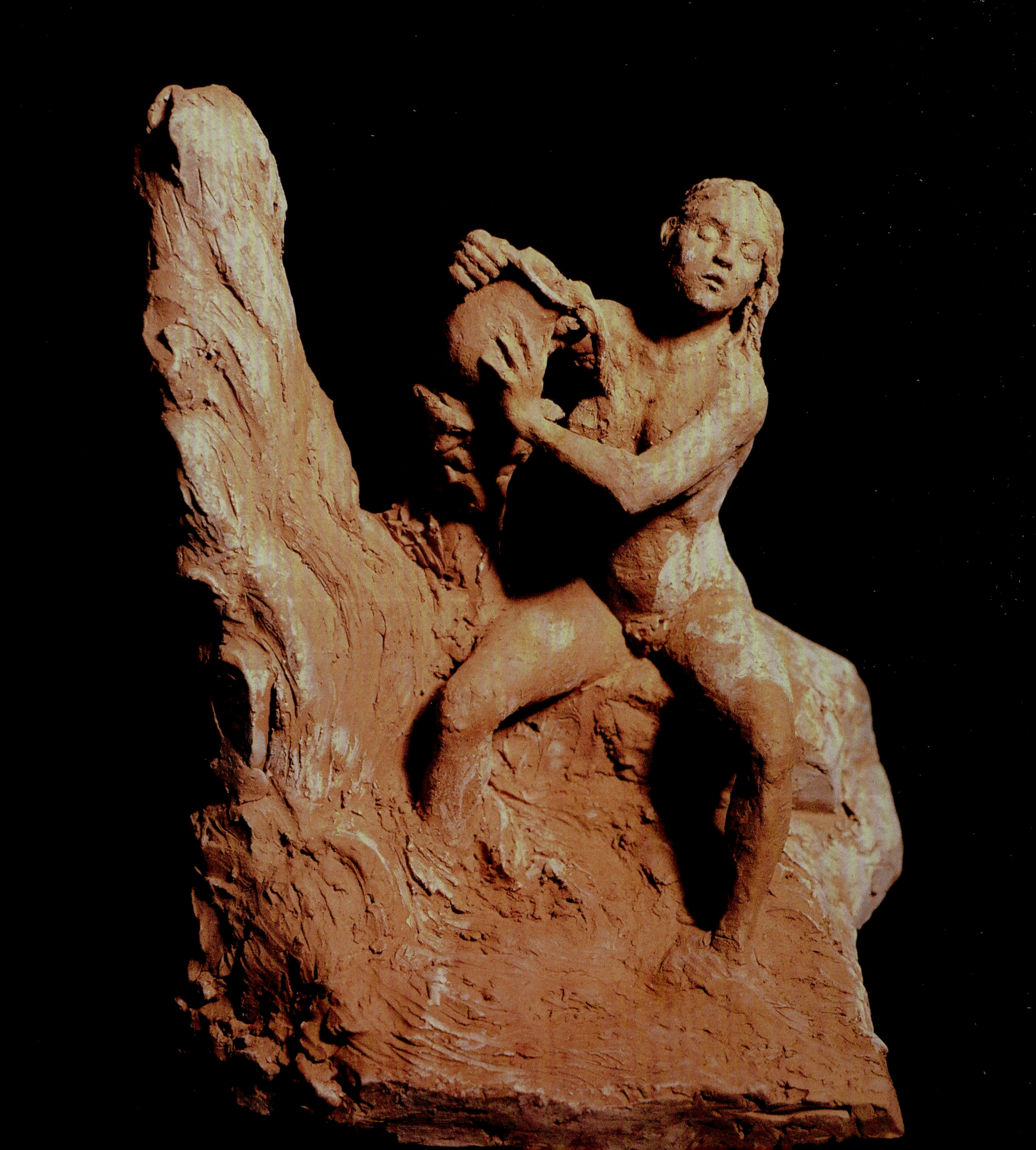

Donatello and Michelangelo each
had a *terribilita* which was an identifiable,
sympathetic depiction of humanity
and a *furia* that contained the deep
human psyche under muscular tension.
These forces have been very inspirational
in the forming of concepts in my work.
In Donatello, it is associated with the
beauty of his fear invoking realism.
It is associated with Michelangelo
in the *gigantismo* or anatomical
exaggeration of his work.

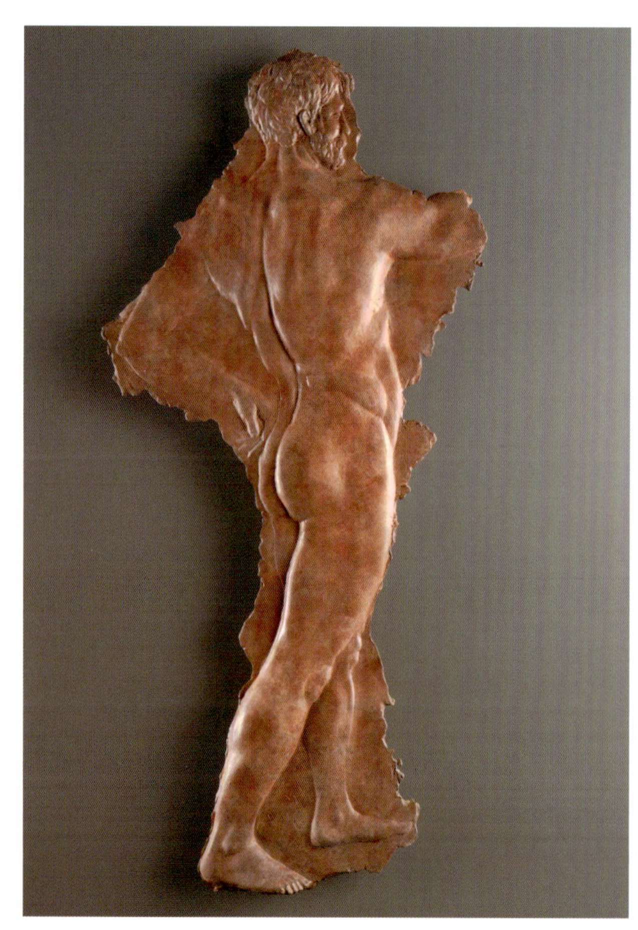

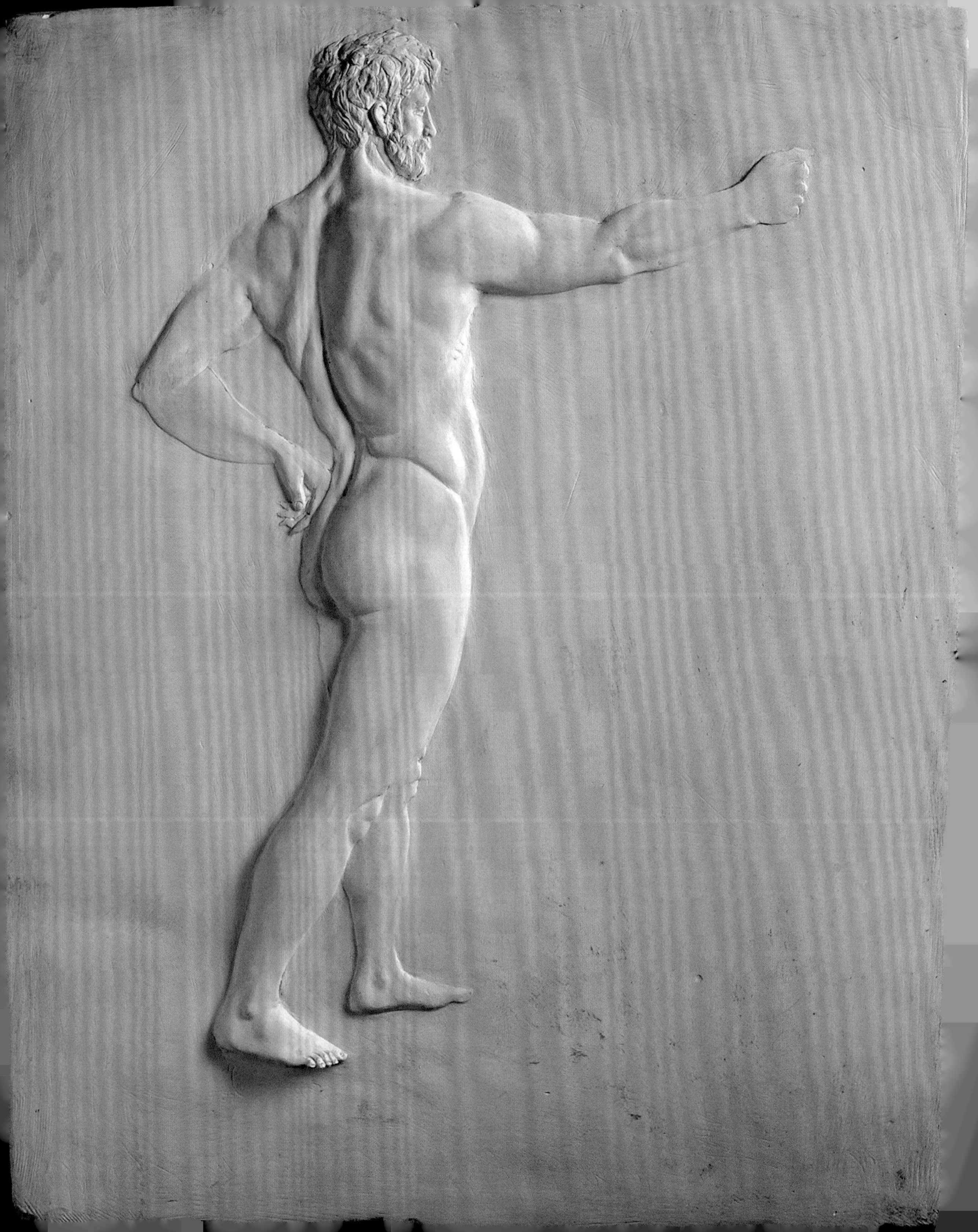

Rodin provided the fabulous blend of the *terribilita* of Donatello and the *furia* of Michelangelo. He also presented the sensuousness of women, the eroticism of human form....

His use of stone and figure is incredible. The contrast of rough stone with smooth figure is beautiful. He creates a space or an environment for the figure to exist in and this is what I find so striking about them. The only way this is achieved is knowing exactly where the figure lies within the marble and entering into it with confidence and assertiveness. Strength and beauty-contrast, Rodin is full of contrasts.

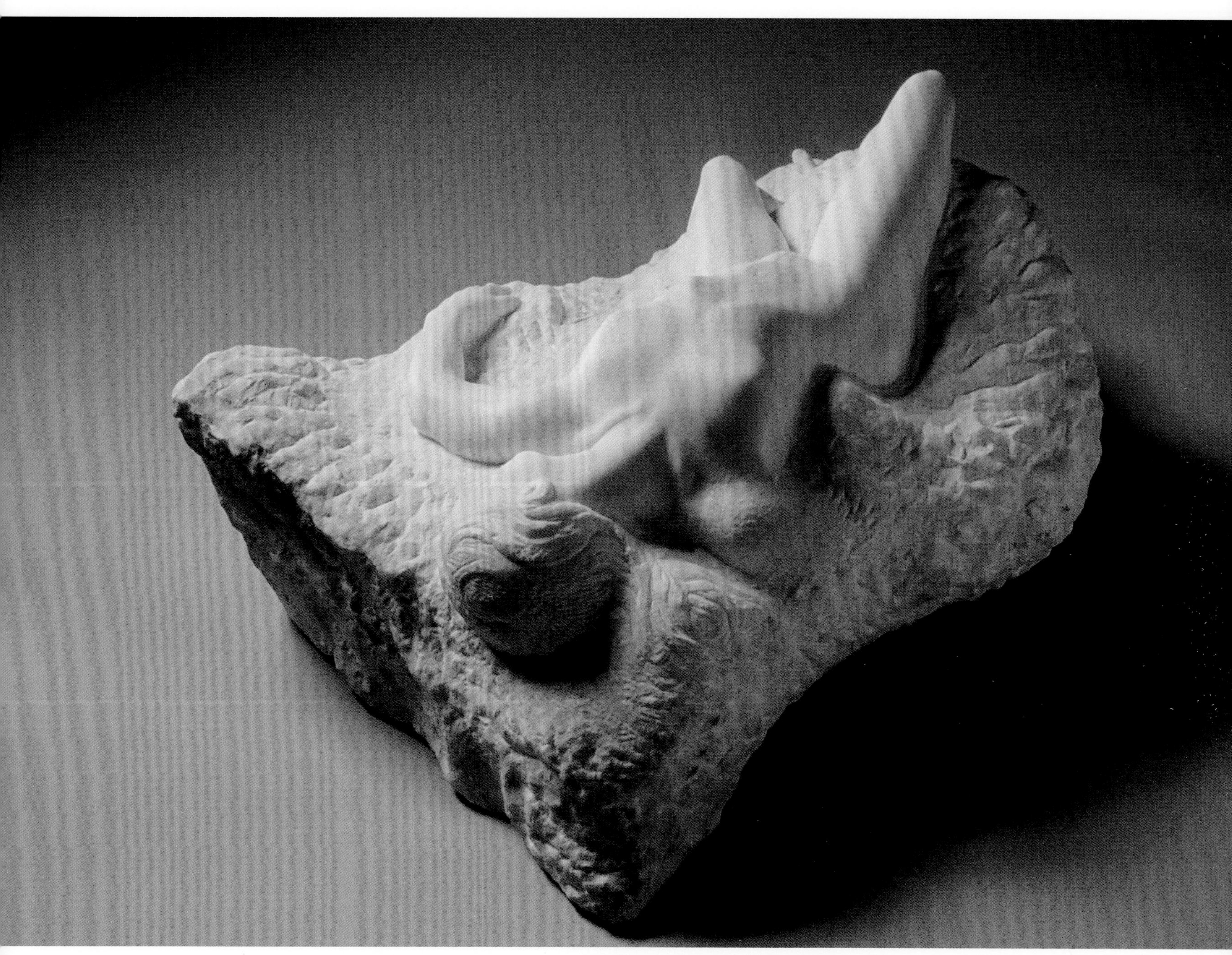

I AM A CHISEL

I am a chisel
as I cycle the undulating road.
I hammer at the uphills
and glide through the graded curves.
With my strength I carve
the formation of the land.
Two wheels, two legs
and my heart in command.
With breath I breathe the air
through nature's guiding hand
but it is she not me
who drives the hammer
and is truly in command.

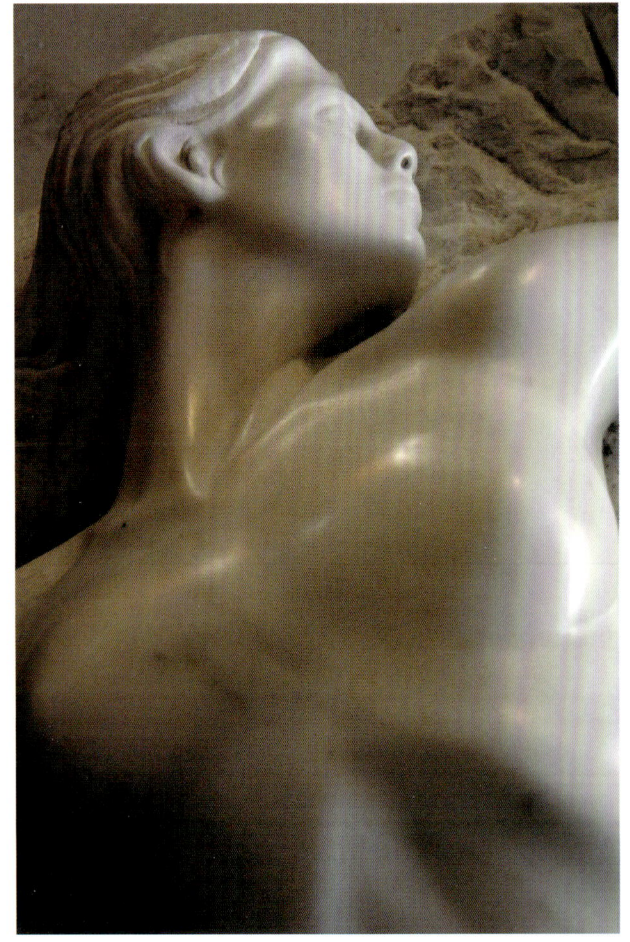

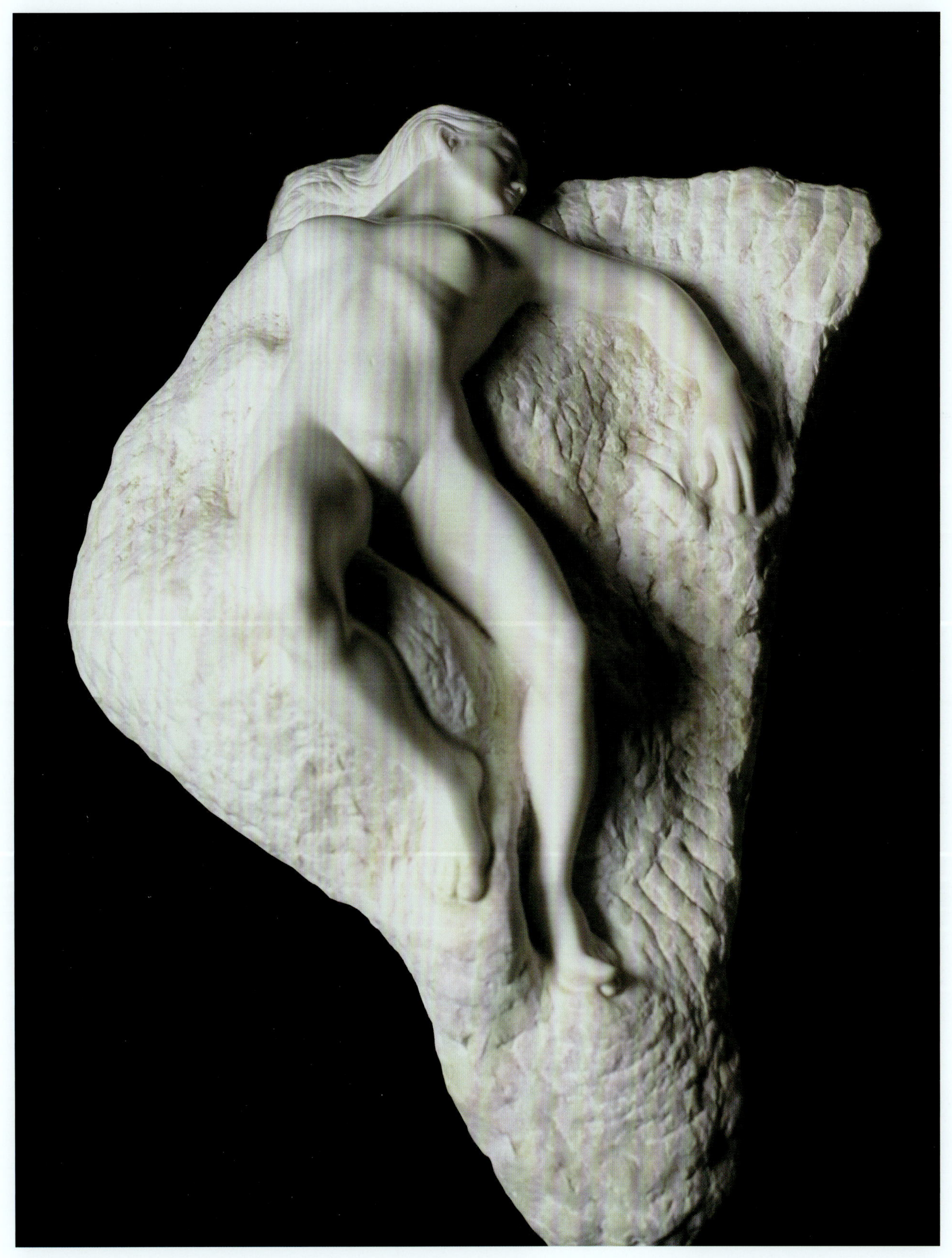

These are my brethren, my spiral of antecedents. I have studied their images and beliefs and integrated my own instincts. We share a common interest in depicting the human form. We share a devotion, though we are not of the same religion. We share the same physical act of creating sculpture with the same materials and methods. I am an heir by choice and I have been chosen.

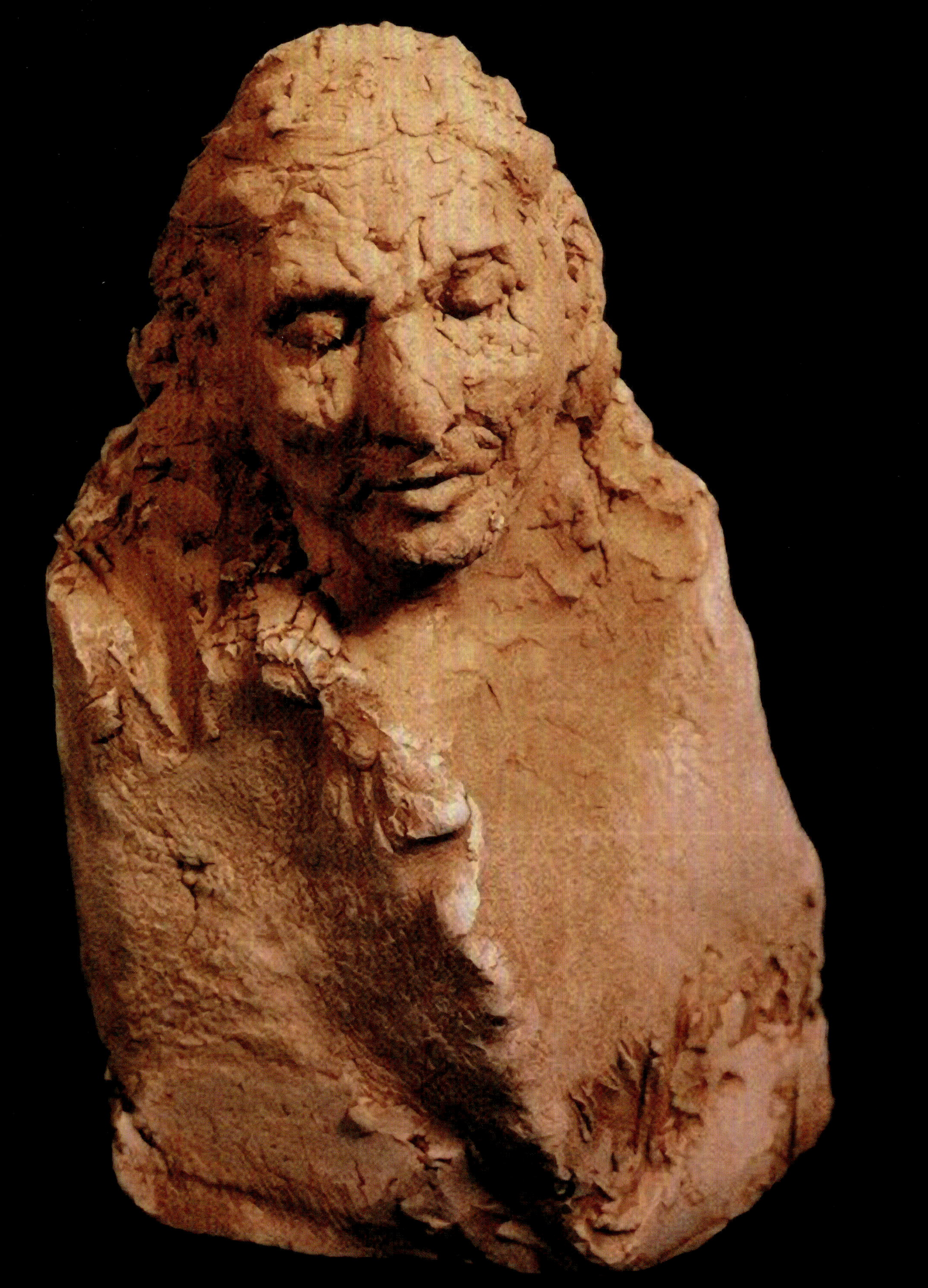

THE SCULPTOR

He makes up people
that don't exist
an image maker—a sculptor
through pencil pen paint
clay marble and brush
he builds a world within himself
an additive-subtractive interaction
with people he cannot touch
Alone
an actor between curtains
where
no one calls
a stage set
choreographed
behind the scenes
carving character
modeling form
a spectator he is not
an audience he seeks
an orchestra–
he plays.

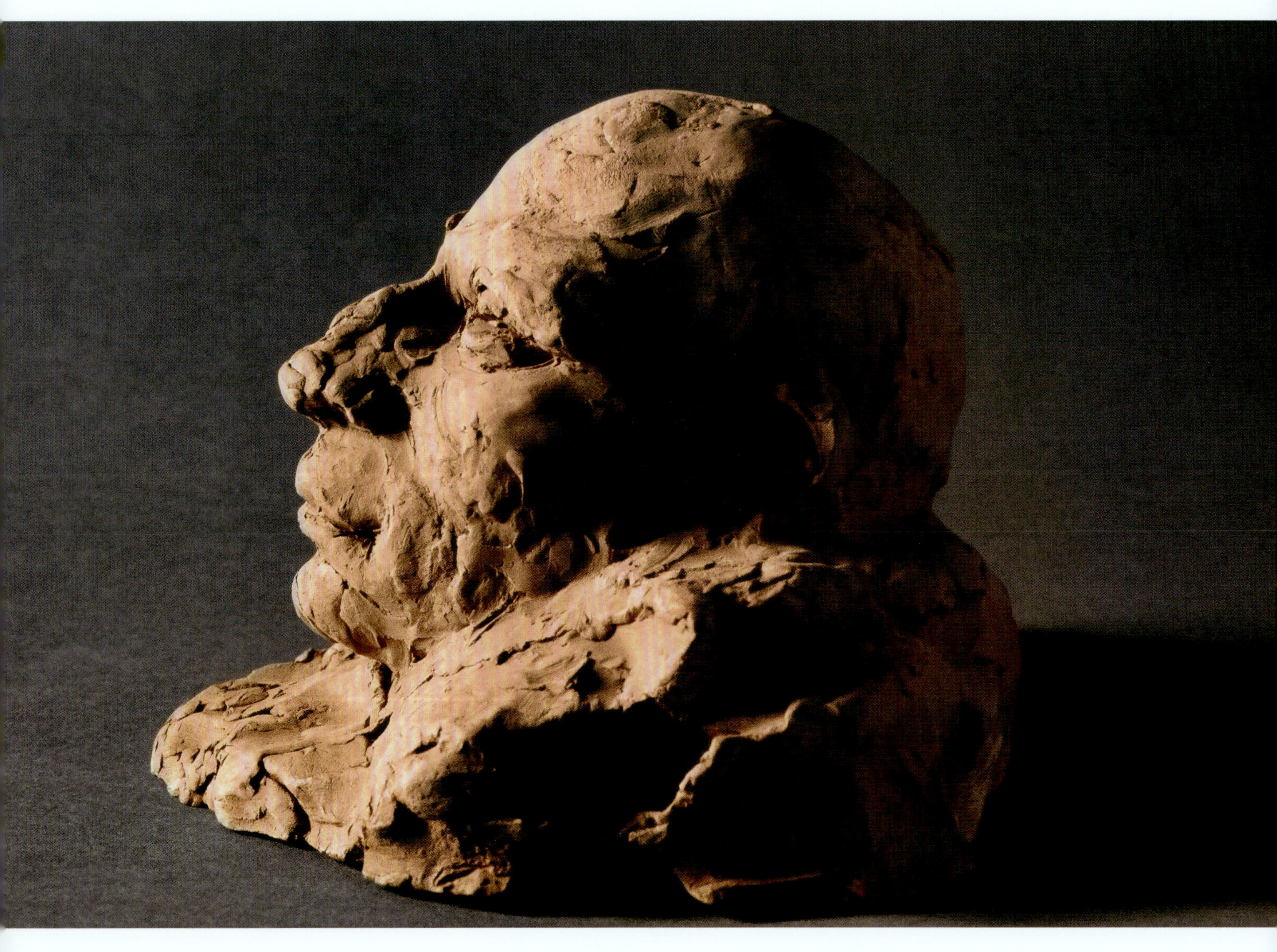

My art is a spiritual practice.
Spi-*ritual* by its nature, involves ritual.
The act of sculpting or drawing or writing
is a form of ritual meditation. Involvement
in the arts awakens, enlightens and liberates
my being. The process of working brings me
close to the nature of being, to my antecedents,
and the God/dess force of creativity. That is why
I work with earthen materials and like to work
most on Sundays. I meet my maker.

Cameron says, "creativity is a tribal experience.... Tribal elders will initiate the gifted youngsters who cross their path." Manzu wrote "my work was "*bella e significativa*," or beautiful and significant. My brethren are my tribal elders. It is no accident.

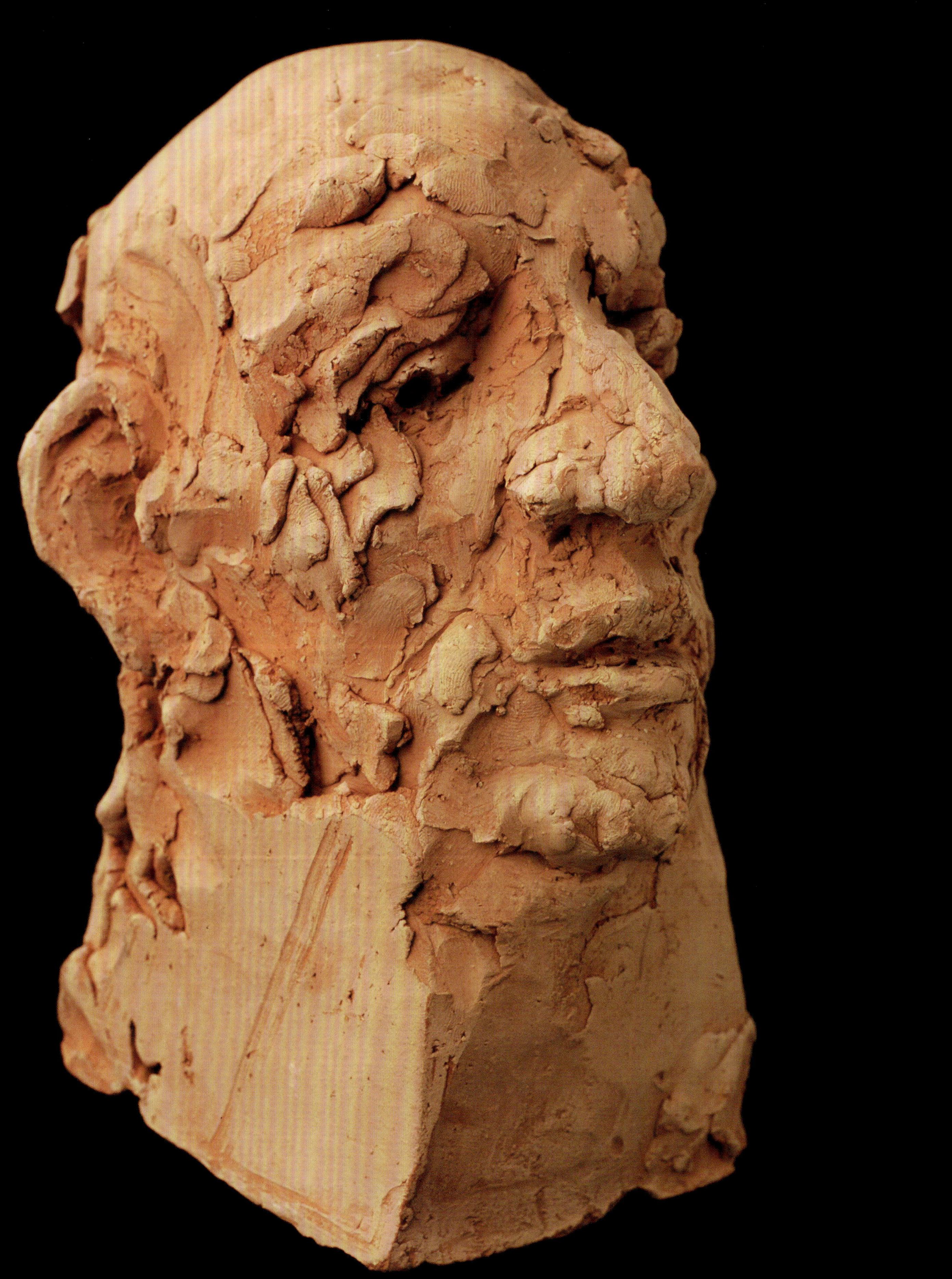

Why do I make art? I have a strong creative drive and an ability to communicate with a visual language. I grew up in an aesthetic environment, my mother, sister and brother being artists. This helped nurture my own instincts to beautify my environment and the environment of others. My decision to be an artist was a logical progression from my love of archaeology.

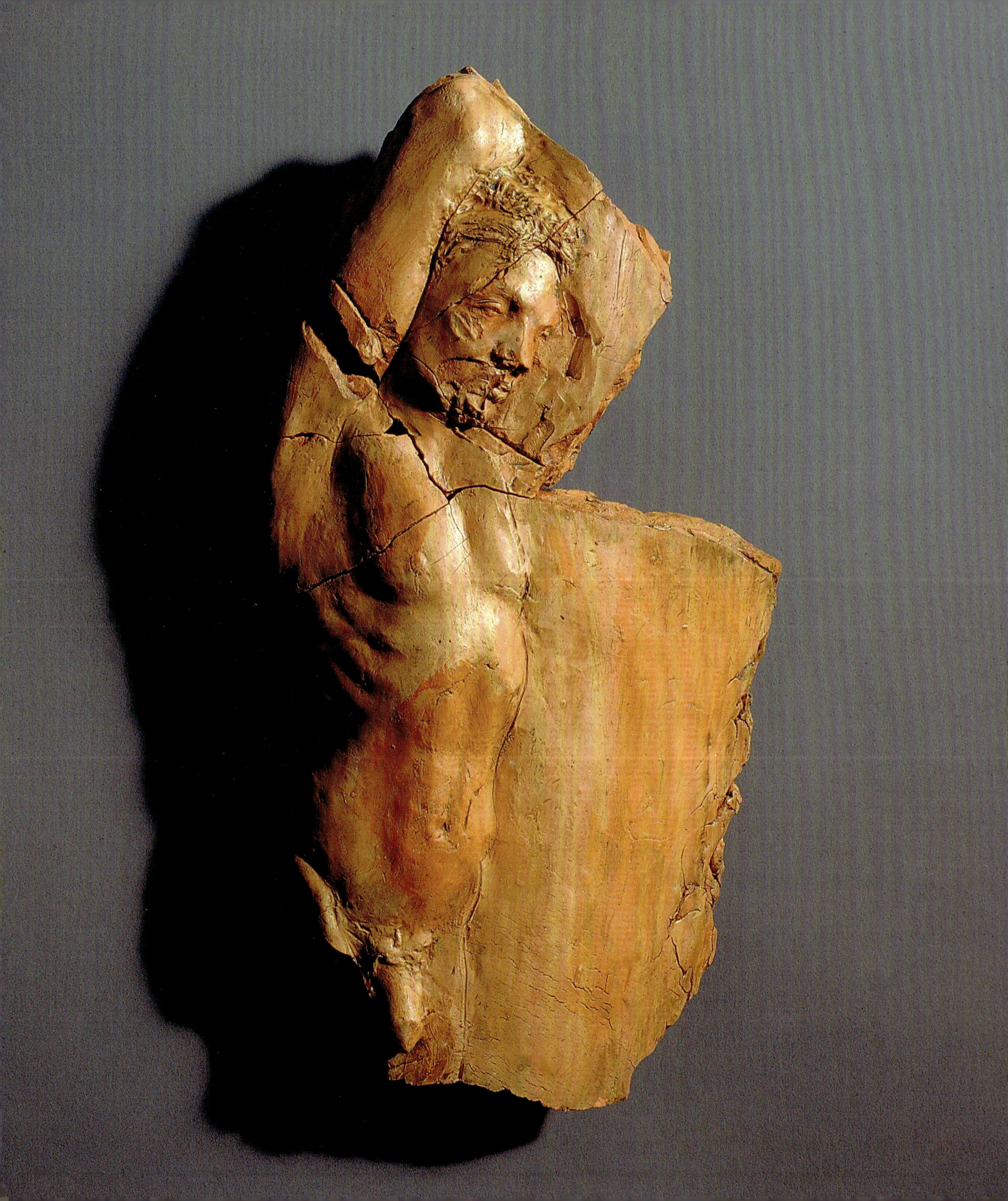

My fascination with ancient cultures, especially those of Italy and Greece, and the eternal beauty of the human form, lured me to the imagery and materials of the ancients. My aesthetic adventure, my own quest of my creativity has been a desire for discovery, the search for beauty and expressive content in the human figure.

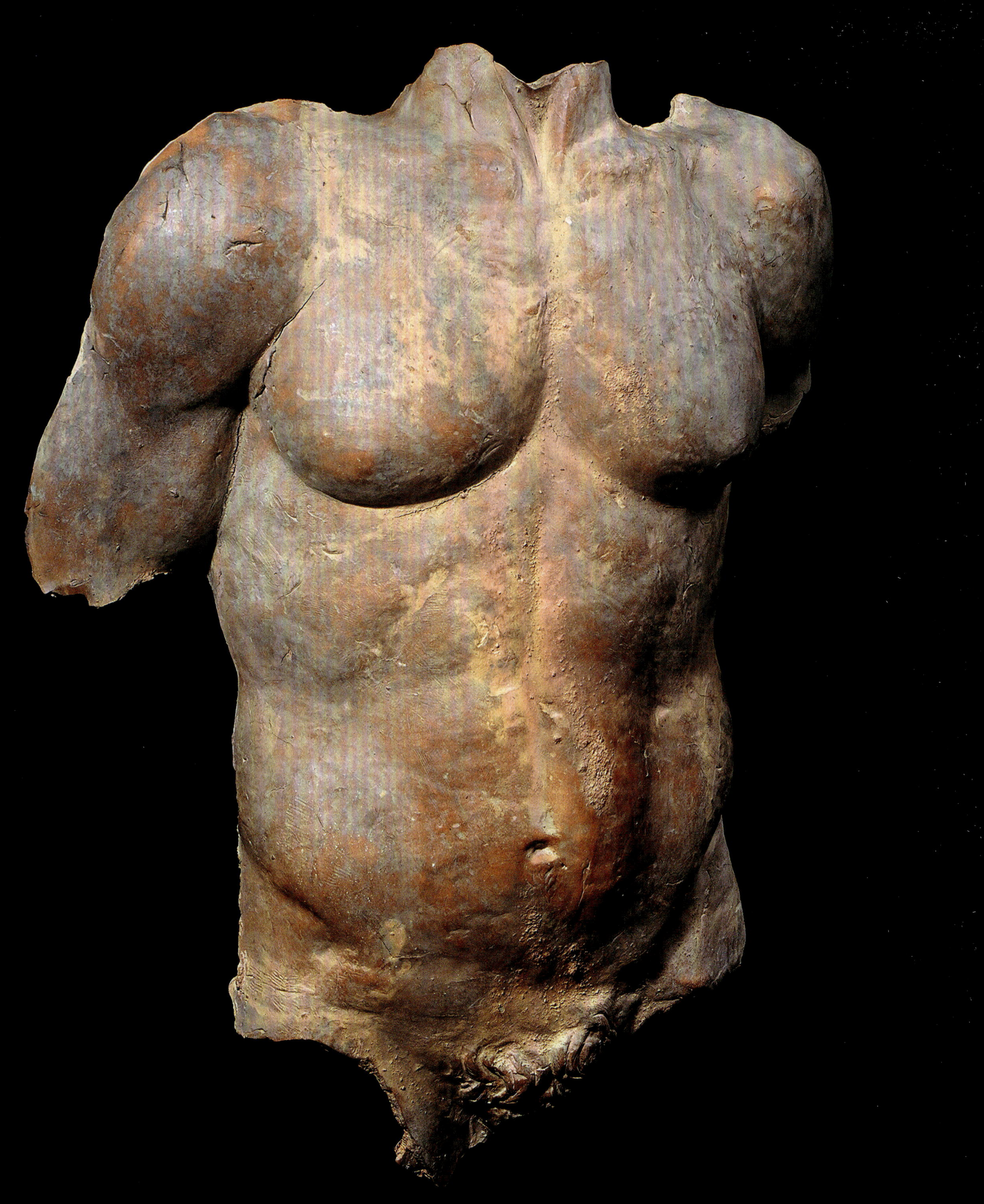

In my imagery I seek an equilibrium, a way to bring classical aesthetics to a contemporary longing for humanism. The human form, with its beauty, harmony, intellect, dignity and spirituality, creates reassurance and motivation no matter how dehumanizing our society has become. I pay homage to this universal truth in a form that all of us are in possession of, our bodies.

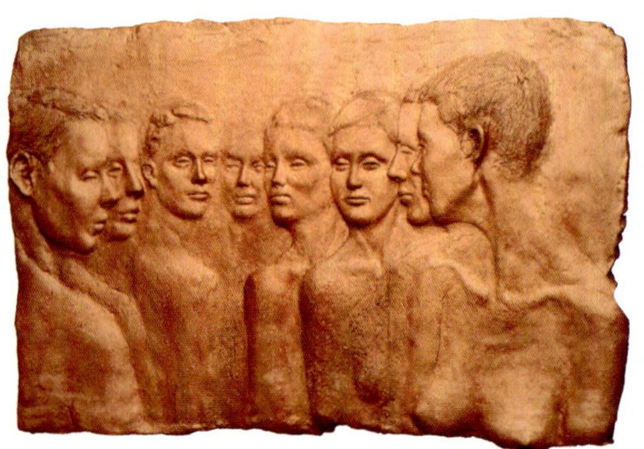

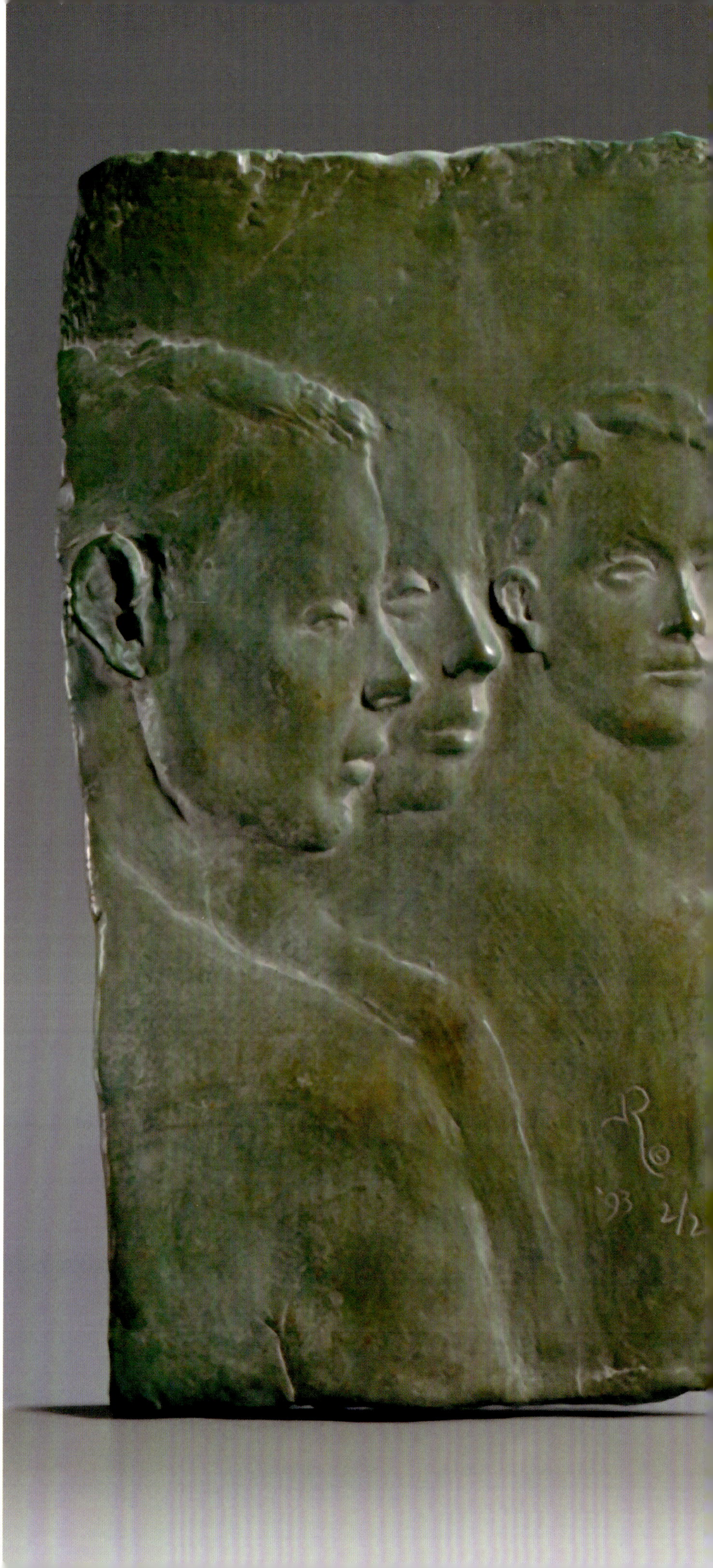

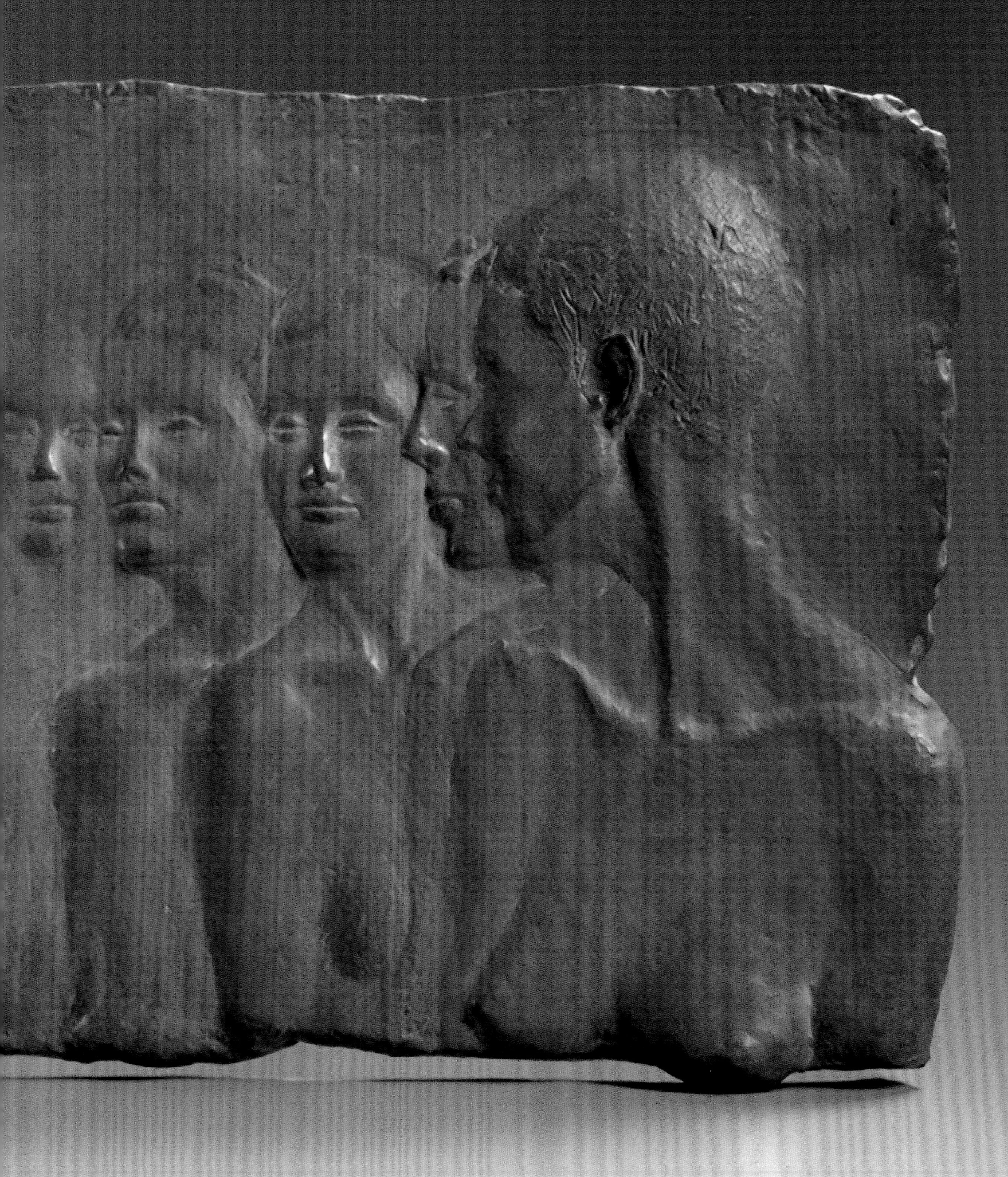

Great art exists in the archetype
of beauty independent from the
critical, temporal, social context.
I believe the human form is infinitely
beautiful, inspirational, expressive
and emotive. To deny this is to
disregard the fact that
you are human.

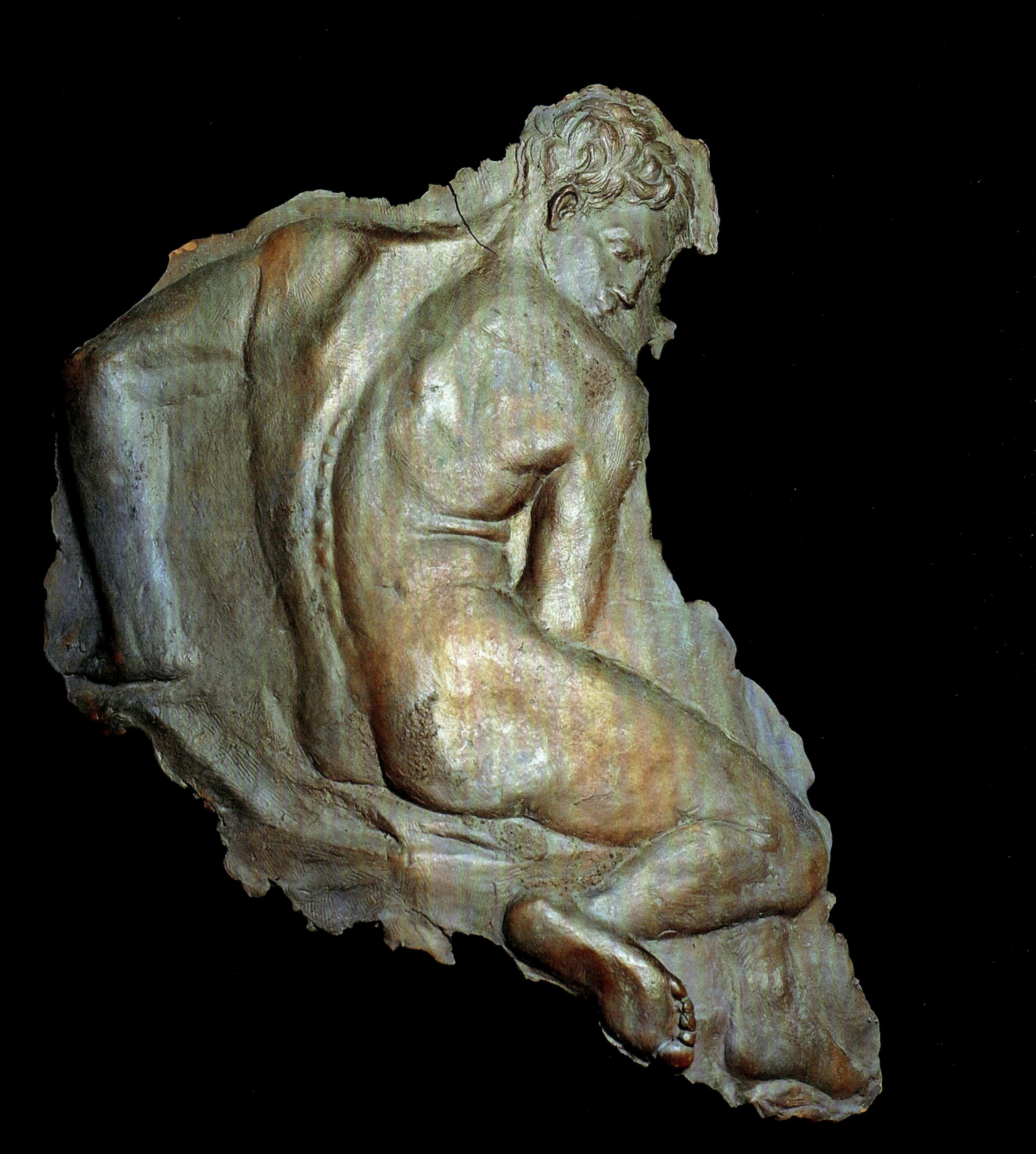

I can remember visiting the Rodin Museum in Philadelphia with my father. We were in front of Mignon. I entered that space where true reverence meets creative genius. My father said quietly, "I'll leave you with Mignon." My father knew. He had seen me with the David eleven years before.

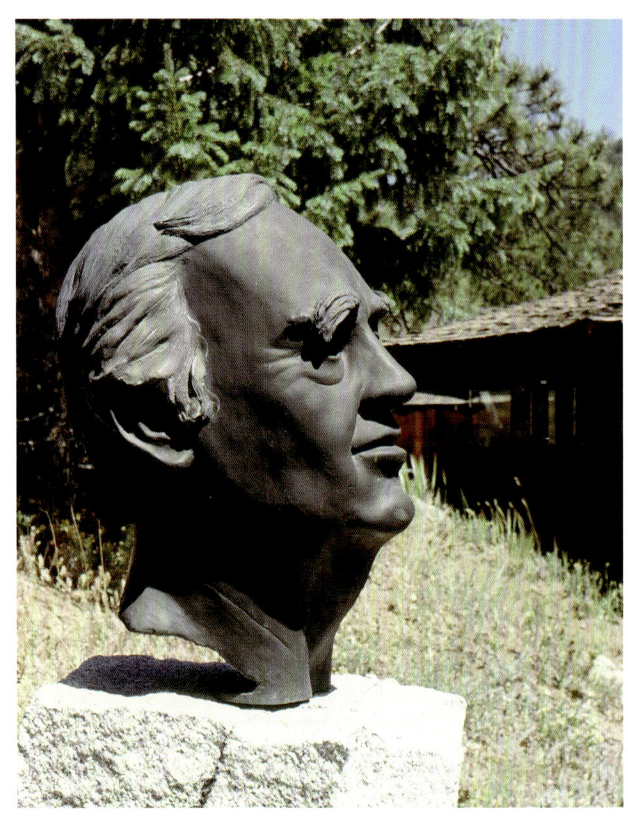

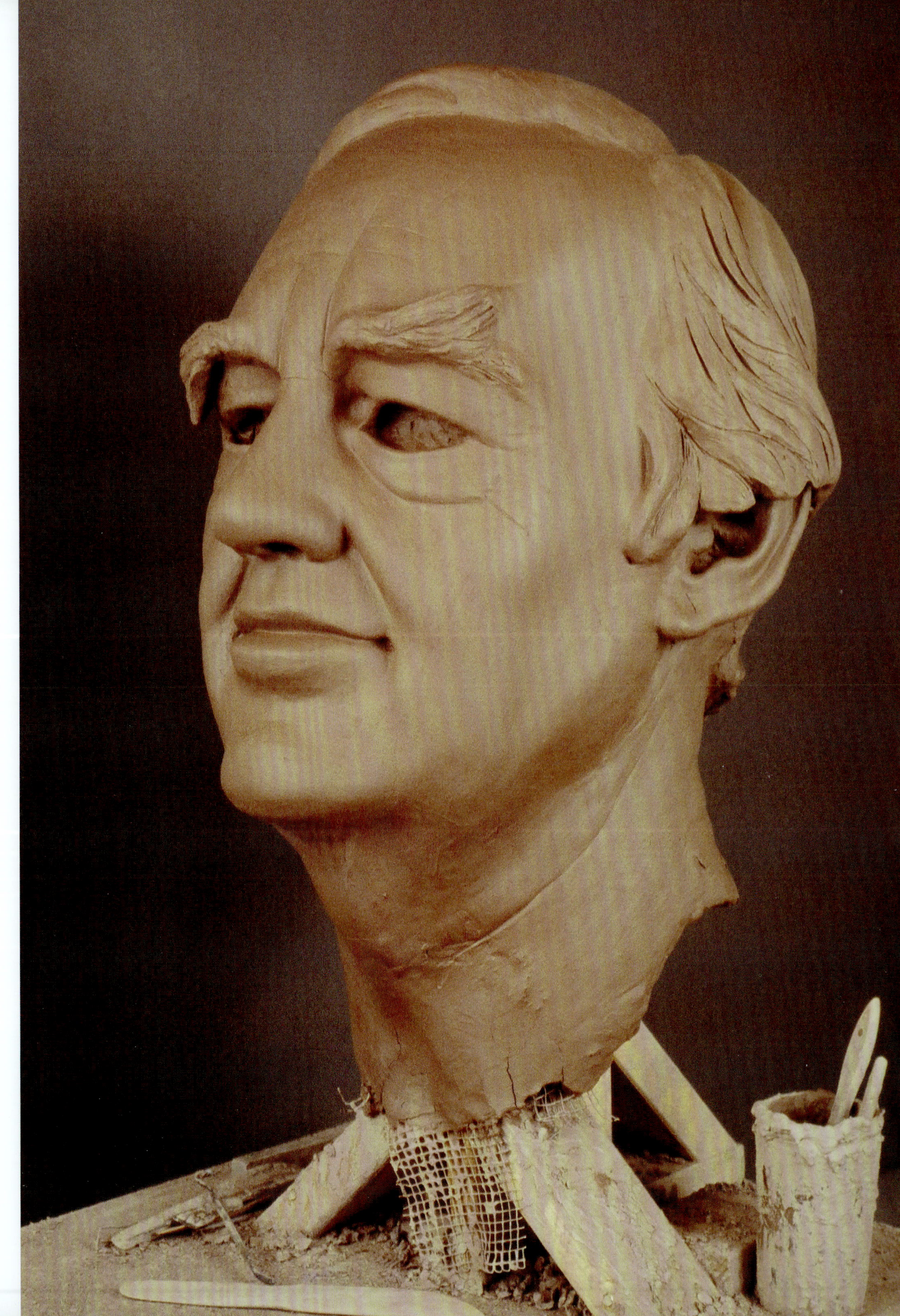

I went to the Met and drew from Greek and Roman stones. The ancients had it. I then came back and sculpted George. I broke through the stone and began to see the head. I worked possessed and things began to happen. It is now an oriental head and will begin as transformation of races until I reach George.

IMAGES BY HAND

images by hand
ancestral passage
collective linear graphic
heart beat of marble
rhythm

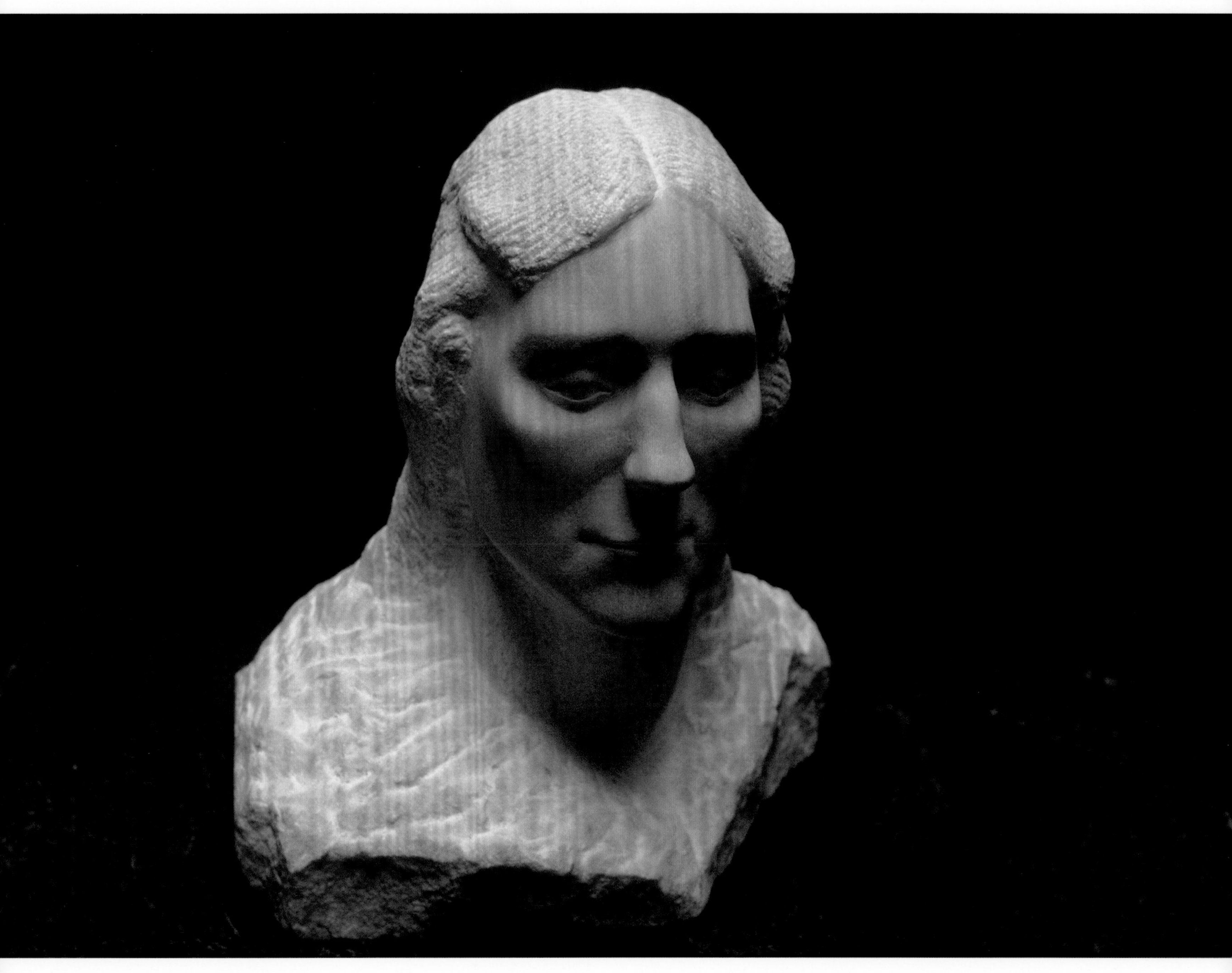

I'm in Azzano ... La Cappella. I'm working on a fairly large piece of stone. The sculpture will be a woman's head looking up from her first kiss. I had a girlfriend in Rome, Carla Angeletti. She worked at the museum with me. I got a good taste of Italian culture, especially understanding the Italian family. We had good times together. We went to the Forum, heard piano concerts and Beethoven's *Fifth Sinfonia*, walked around Rome, etc. The sculpture I'm working on now is inspired by her. The first time I kissed her ...
I looked down at her and waited
for her to open her eyes.

When she opened her eyes I saw a sparkle, and I saw deep down into her soul. She looked so beautiful ... a unique moment, the moment when a woman is first kissed, and the moment when she first opens her eyes. You see all the love, hope and fear, and the trust she is looking for.

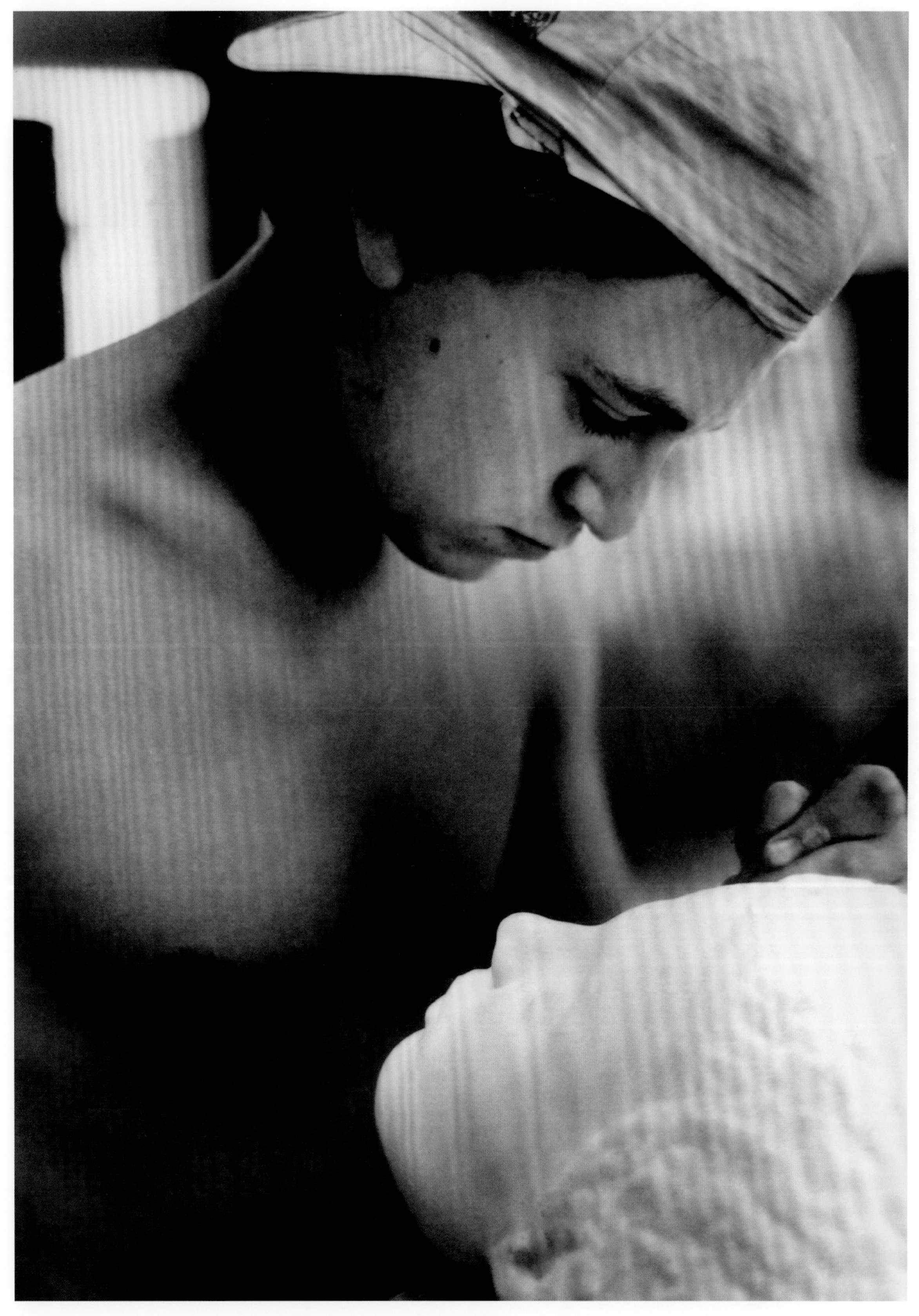

THE FOUNTAIN OF YOUTH

I drank of your fertile spring,
returned to your lips
to taste the kiss where
life produced its course.
Strung out on rope's end
I recovered, a castaway,
guzzling fresh water
within your cup,
building, rebuilding, rejuvenating
the source.
I taste this now—
my mind—the memory,
the tingling spark.
The fountain of youth
the source of life,
I drank of your fertile spring,
and returned to your lips
to taste the kiss
and moisten an arid dream.

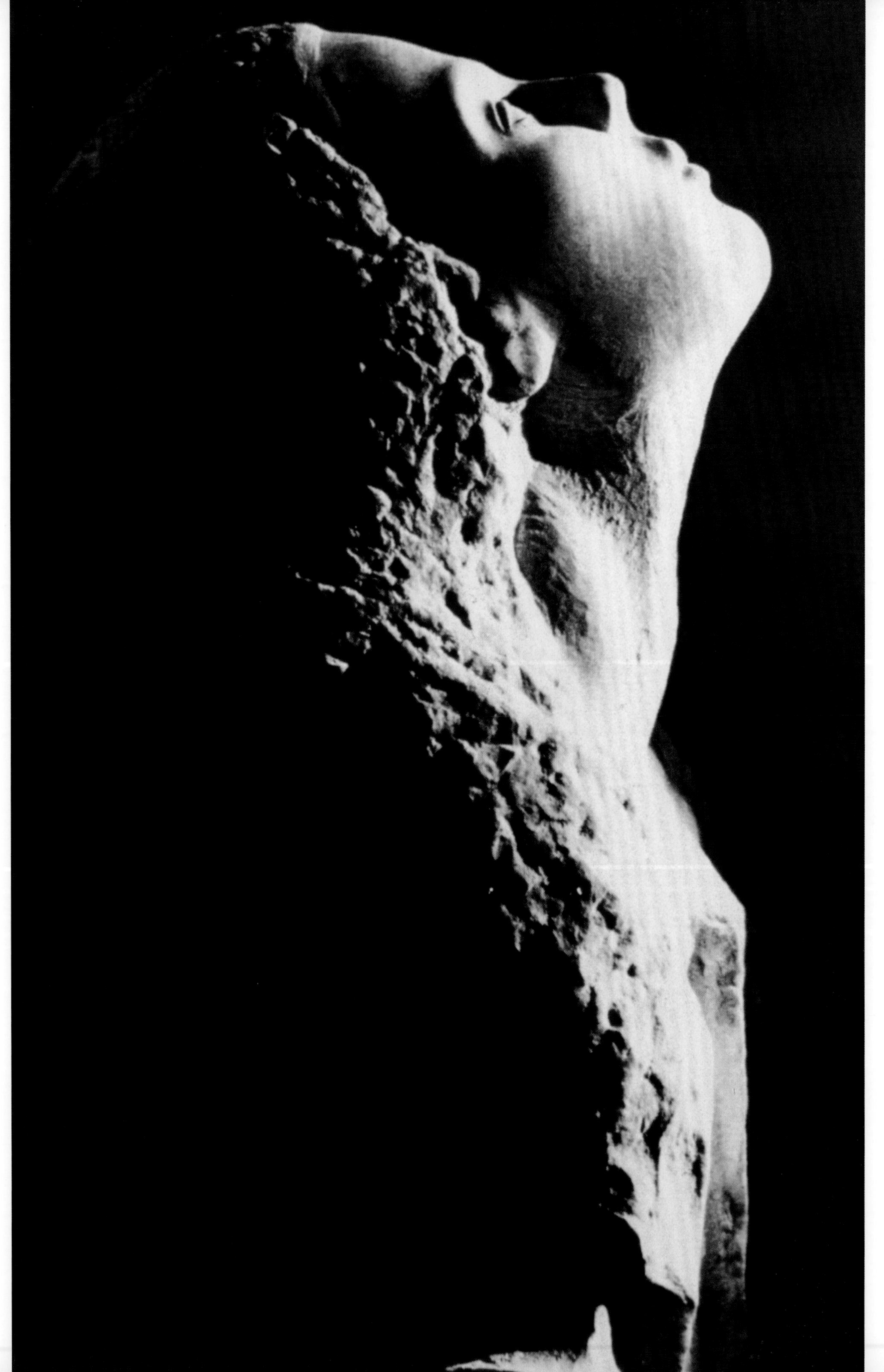

Classical ideation has no sense of time as well as a great sense of time. In my mind I have a little adage in which I say "think antique," and it's a kind of bumper sticker in my brain to get into this fantasy of something that is ancient. The reason for my classical work stems back to my love of archaeology and anthropology. Rather than digging up the work I make it myself ... so I kind of play with the idea of time.

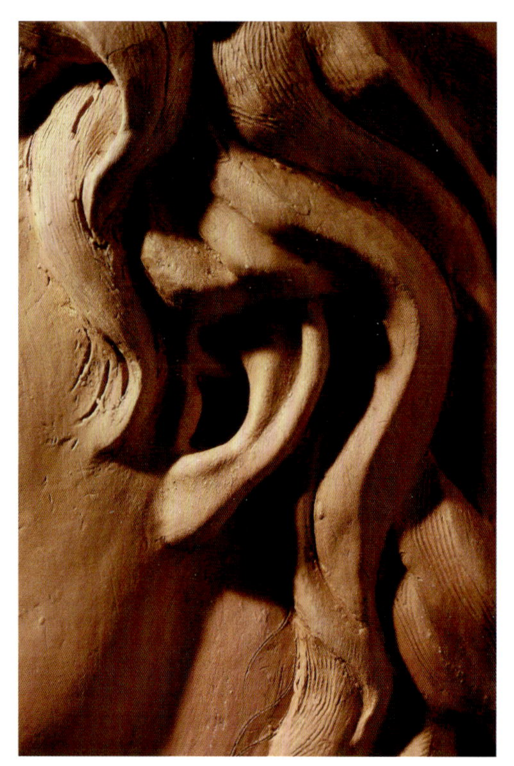

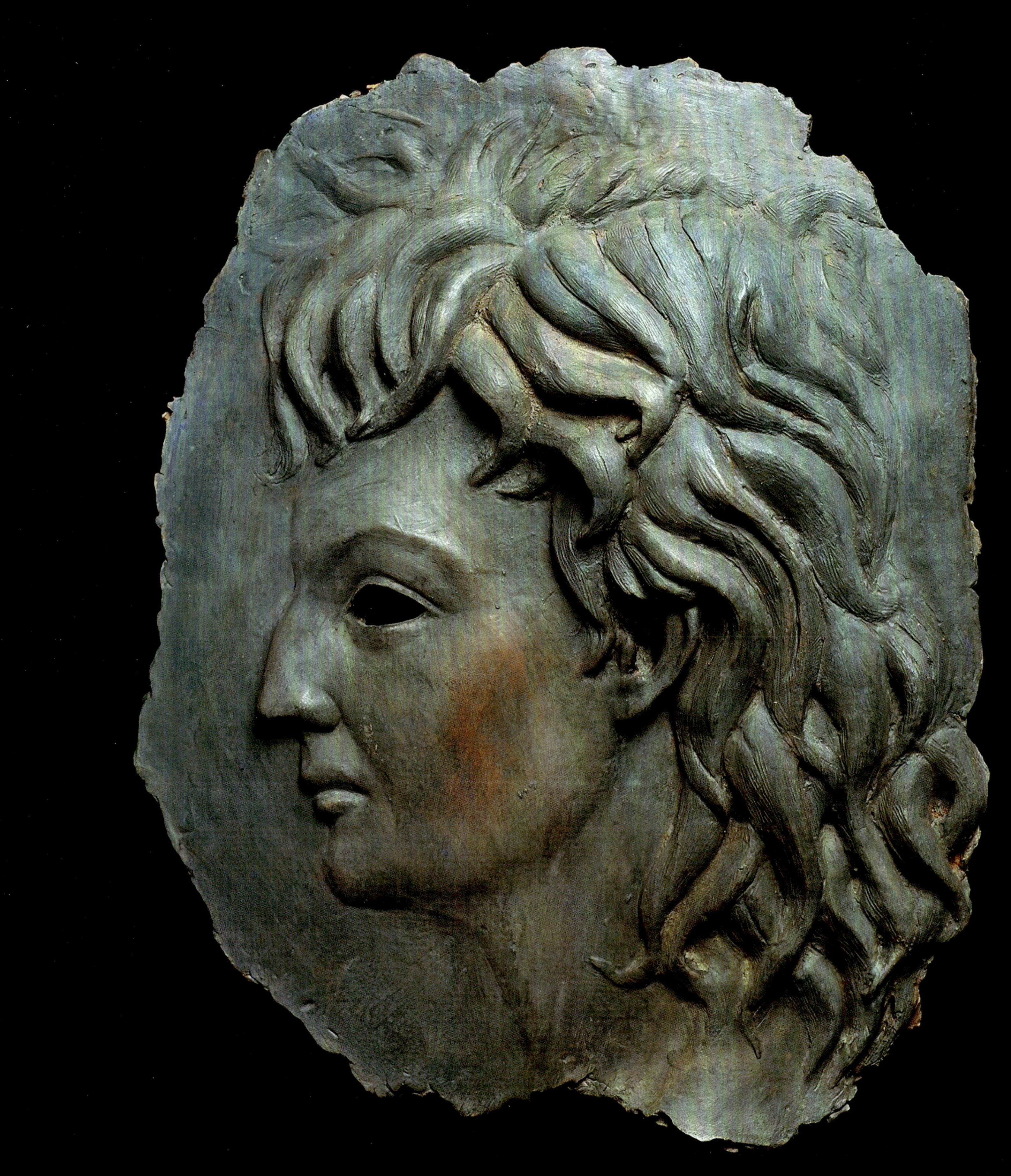

With the *frammenti*, I pay homage to antiquity as the continual source of inspiration to my imagery. The *frammenti* are like found objects from the earth or from the sea that have survived thousands of years.... The *frammenti* ... make us aware of the fragility of life itself and the life of our civilization that will, one day, be understood only by the fragments to be found.

They are filled with archaeological echoes. They are like found objects from the earth or from the sea that have survived through the centuries to be placed on your wall as an artifact of a lost civilization. They evoke an ancient feeling, yet they never existed five years ago.

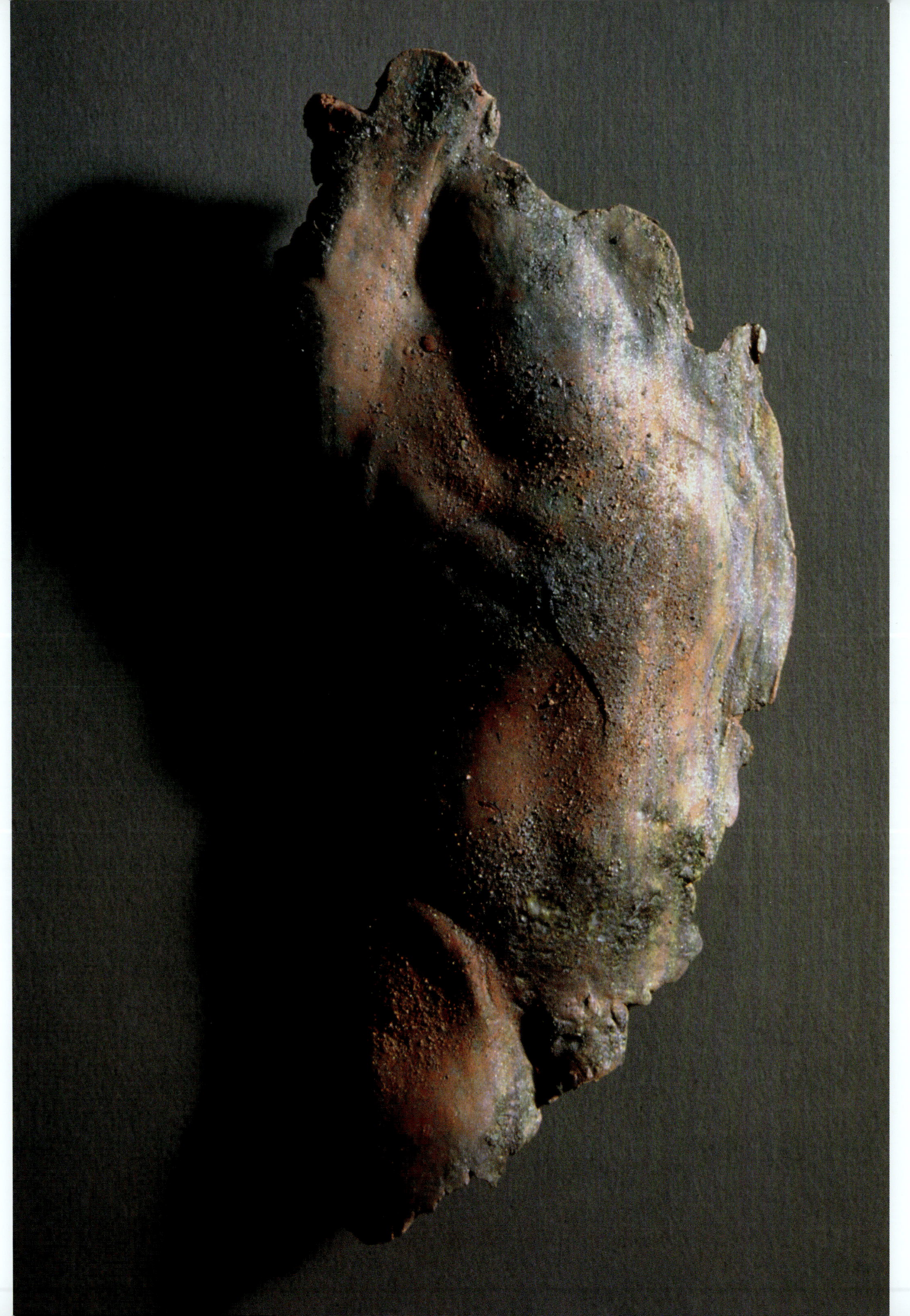

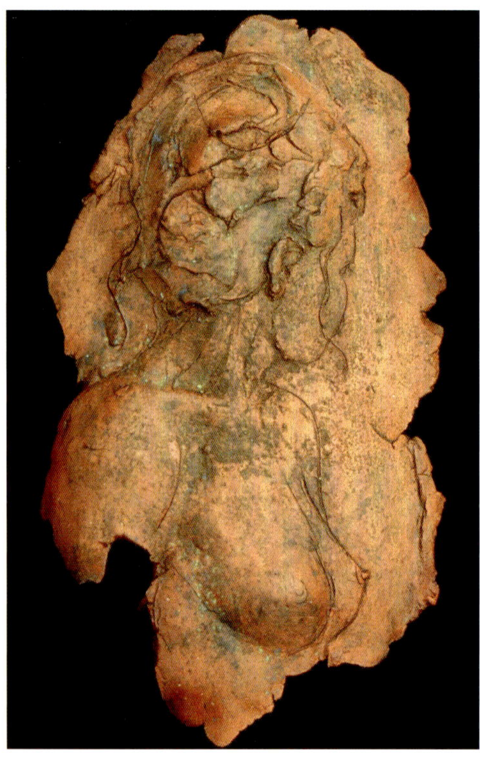
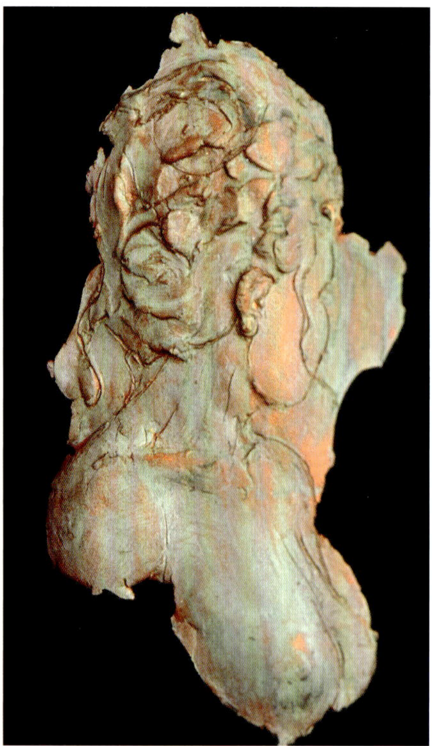
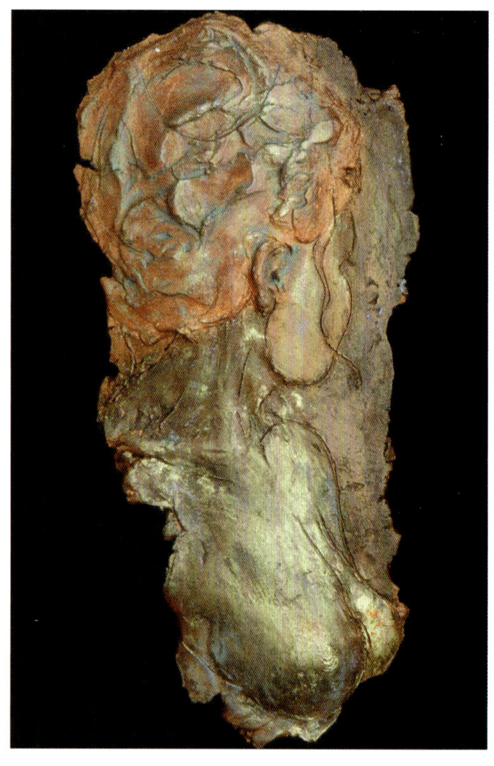

I AM OF THE EARTH

My heart is as big as the world.
It's made of silver, diamonds and gold.
It's been mined for its minerals
excavated for its wealth
consumed polluted
threatened its health.
Yet beauty remains for those who seek it
in every square centimeter peace can be found
day to night month to year
spinning spinning spinning 'round.
Season's change,
my heart grows cold
bitter a battle to stay warm,
greens turn to browns
I drop my foliage
and bare the cold lonely winter.

Spring—new hope new life
buds are blooming
new energy-new strife ...
Summer scorches the surface crust
dig deeper you will find the jewels,
a treasure box to seek—
but never use ...
Autumn comes again at last
the harvest the colors
and in its passing–
the cyclic fast.
Grow, turn onward, revolve 'round the sun
spinning into infinity
love's pain longing ecstasy song.
Tears fears souvenirs.
a life/love
battle lost/gained.
I am of the Earth, Wind and Rain.

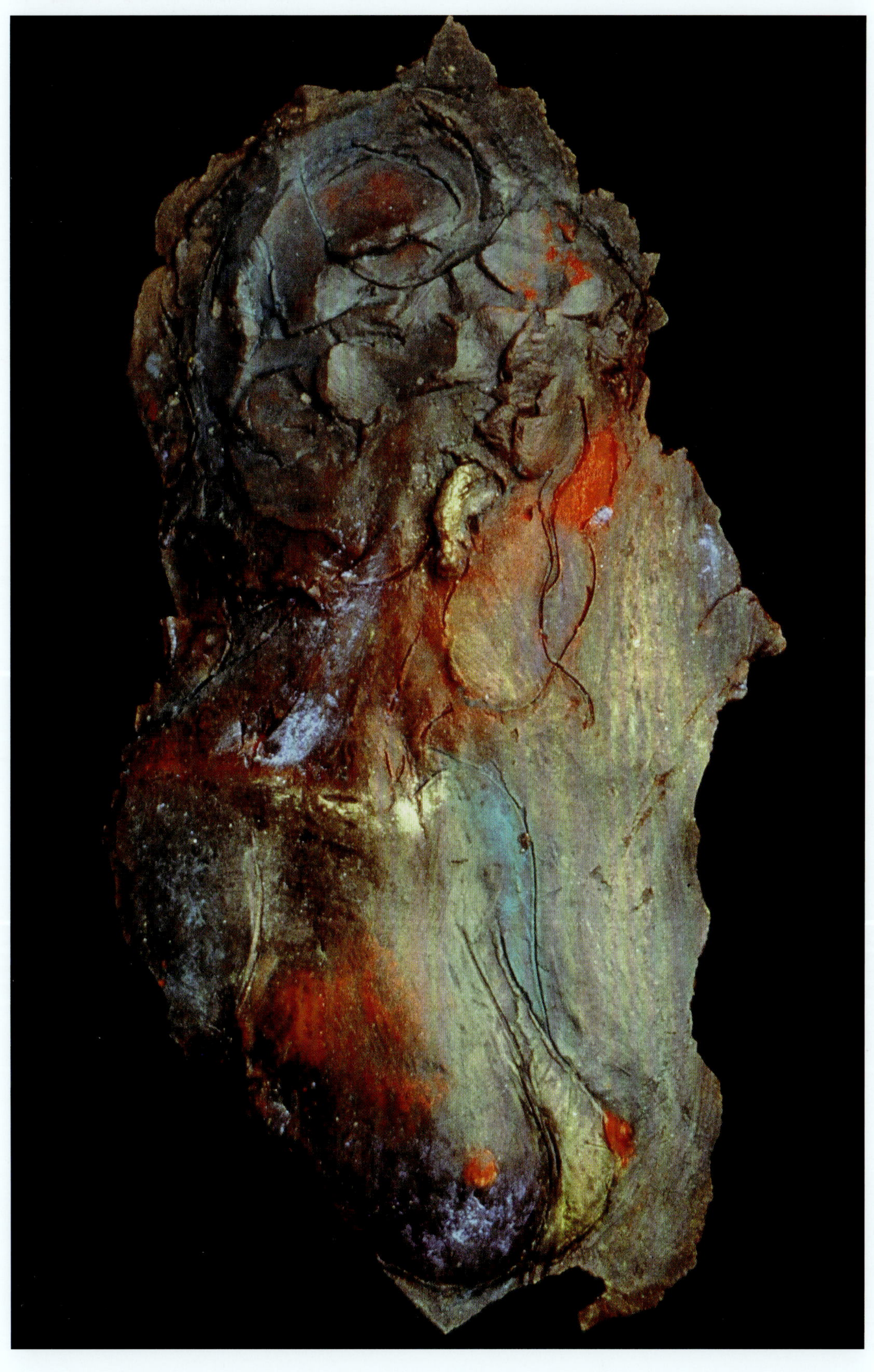

UNTITLED

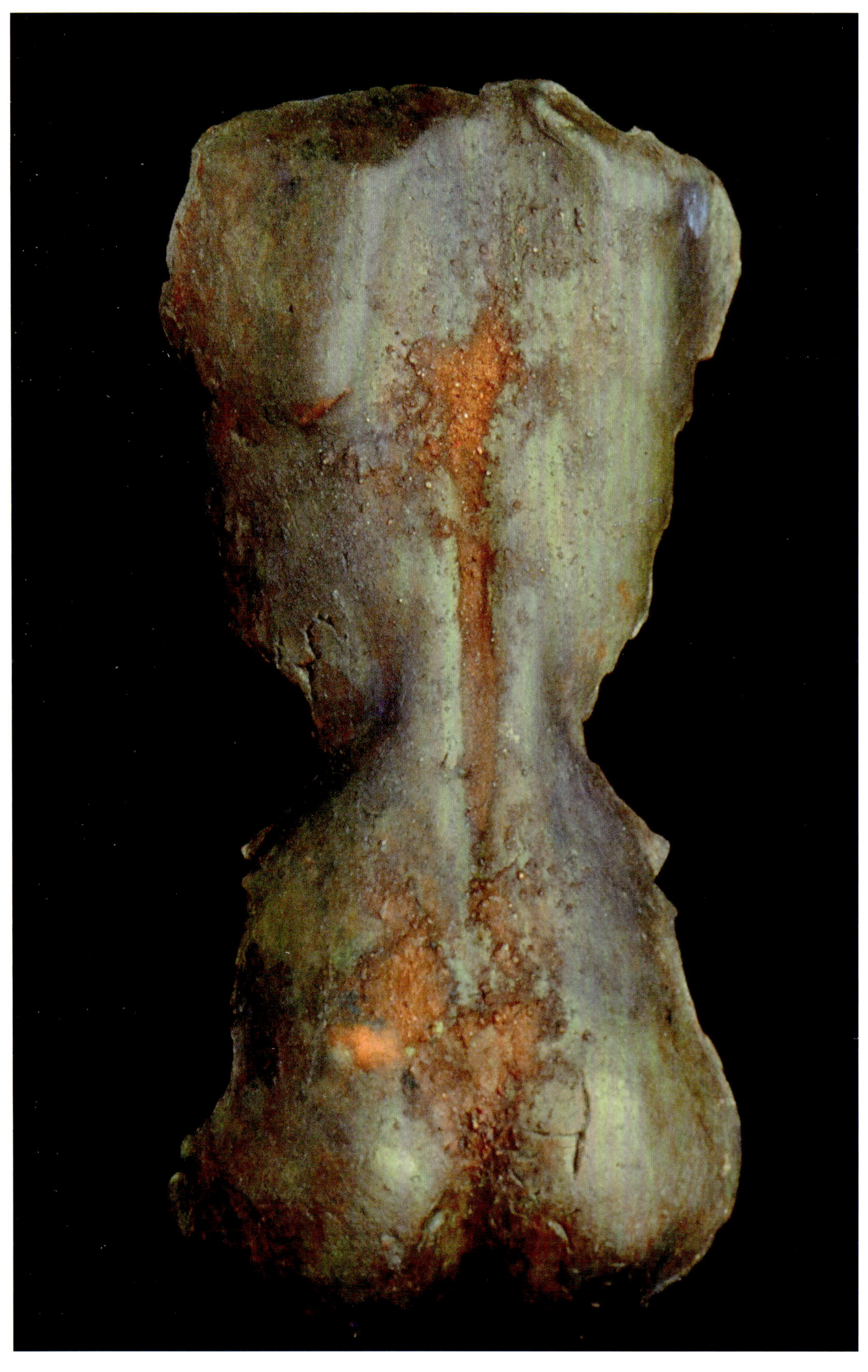

SCHIENA

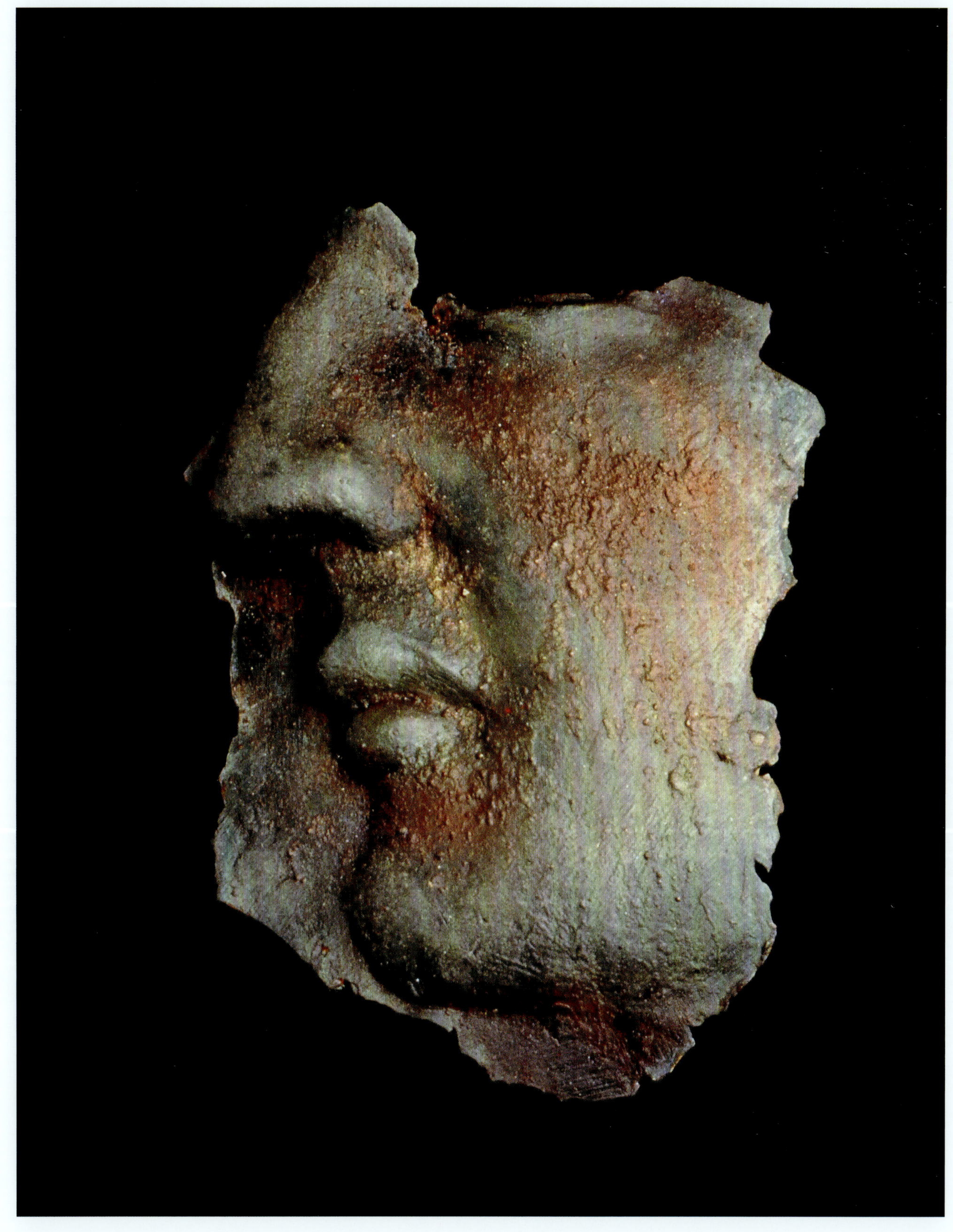

MASCHERA

The figure has been worshipped and revered for over 15,000 years.... Since the earliest cave paintings and sculptures, the nude has been a focal point. I believe, as was the belief in the Renaissance, that to step backward is to step forward. An understanding of history and artists that came before you is essential, simply because art begets art.

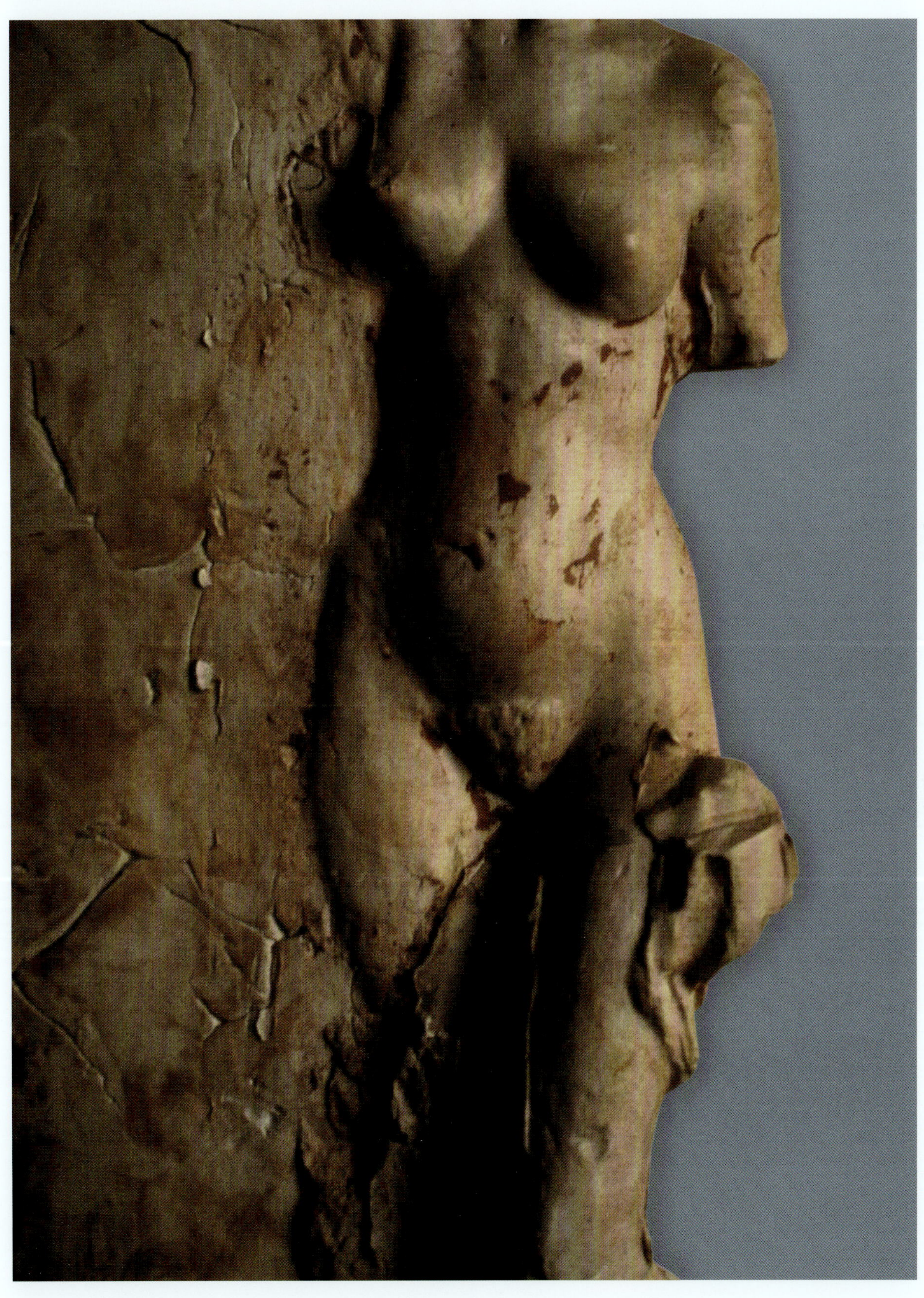

Frammento Donna della Colonna

THE POET'S DAWN

I awoke from sleep in bas-relief.
The first light of day
I modeled in clay.
The rosy dawn and I
arose slowly, on the low plane, and I, like
the fiery half-globe on the horizon,
became more volumetric towards consciousness.
I awoke from sleep in bas-relief
a prisoner of Buonarroti
in the marble black of dreams,
struggling to cast off sleep,
to peel the layers
and release the form
of a new day dawning.
I awoke from sleep in bas-relief
carving more shadow more light
revealing
in the sun's arm rays from mass to vibrant
detail,
a new man
and
a new woman.

Uomo della Colonna
y Donna della Colonna

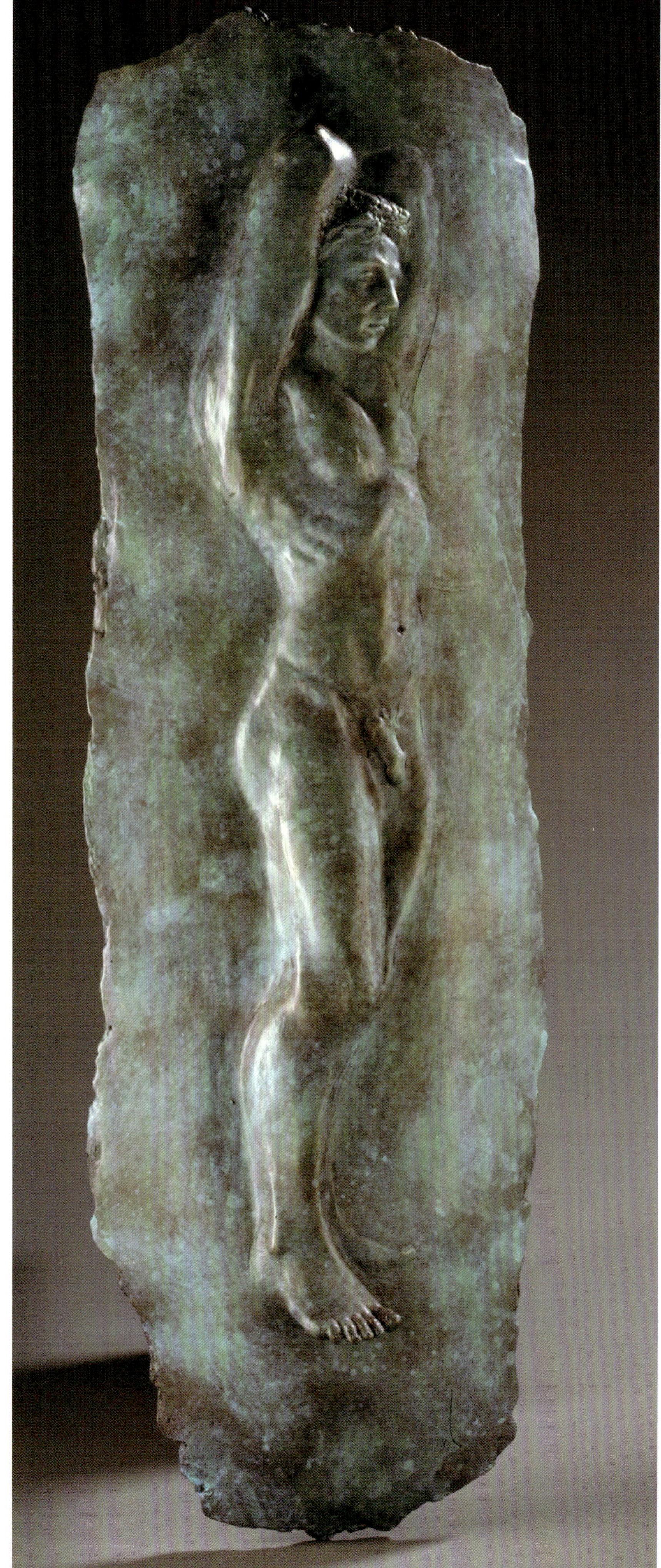

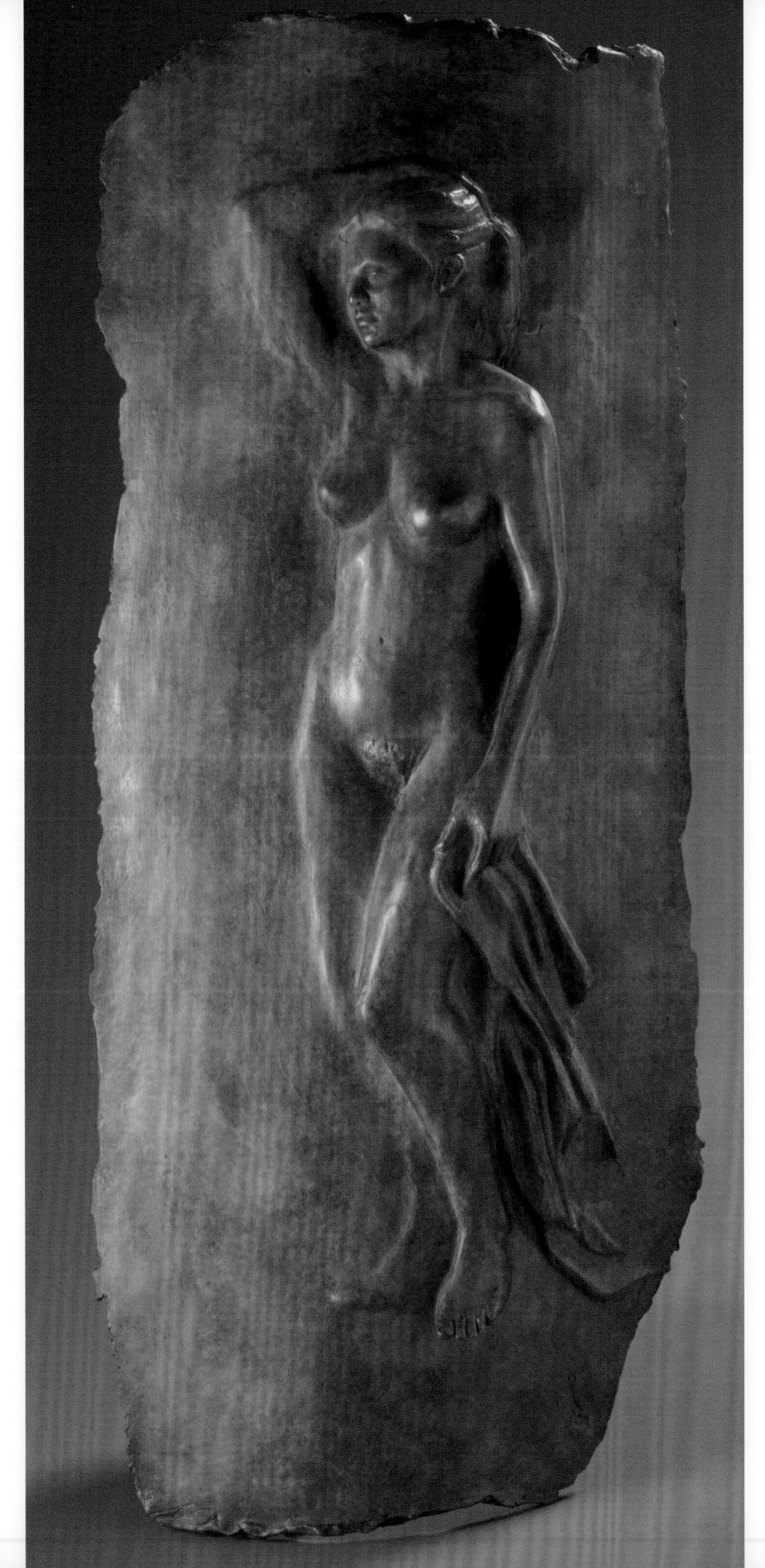

Tonight I finished the most refined sculpture I've done, a formal body.... The hair I worked out with a series of tools—masses first then lines of finer tools. I also used a lot of *colla* as I went, to arrive at the smooth surface....

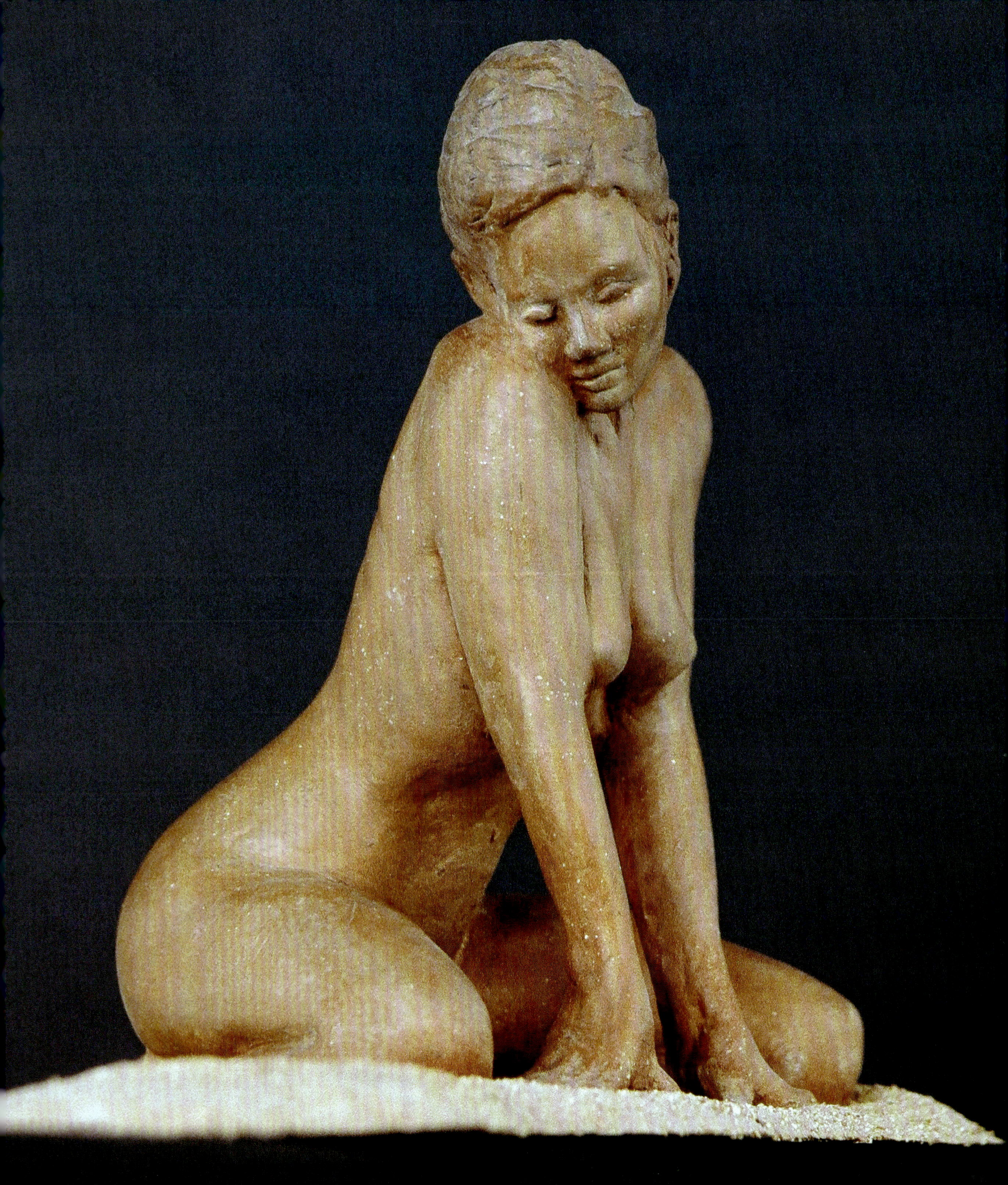

YOU ARE SO BEAUTIFUL

You are so beautiful
in the candle light,
three nights I hold you
in the fiery flame.
Your flesh caressed by hands
of shadow and soft light,
patterns of subtle rhythm pulsing
a beacon
reflective
on the shores of my embrace.
The sirens lulling melodies
whispering a panorama
in my heart to your ear
circumvented
in an aura
of love's glowing light.

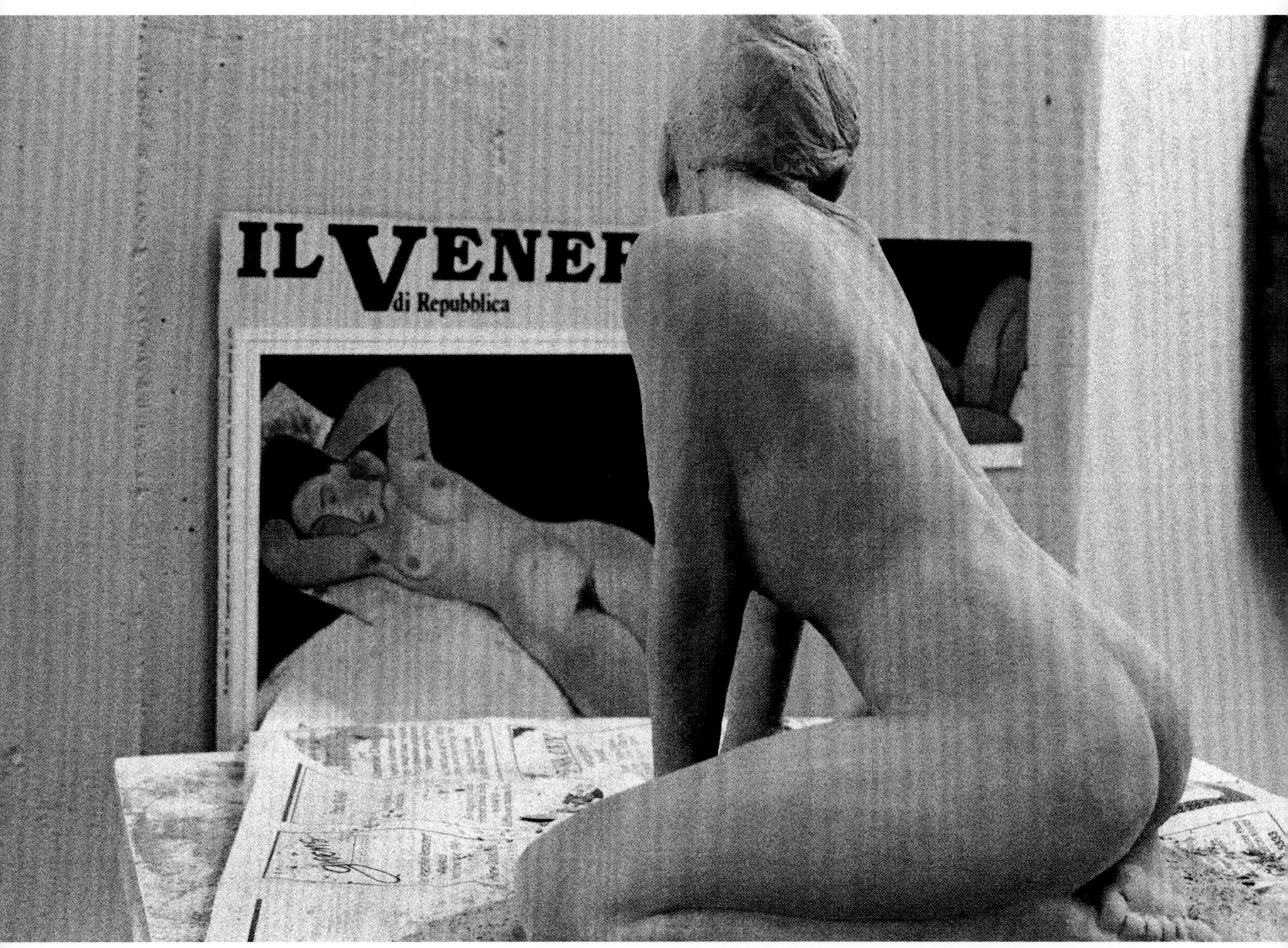
IL VENER
di Repubblica

Quite a beauty with lizard eyes and a heart of an island flower. She has a history of Rome and a thousand years and a practical wisdom and patience to withstand my turbulent sea even if she suffers from seasickness....

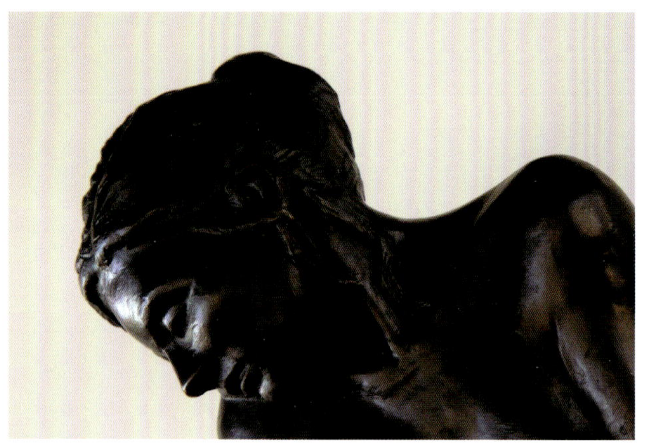

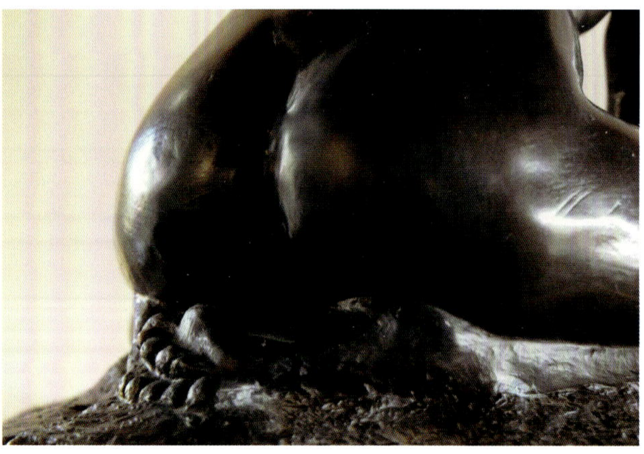

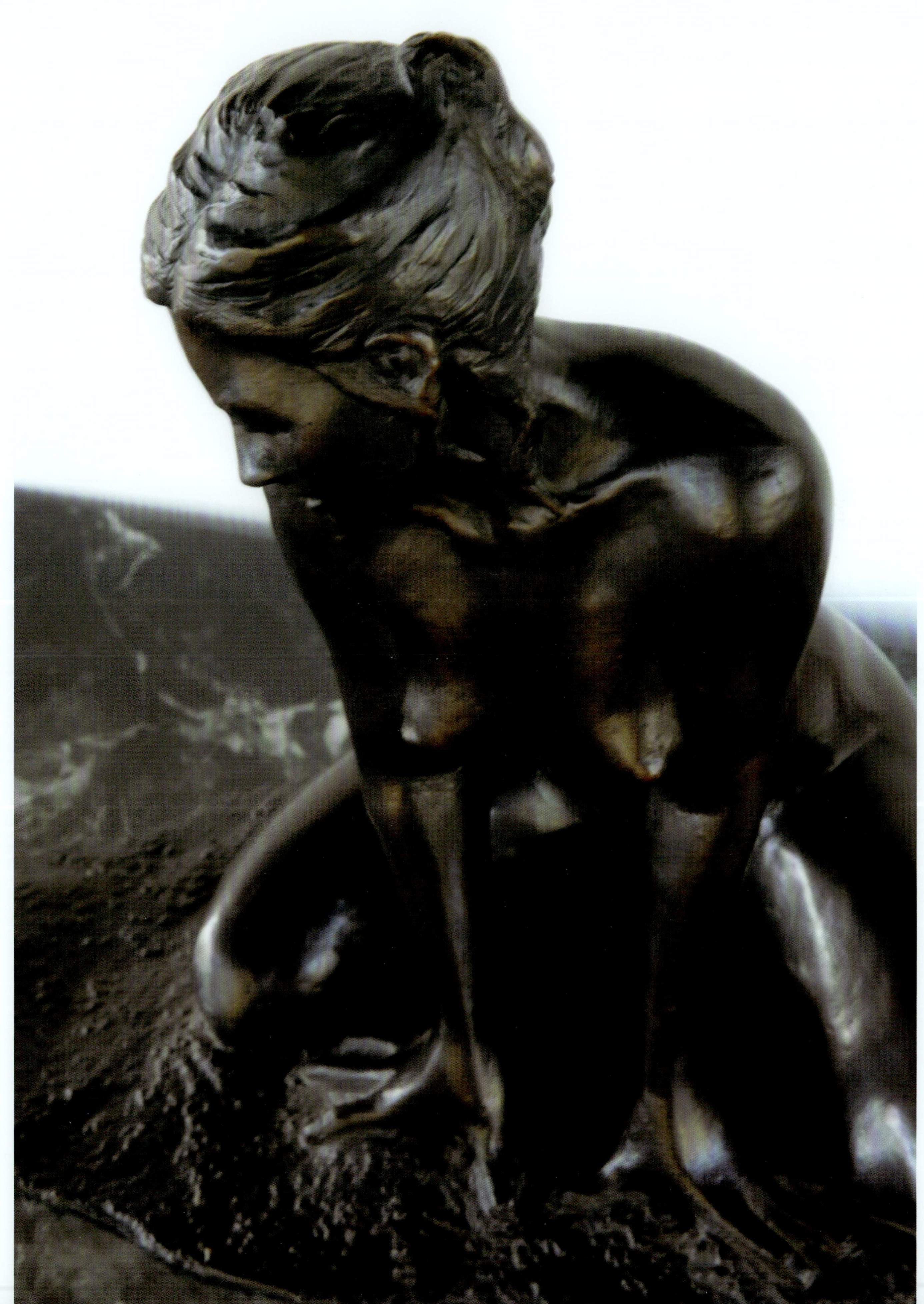

It is my belief that the sculptor's personal motive in doing a portrait … is a desire to bring life to the medium. As he draws closer and closer to a perceived likeness of his subject, the sculptor … juggles a constant three-way dialogue between his ability to see and perceive his subject; his artistic capability to render the perceived similitude; and the actual physical, psychological, emotional, and spiritual characteristics of the subject. The sculptor strives for harmony within this triangle.…

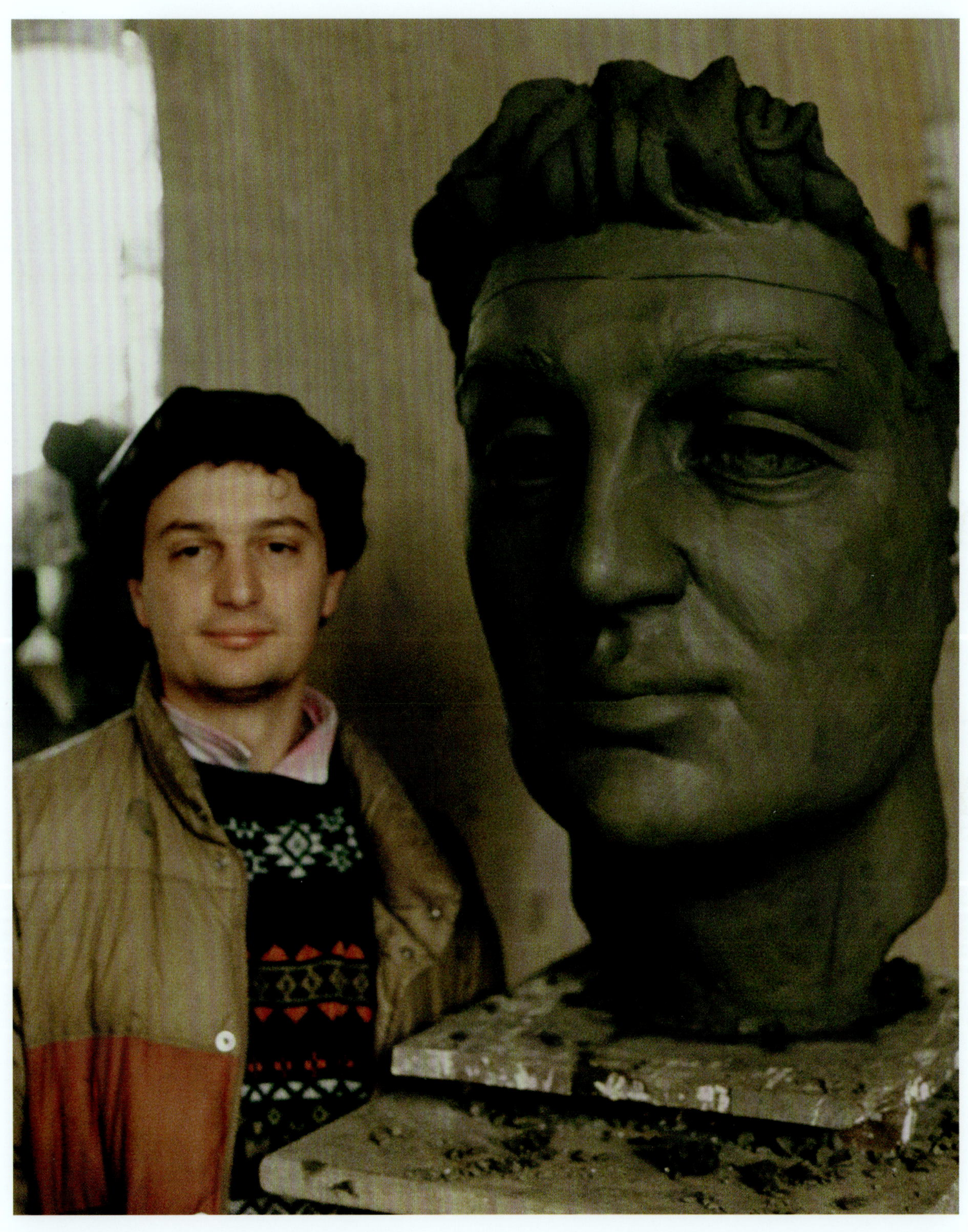

Marcello Giorgi with portrait, Pietrasanta, Italy, 1991

My work begins to take on personality
when I work on faces. They become
individual, emotional and expressive....
Portraits are ultimately what I am
interested in, and personality is
an important color to the canvas
or stroke of the chisel.

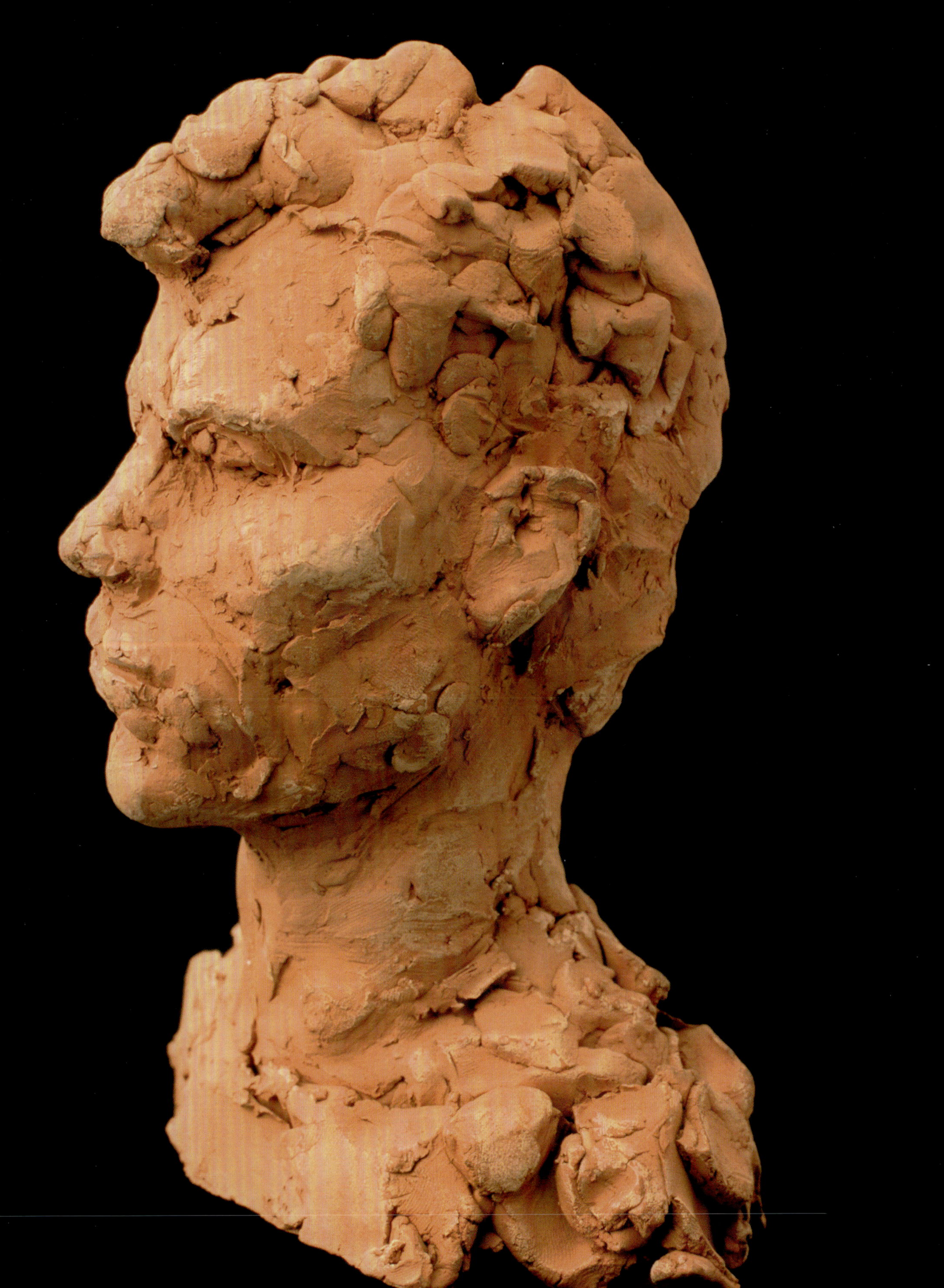

The artist must be in an isolated
mental state free of distractions so
that there is concentrated, focused
seeing.... It is this state of mind
my parents germinated within me,
to go beyond the physical, to search
for the heart and soul of humanity.

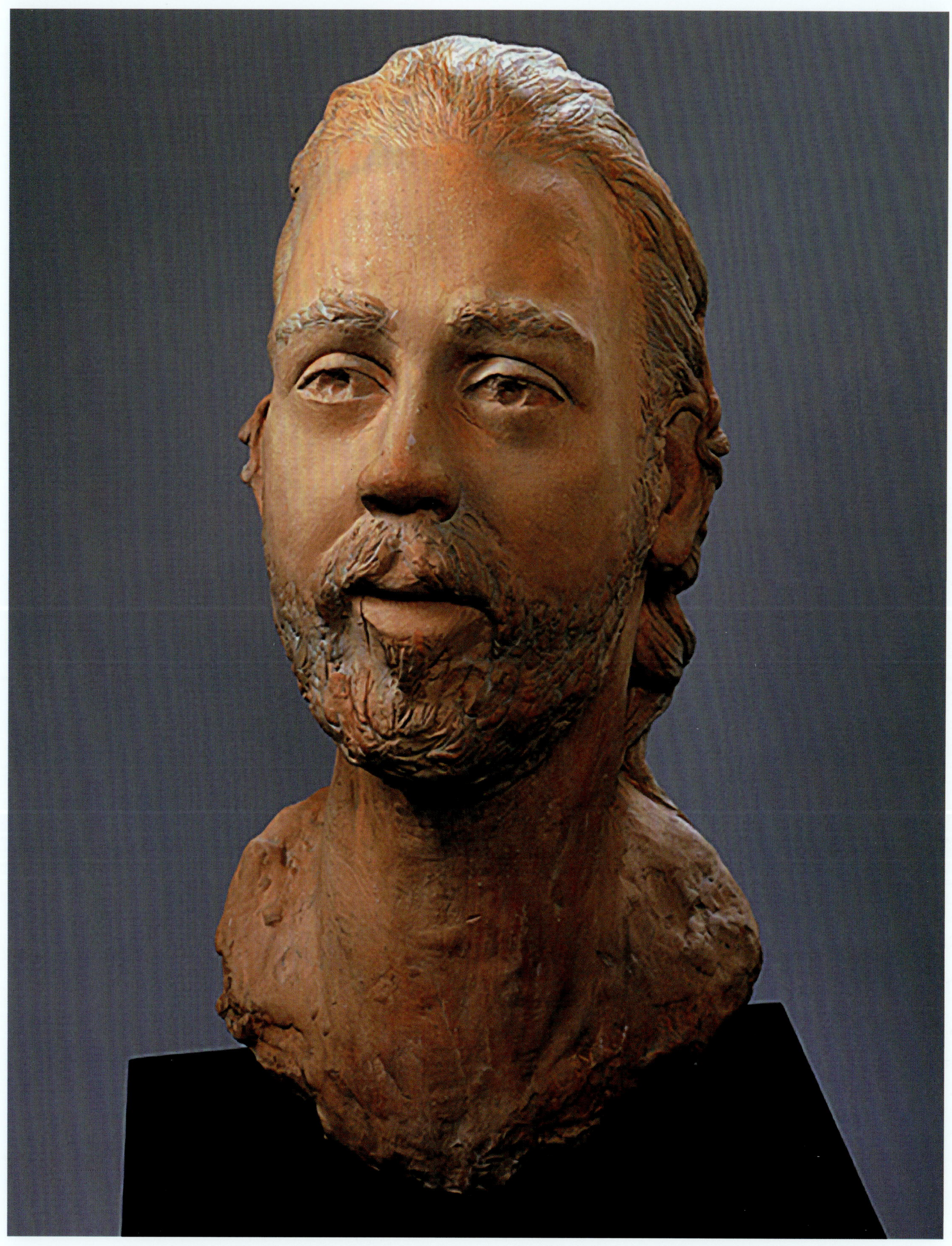

…I'm also planning to sculpt a portrait of Vicky, an English friend of Carla's. I saw her face and said that's a head for marble. So if I fix her garden, I'll have an outdoor studio and a model.

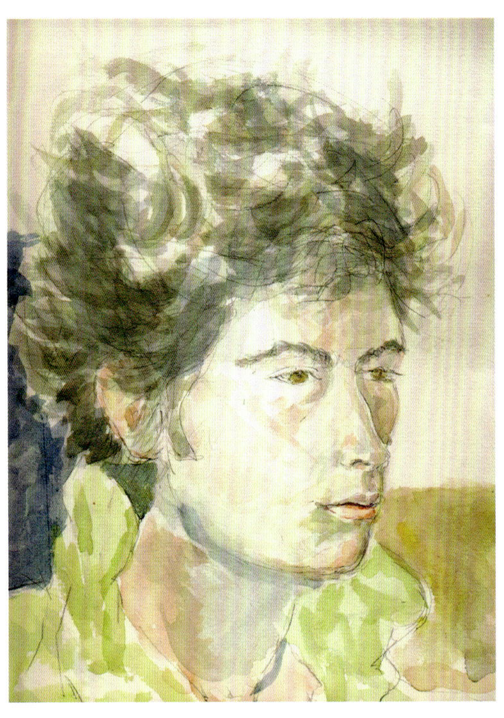

…I am carving a portrait in statuary marble using a plaster cast as a guide, watercolors and drawings from my subject, and drawings from Michelangelo's *Brutus* which I had ridden to see last week in Florence.

…The portrait of Vicky I changed from the *bozetto* because the marble said, "the head should be turned on the shoulders." It is for that reason I prefer to live with the stone a while and then make the *bozetto* to fit the marble rather than the other way around.

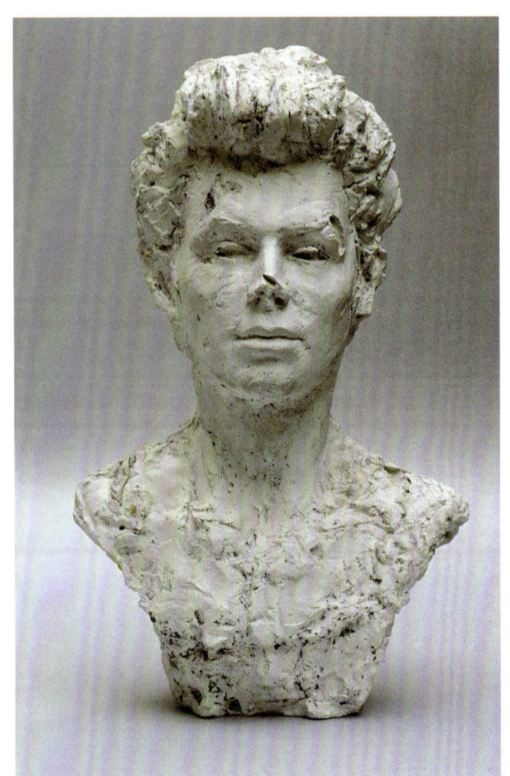

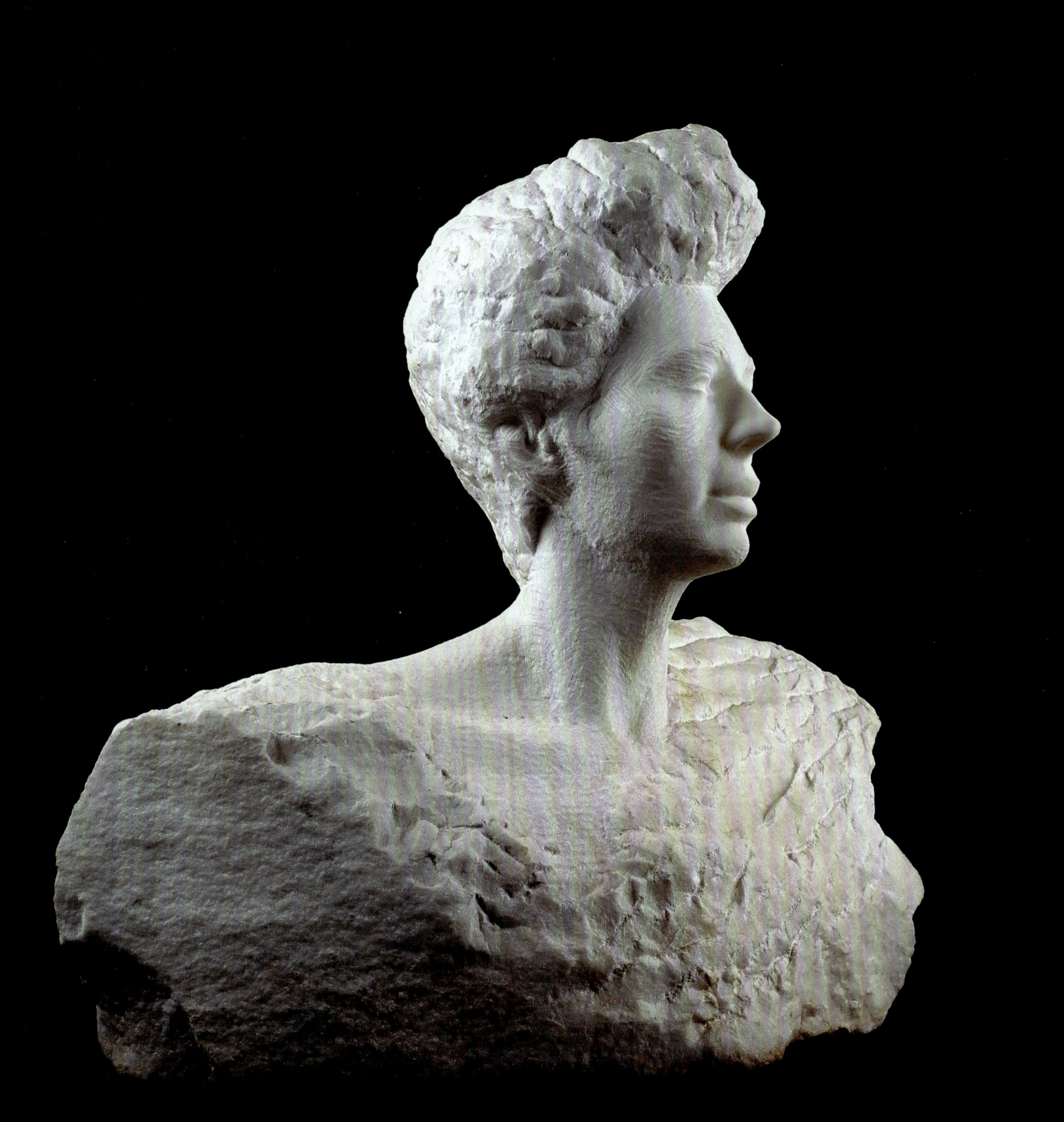

I moved to Azzano to carve her at
La Capella where I had sculpted *Il Bacio*
eight years before. I worked from memory,
the plaster cast, and from imagination,
when I reached a standstill.... For months
we had talked of her coming up to
breathe life into the stone and finish
the portrait.... She drove up the weekend
I moved to Pietrasanta and it was
a blessing.

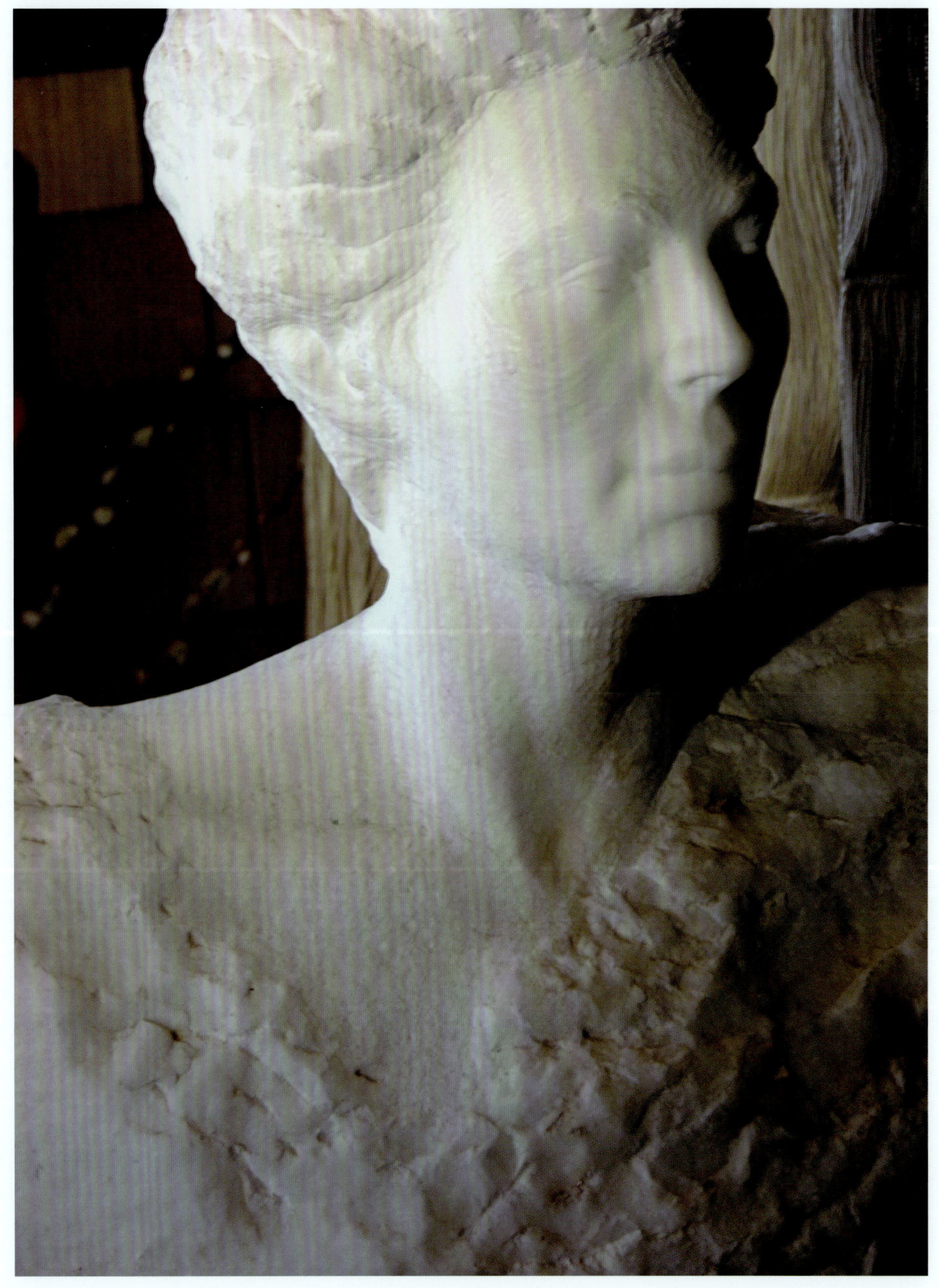

I'm back in my marble *ufficio*/home in my flat after my trips to Rome and Milano. It's good to return to my solitude of work and the warmth of good friends. Today, Freya returned from Germany with her beautiful smile (a smile to cure the world).... It's great to have her back. I cooked dinner for her and Khaled, the Egyptian, who have become my best friends.

...My neighbor Freya has returned to Germany. She was here only a week, but I "finished" her portrait in clay. She writes river letters, page after page in rapids they flow.

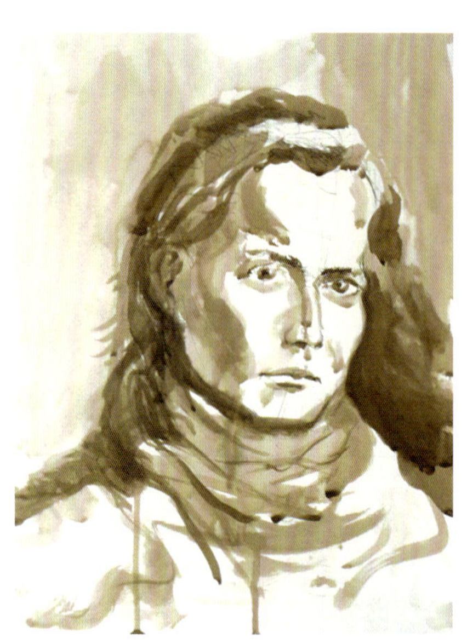

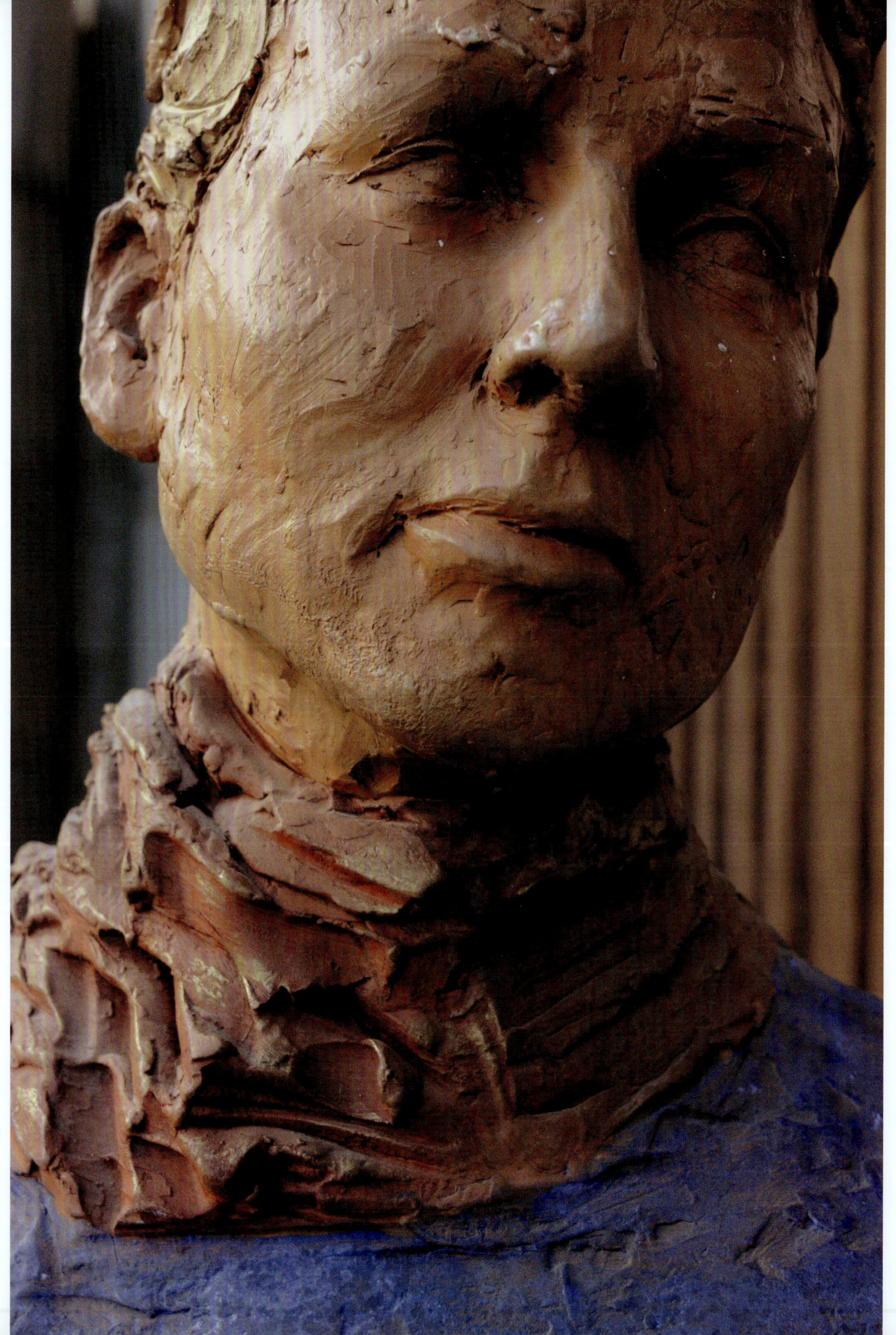

In my art I only want to work from life. There is such a difference in my work when I do so. It lives from life, but looks stiff and studied without it. But models are not easy to find.

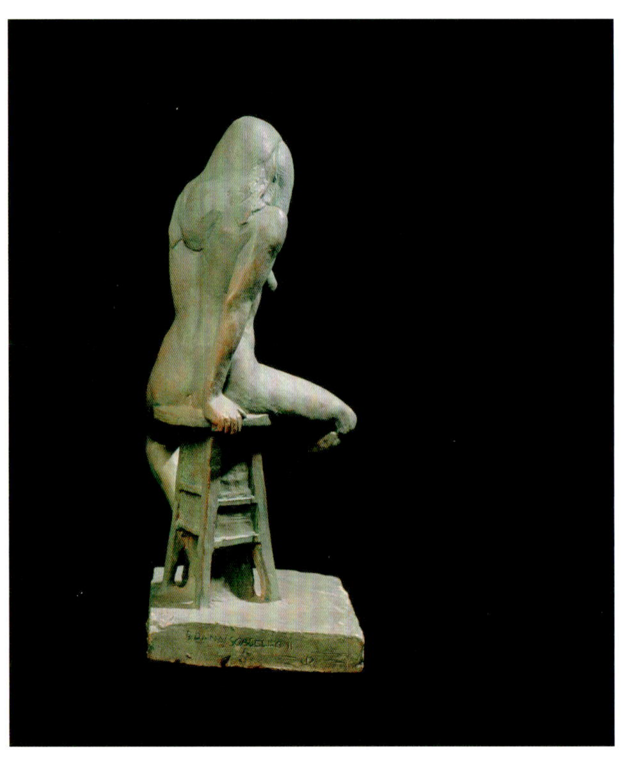

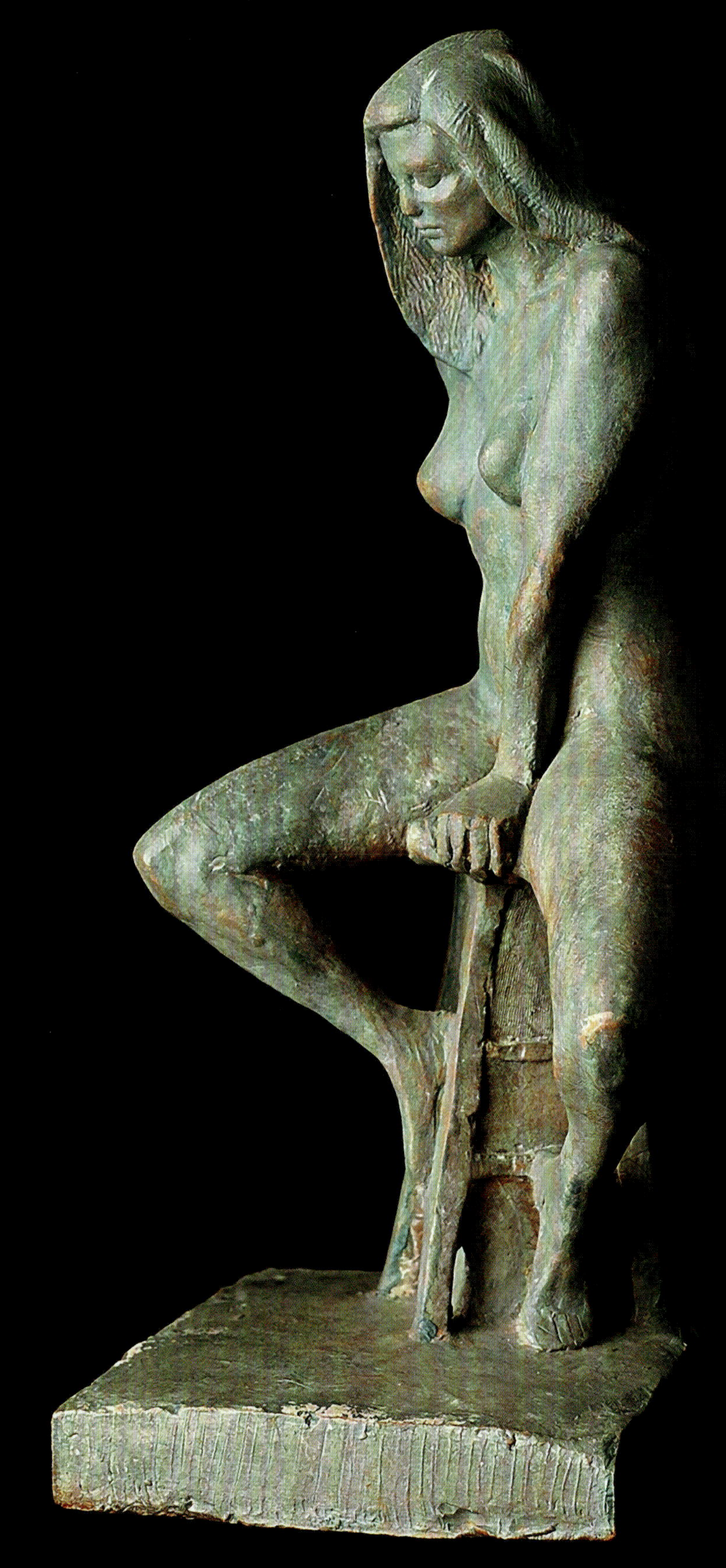

"Hi, my name is Mary. I'm the model for this work of art. Normally you would not hear from me, since traditionally the model remained anonymous (as if I played no part in the creative process), but since the advent of post-modernism and the use of text in art I've been given a voice. Since I cannot speak, I will not be able to answer any of your questions but perhaps, if you're having a pressing question, write it on my body and I'll try to answer it in the next piece. I want to write you what it is like to be a model and to pose for an artist. First of all I work for trade. I heard of this sculptor through a friend of mine. He was looking for a model, but could not afford to pay for one. I met him and agreed to work in trade for a cast of what we worked on together. Fair enough, he was kind to me, treated me with respect and not once did he try to seduce me or touch me in any way other than to understand the form. I felt comfortable. He didn't talk much, mostly worked while I slept. At first I was apologetic. I was so tired from working my other jobs, that every time I posed, I fell asleep. He didn't mind, however (in fact I think he liked it). He was just happy I didn't move. Sometimes when I woke up I would tell him my dreams. We had a friendship that was not spoken, a love that was not fulfilled. He worked hard, he was very committed. I slept through every session. That is why Jefferson the sculptor, titled this work *Donna Addormentata*, or sleeping woman in Italian. He is fluent in Italian. He says Italians understand art and know how to live. He lived in Italy for four years."

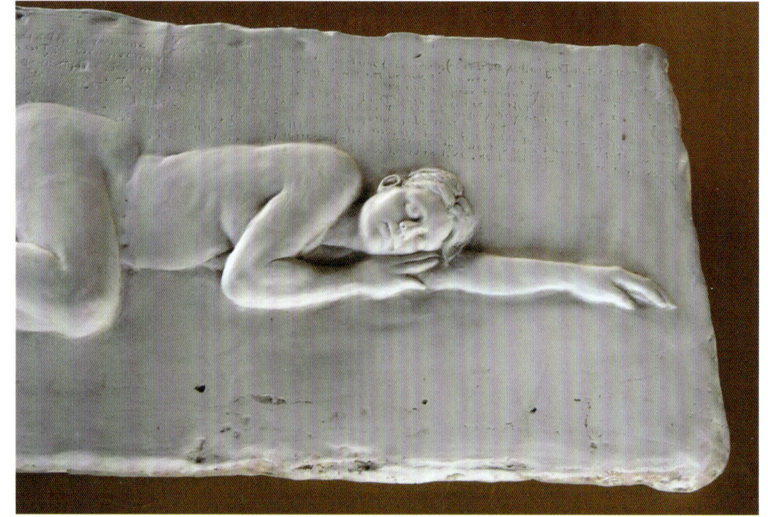

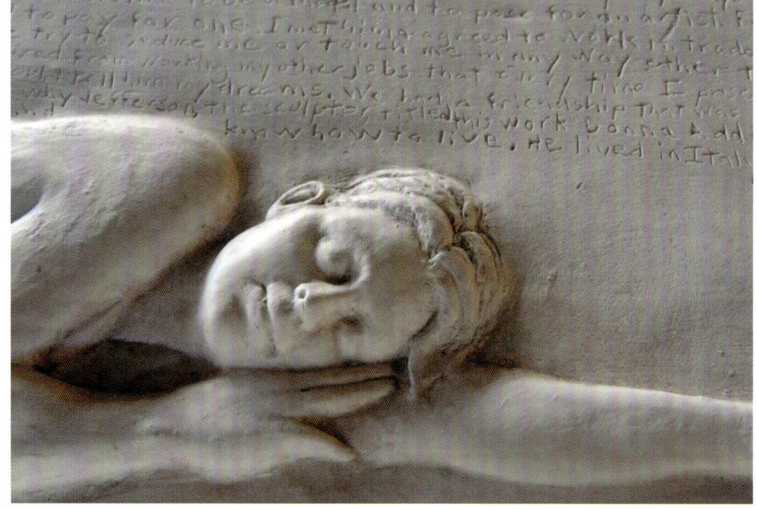

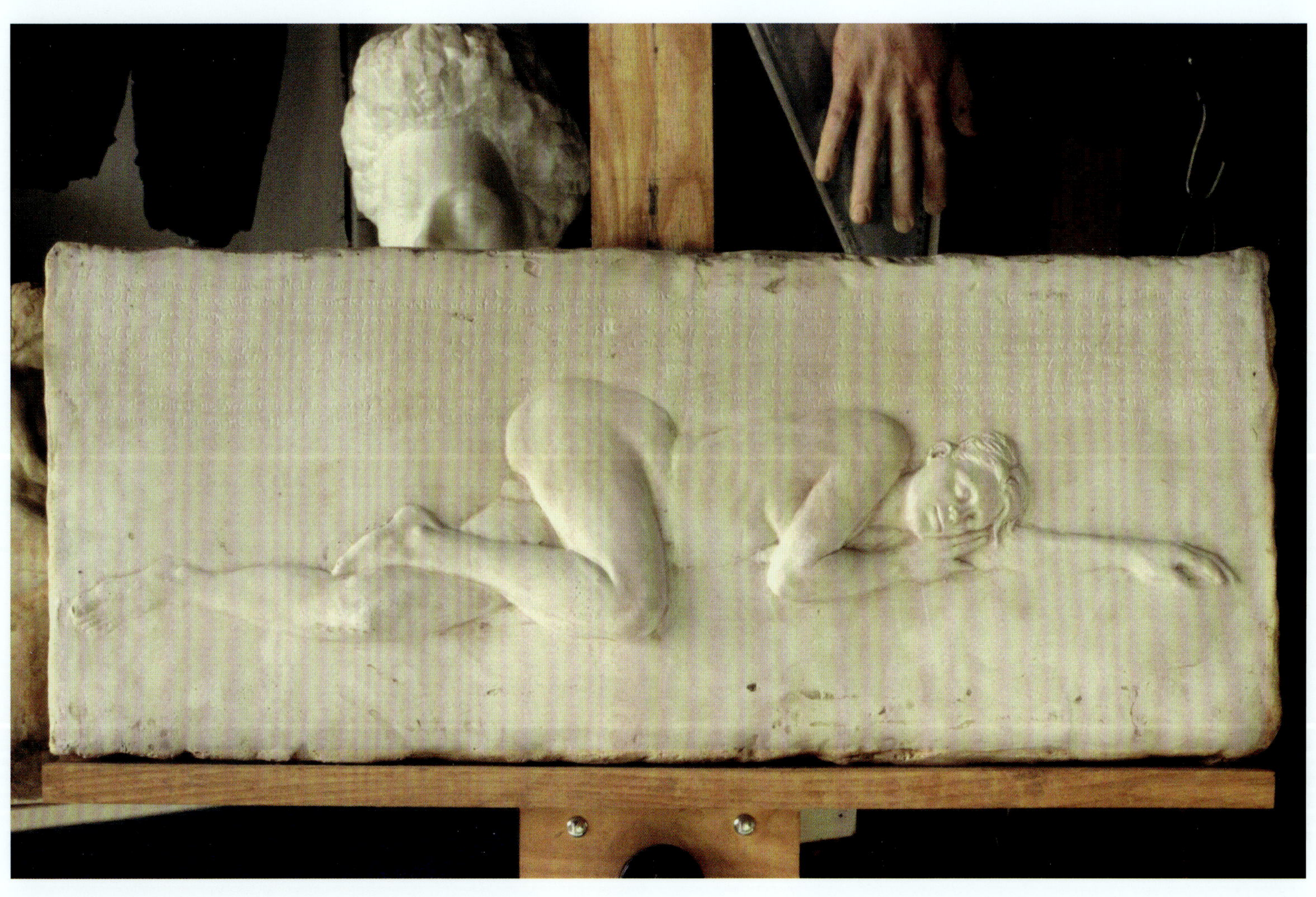

Donna Addormentata, or Mary, was a challenge of perspective, foreshortening and exaggeration. Body as landscape. Yet the head remained the most important … the peacefulness of sleep.

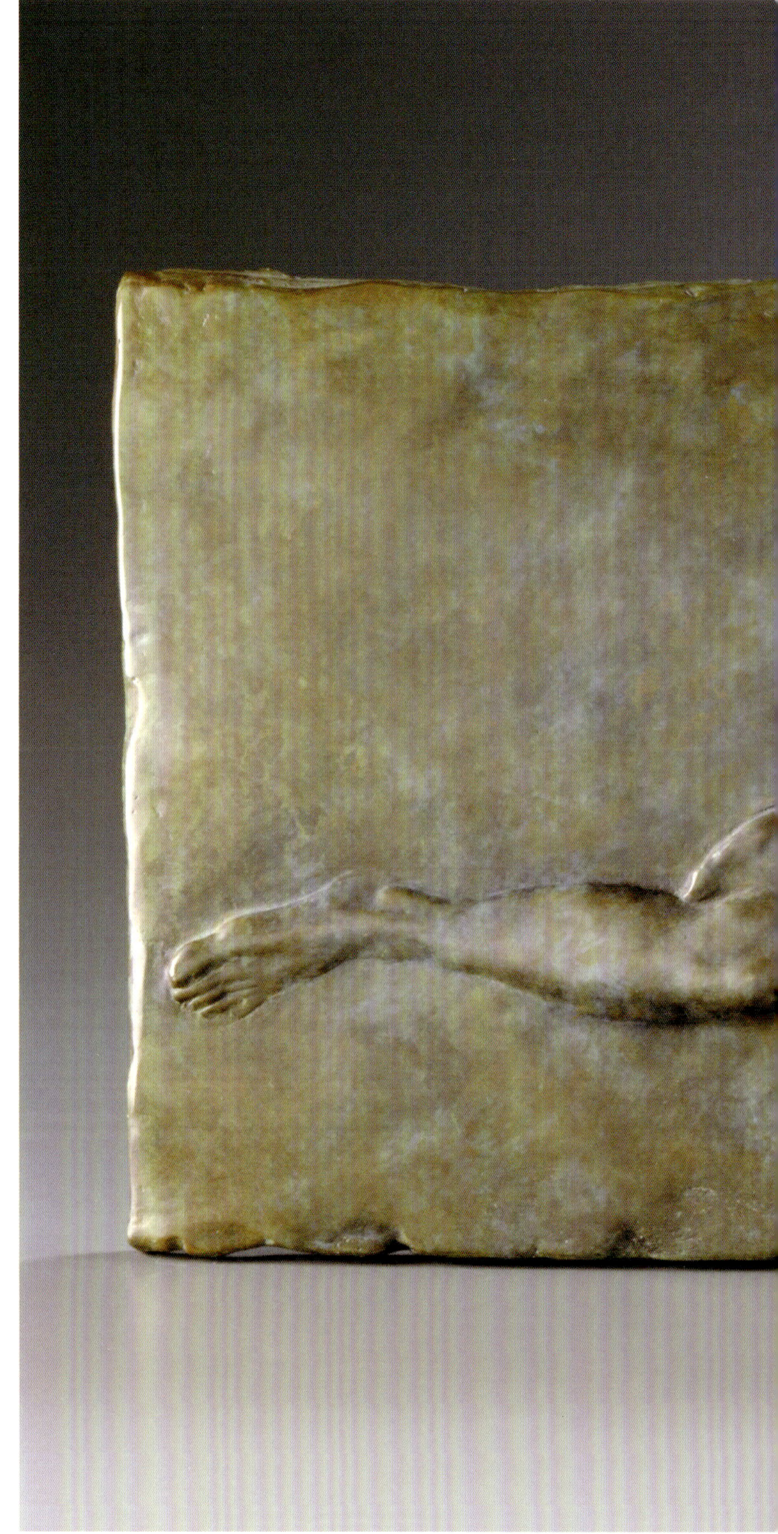

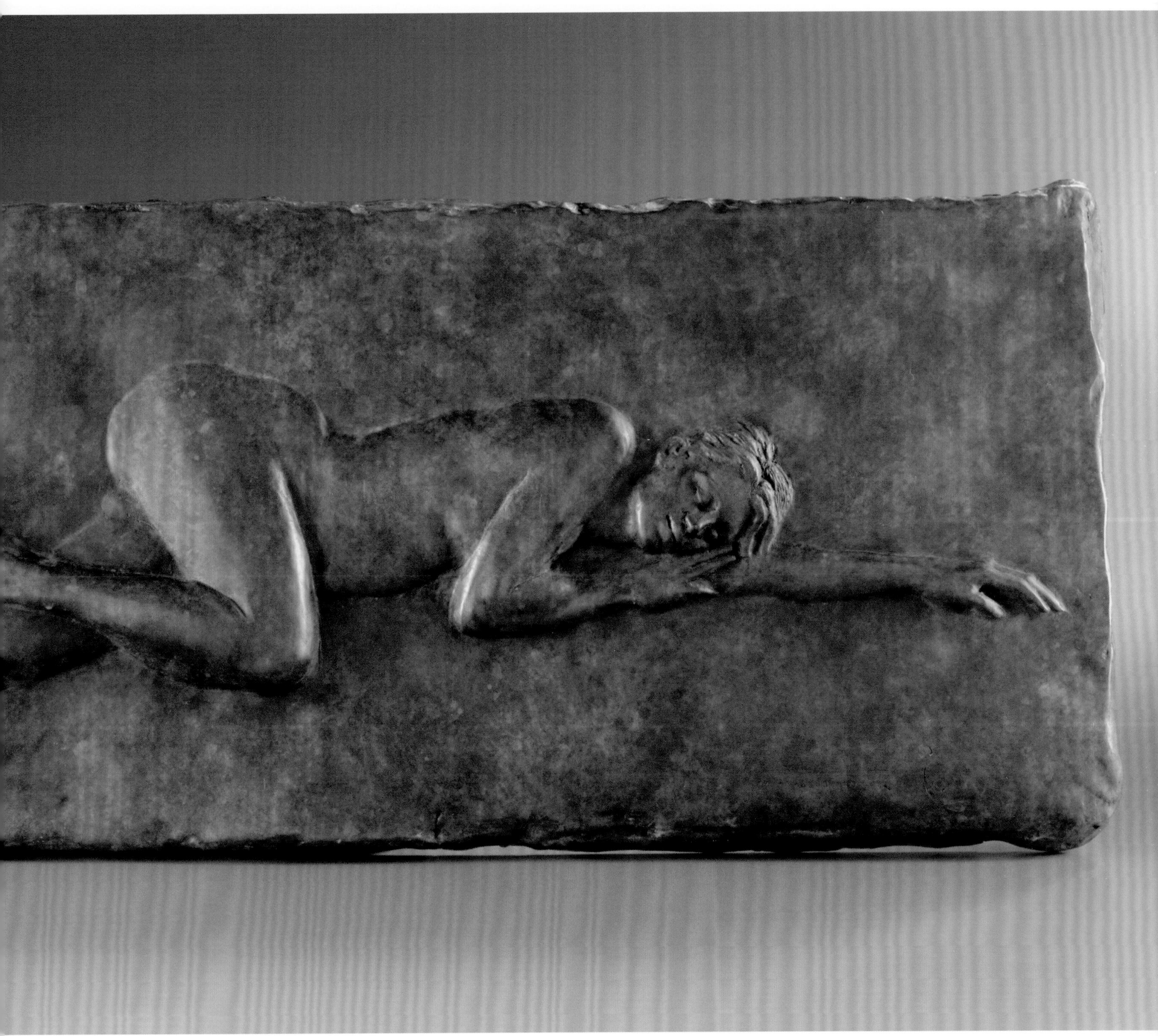

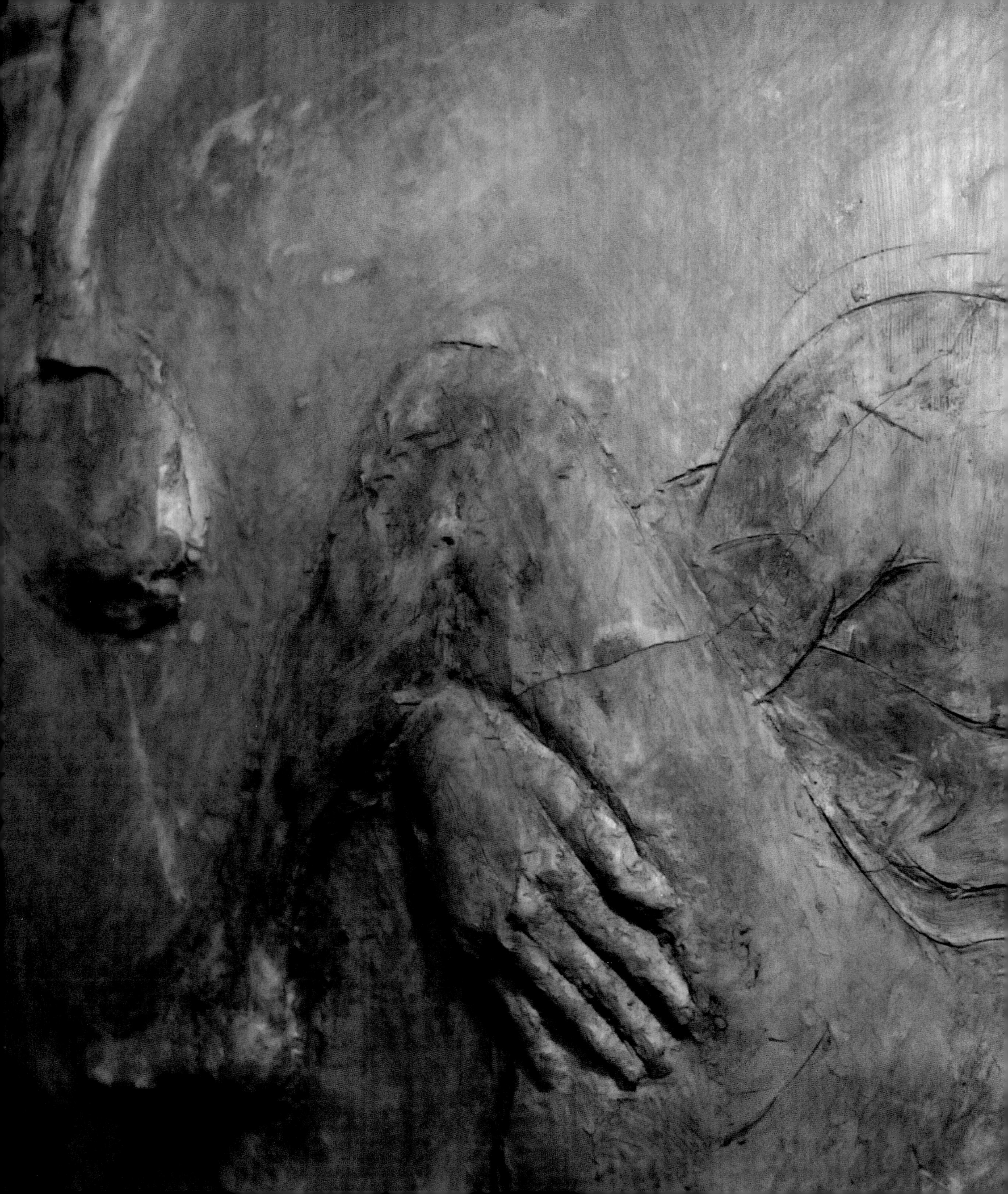

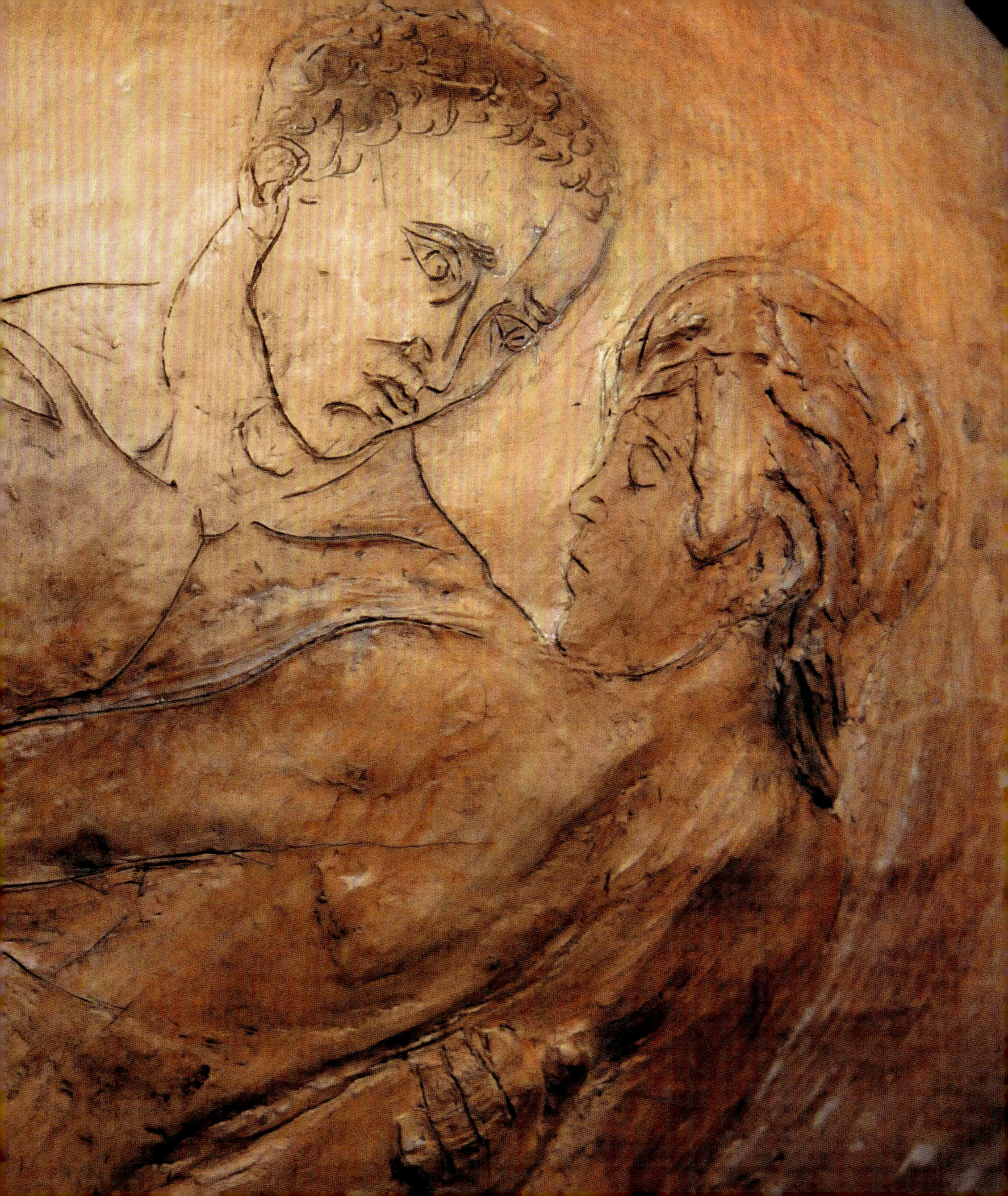

My vases further amplify my interpretation of the human condition portraying the relationships, or lack thereof, between one another and between the sexes.

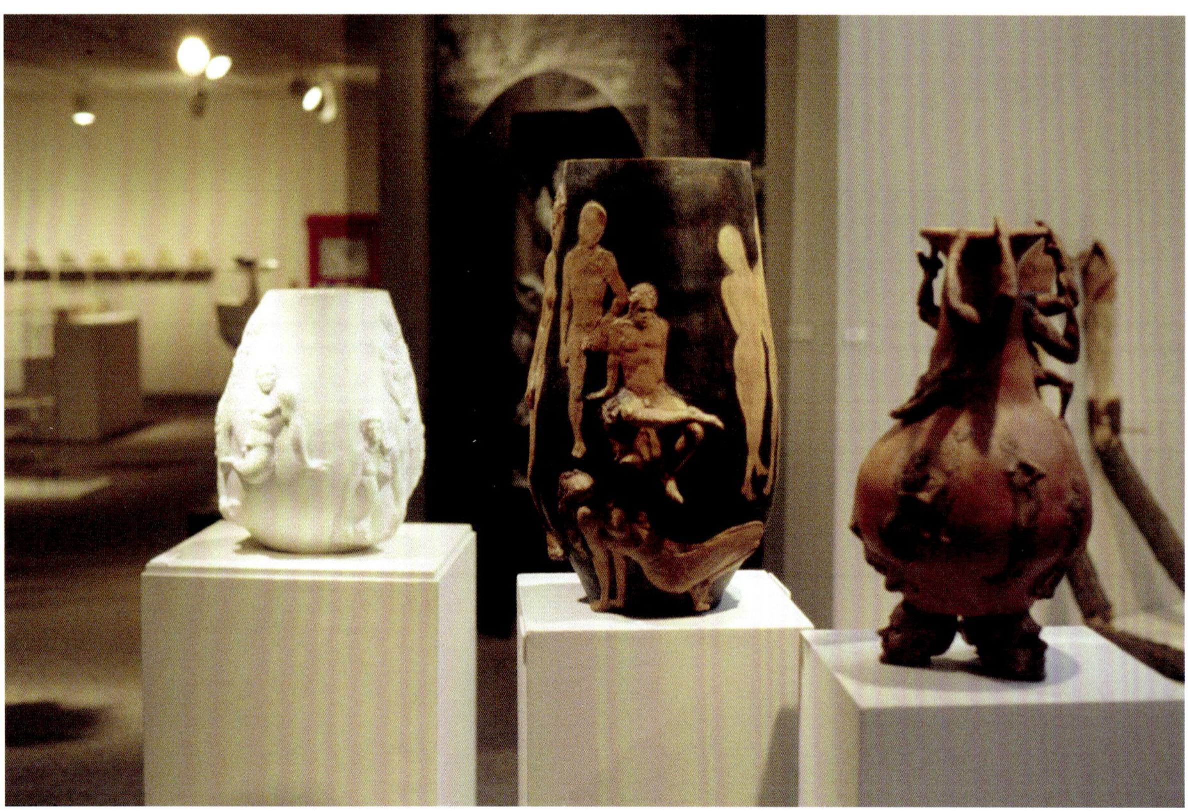

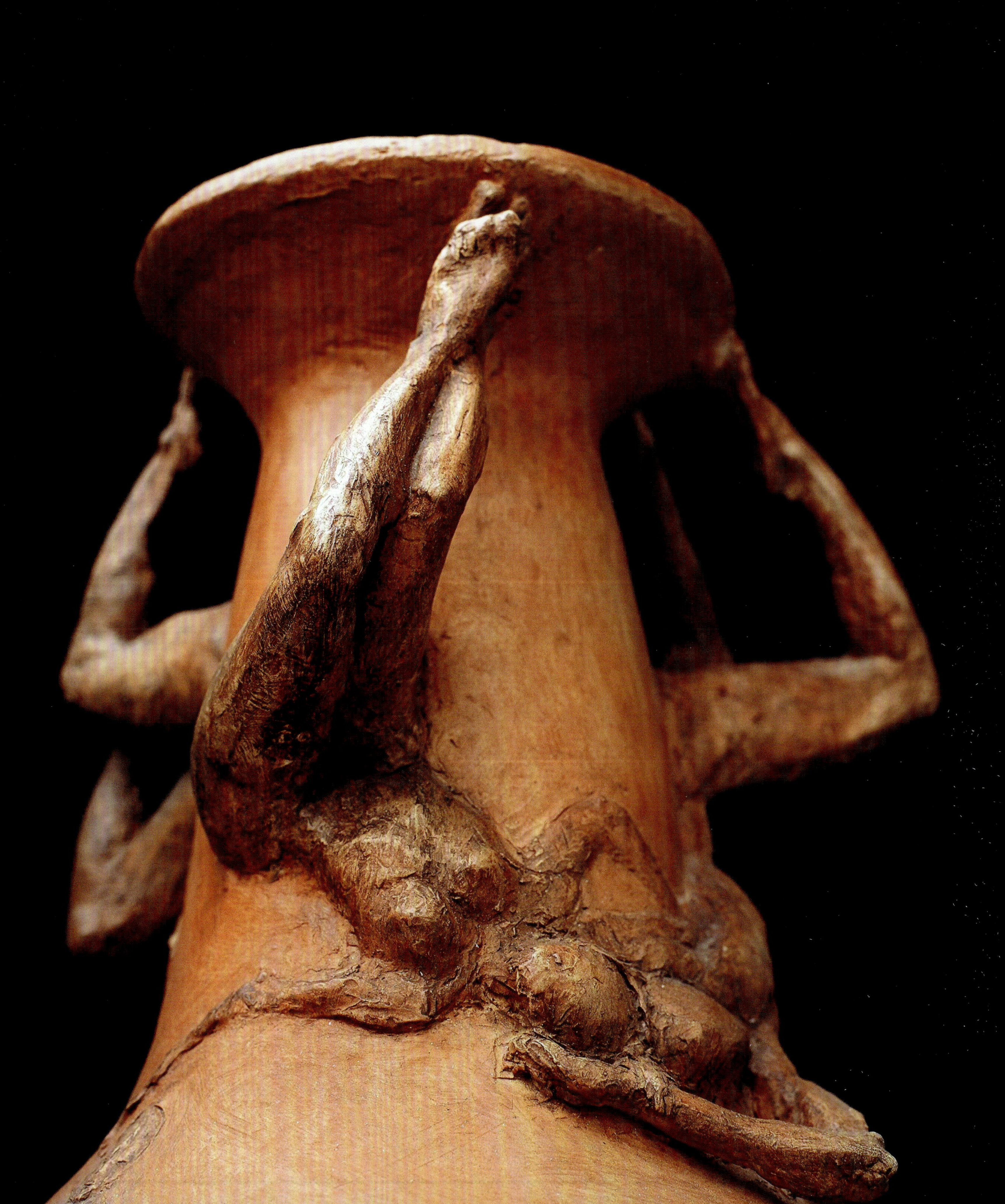

I worked all day in marble. Marble
is a great passion. It warms my heart.
It is ancient and I feel its power
and beauty, deep.... I love hammer and
chisel rhythm. It is how I work best,
how I feel and why the muses can be
heard when they sing softly in the shallow
light.... There are few who embrace
or caress marble as if it were warm
flesh, and there are few who breathe life
into its crystals or move the immovable.
Therein alone lies my challenge, my true
mission. To bring life to any material
I touch, but to follow the material
and expression that move my heartbeat
to race.

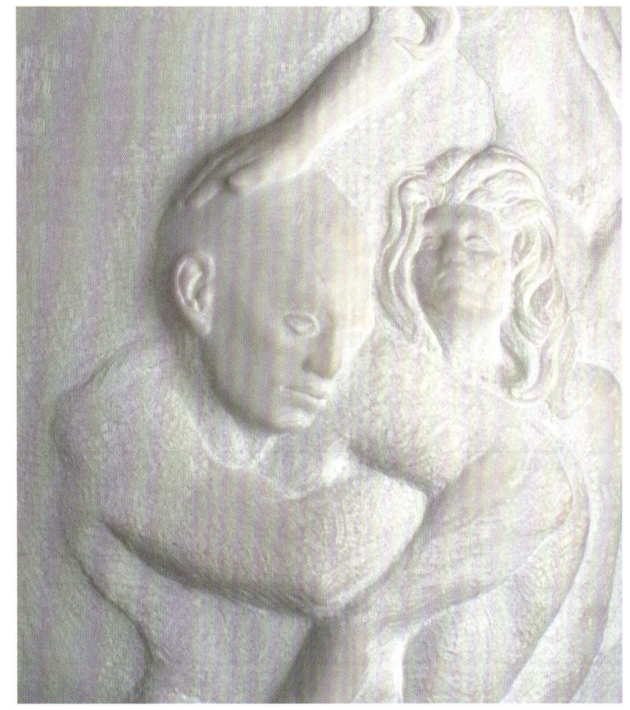

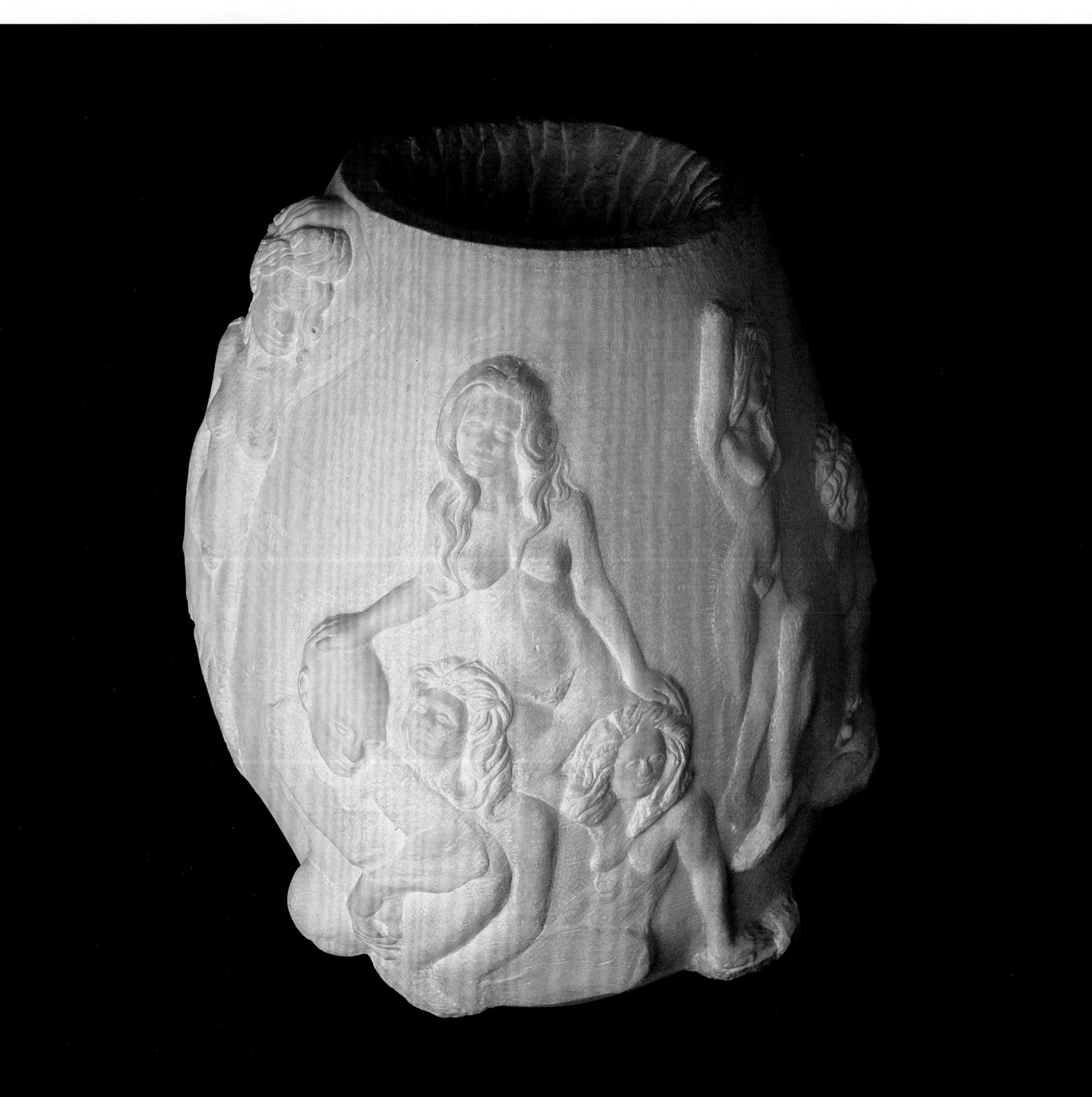

Work at the studio went well. I began to soften the stone ... today things were clicking, as if the muses decided to beautifully emerge themselves. It's moments like this you will suffer countlessly for and what makes it all worthwhile.

Time does not matter; time is eternal in these moments. Working with clear mind, confidence and pure beauty. These moments are rare. Mortal, though I work with the immortal...

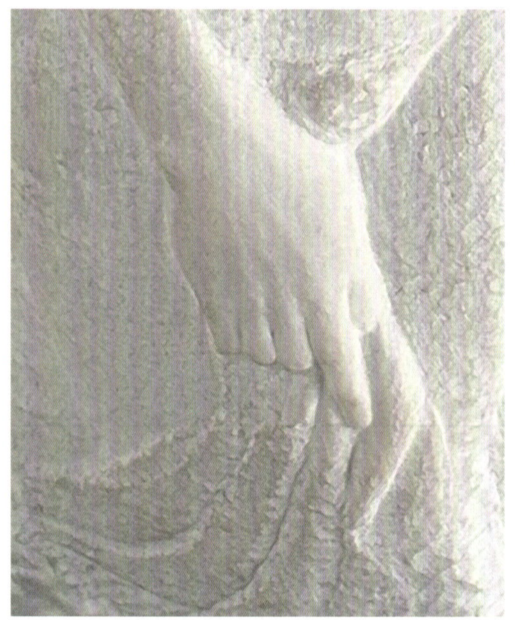

...Worked more on poet and muses. Began working in very low relief on poet, going for "negative space" between eye and nose and at nostrils.

...Changed shape of bottom to make it "float." Worked more on shape of entire vase. ...Began to use rasp on the vase. I used it to clean the surface, to *graffiare*, but I also found it works like *colla* in cleaning and clearing the form and my thoughts.

...Worked on hand of standing muse and face and head of Opera. Moved her hair back ... and dropped curls on the neck. I should have put them in earlier, but they clarify problematic areas.

...I enjoy the free carving, the challenge and the wait, that can be difficult at times, for the figures to instruct me.

...I work best at twilight. Perhaps the muses sing the clearest in this light....

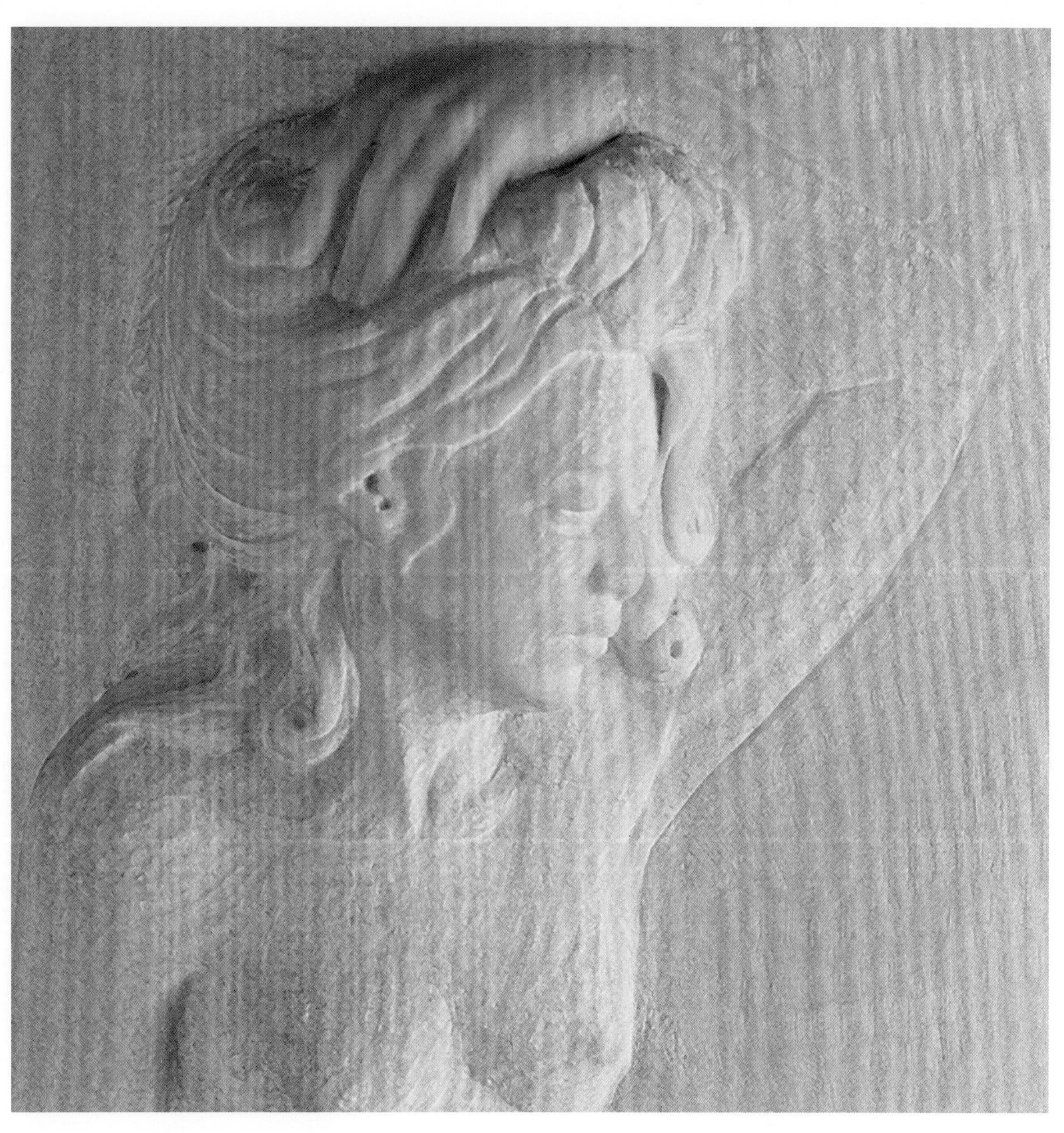

COLOR OF DUNE

Color of dune,
sand,
dried sea water grass
wind blown
Siena earth
in an olive grove
sifting, beneath my palm.
Texture-pressure
the soft petal folds
in the morning rays green house.
and moon lit
obsession
of dew drops forming
in the scent of
tinged
anticipation.

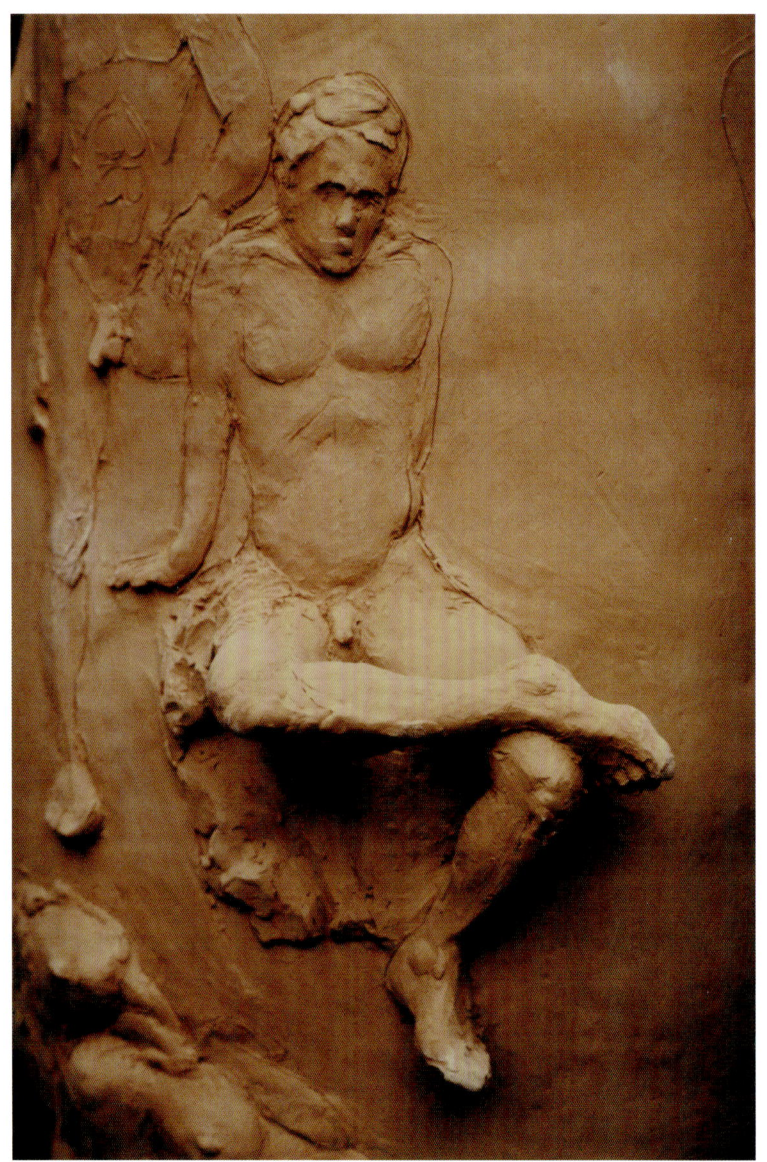

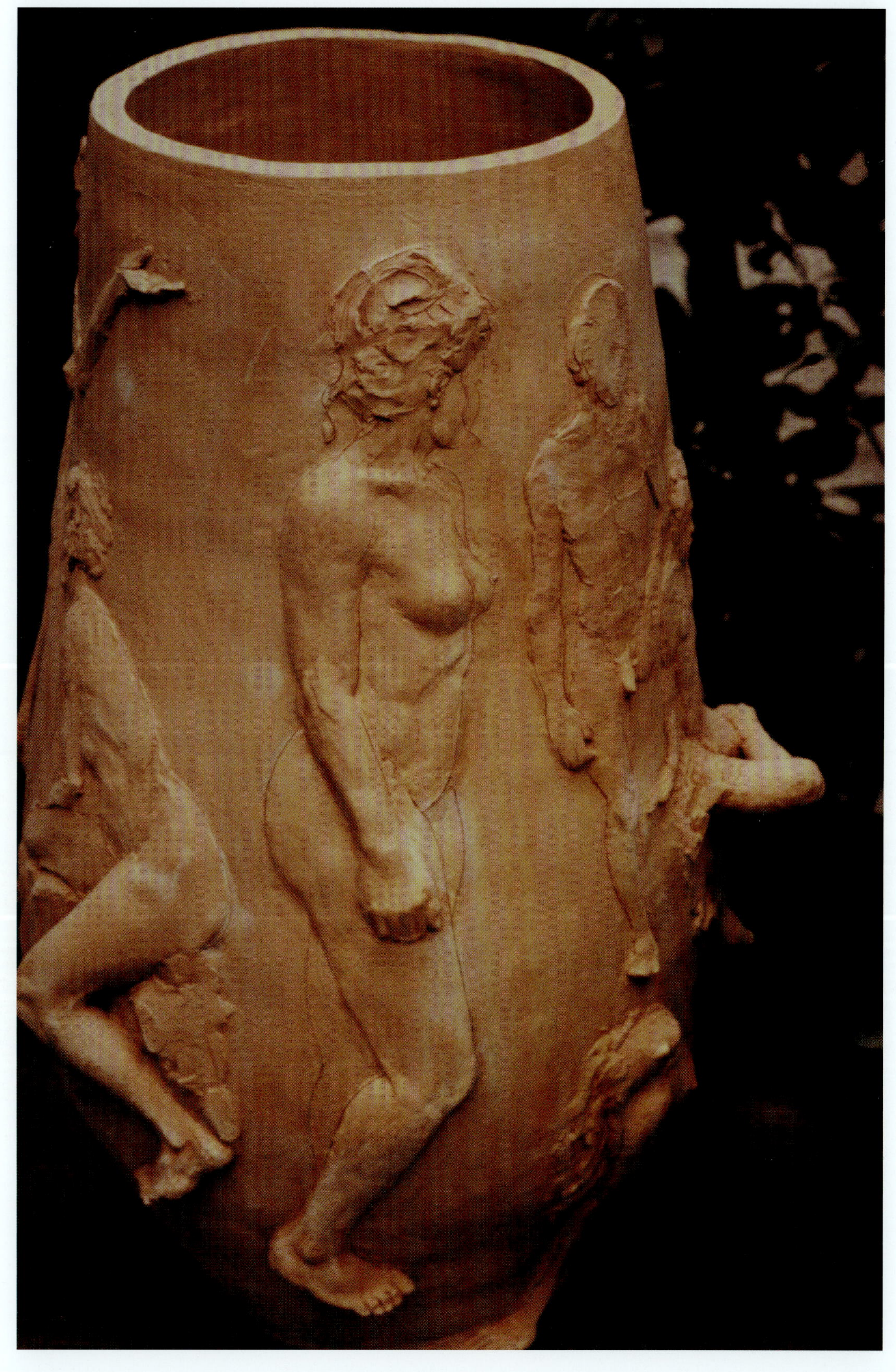

SCULPTED VASE IV

Worked with Musci for vase. I did drawings and watercolors of other poses as well. It's good to work with her, work with her beautiful body that is so sensuous that I can feel crippled in front of her at work. She is never more beautiful than as a model. I told her that and she was shocked and asked: "When I'm naked in front of you making love, isn't that when I'm the most beautiful?" It's different but I would say as a model you are the most beautiful because art has a way of increasing the beauty of that or who you are working with tenfold. It is the forever challenge of life to seek the harmony between the work and nature. Nature being the true artist, the true work that only the artist sees in his nature is always elusive, forever expounding, fluid as a stream. The artist turns round and round caught in an eddy, dizzy, trying to move into mainstream and ride the crest of the wave, which is the union of art and nature. These moments are few; there are always strong undertows and many whirlpools.

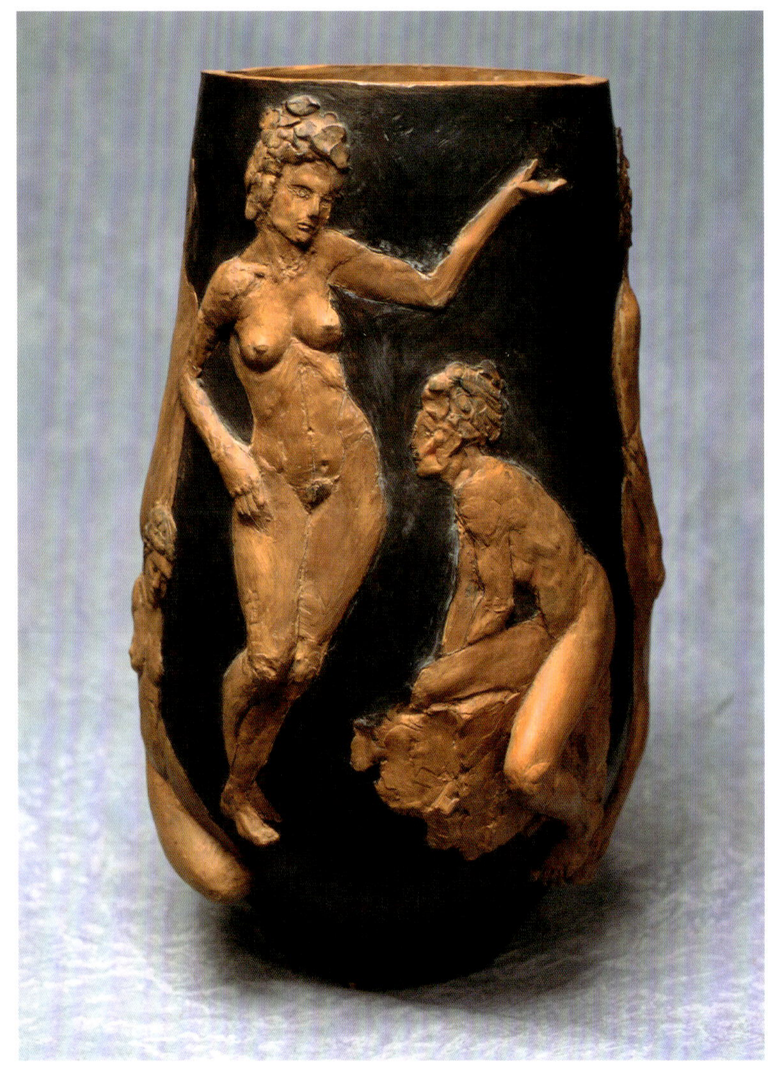

SCULPTED VASE IV

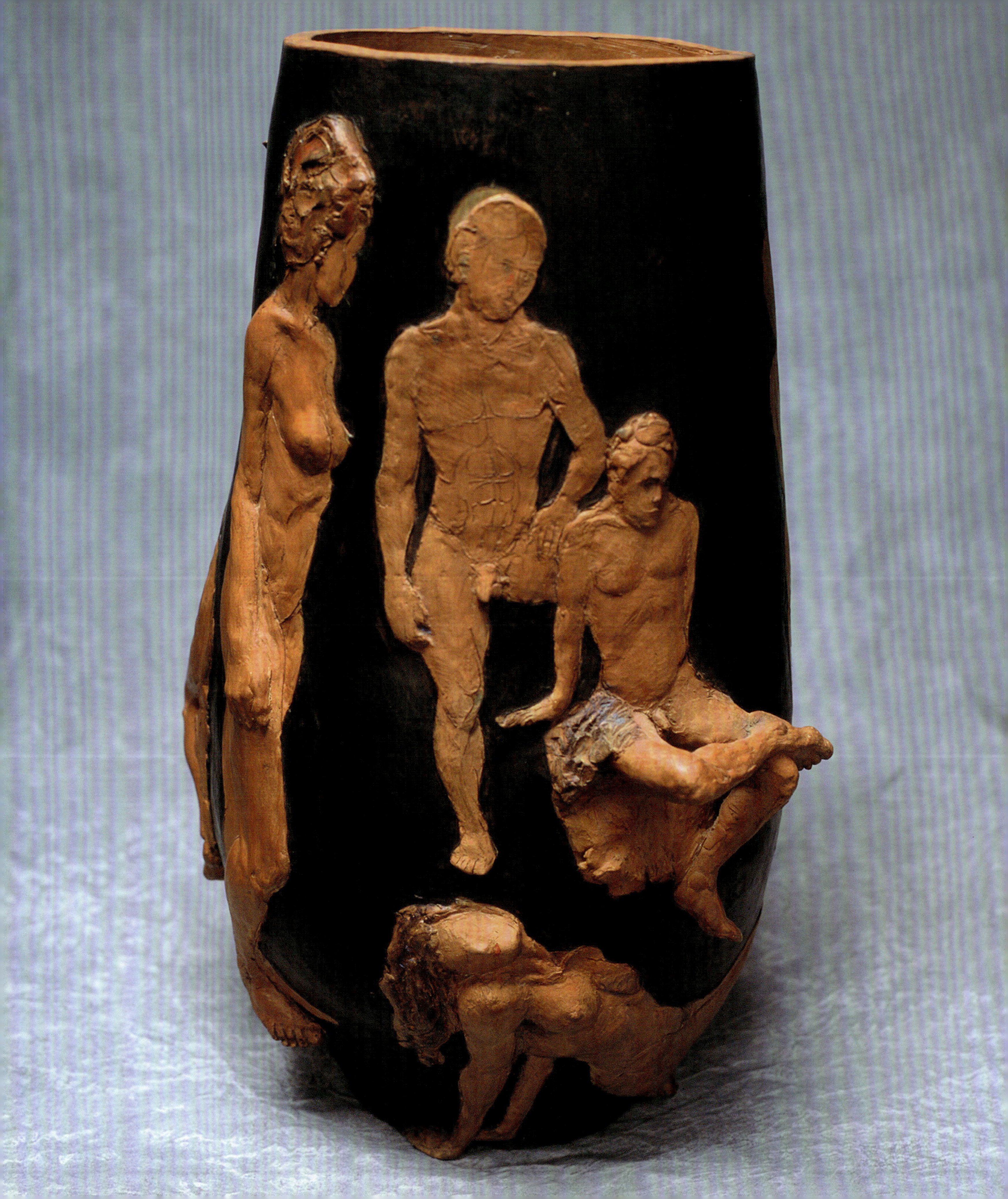

My work tends to get larger & more complex.
My first vase: *Sculpted Vase I* took one week longer than anticipated.

It has 15 figures in *basso-rilievo*, three falling: 2 intertwined/united & supported by three grotesque heads/carytids, & is 54 cm. high.

Sculpted Vase II has 24 figures, five falling: 4 intertwined/united & supported by four grotesque heads/carytids, & is 70 cm. high.

I believe the human form is always contemporary and just as significant today as the moment of its creation. The society and context change but the figure exists in its own spiritual realm in a soulful suspension of humanity's great potential and accomplishments.

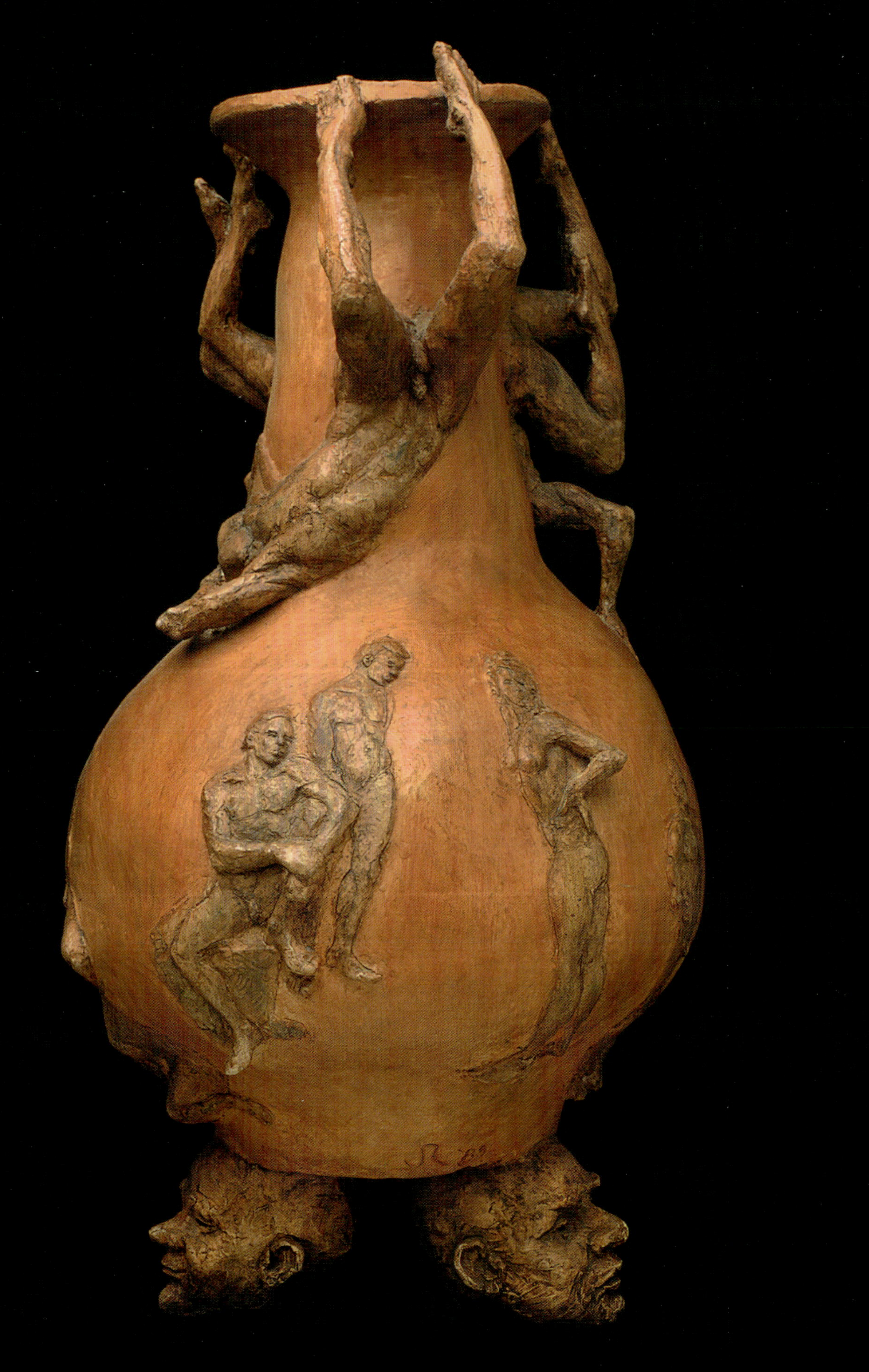

Art does not progress in a linear mode. This explains the revisiting of the classical form and the representational figure during artistic movements. Certainly, the classical artist's center embraces tradition. However, it is this artist's intent not to be bound, as an epigone, but to use history as a springboard for contemporary expression.

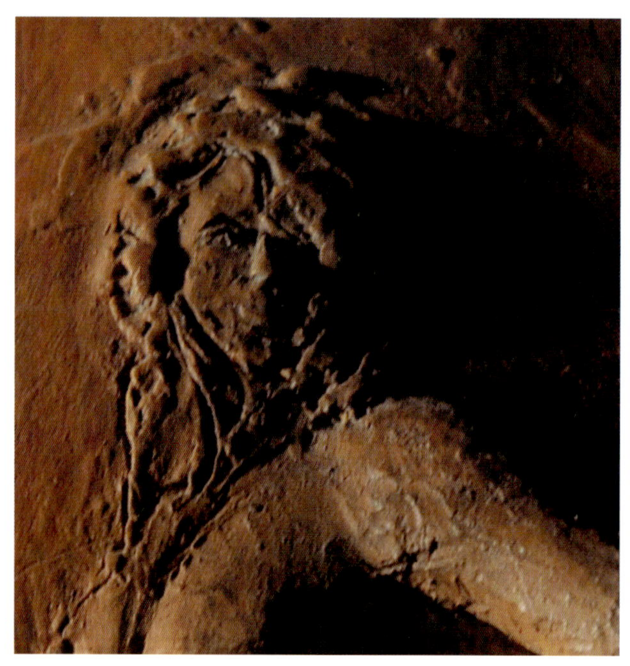

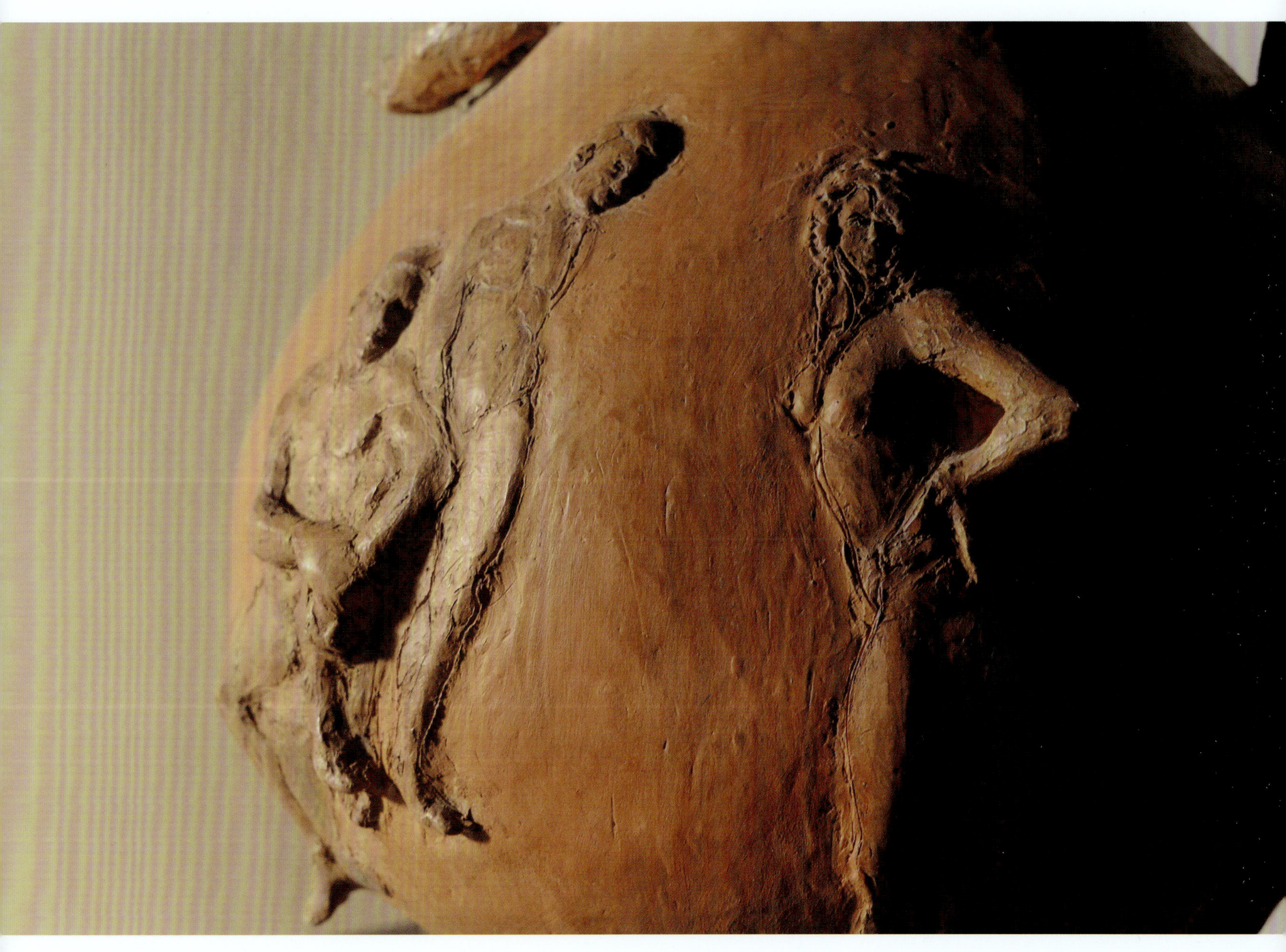

SCULPTED VASE II, DETAIL

I believe in working several sculptures at once. It keeps the mind fresh, or lets time resolve formal problems, but it can also be an excuse.

Right now, for instance, I am working on six sculptures and I have ideas for others. Six is too many, so I'm working on three, and three are abandoned in the middle. Then I get new ideas and want to work on them ... and further abandon.... It's good to go back and forth and move everything on further, as one sculpture feeds the next. On one hand, this method eliminates the post-unveiling blues, but there is not the satisfaction of a completed piece either.

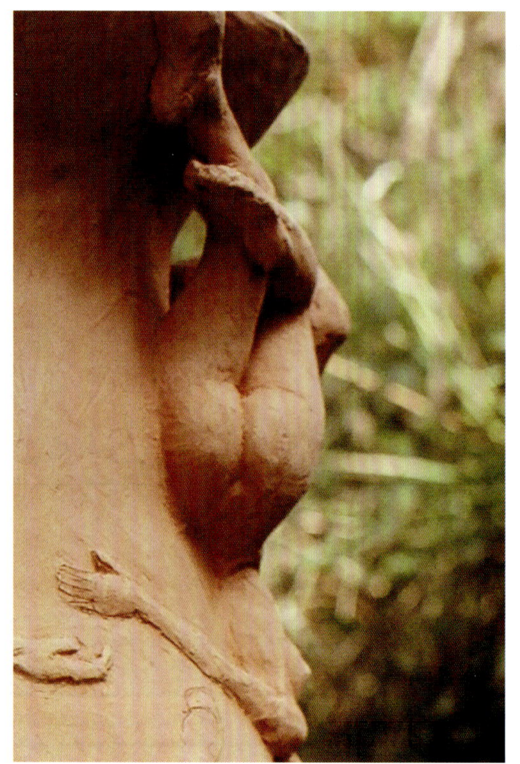

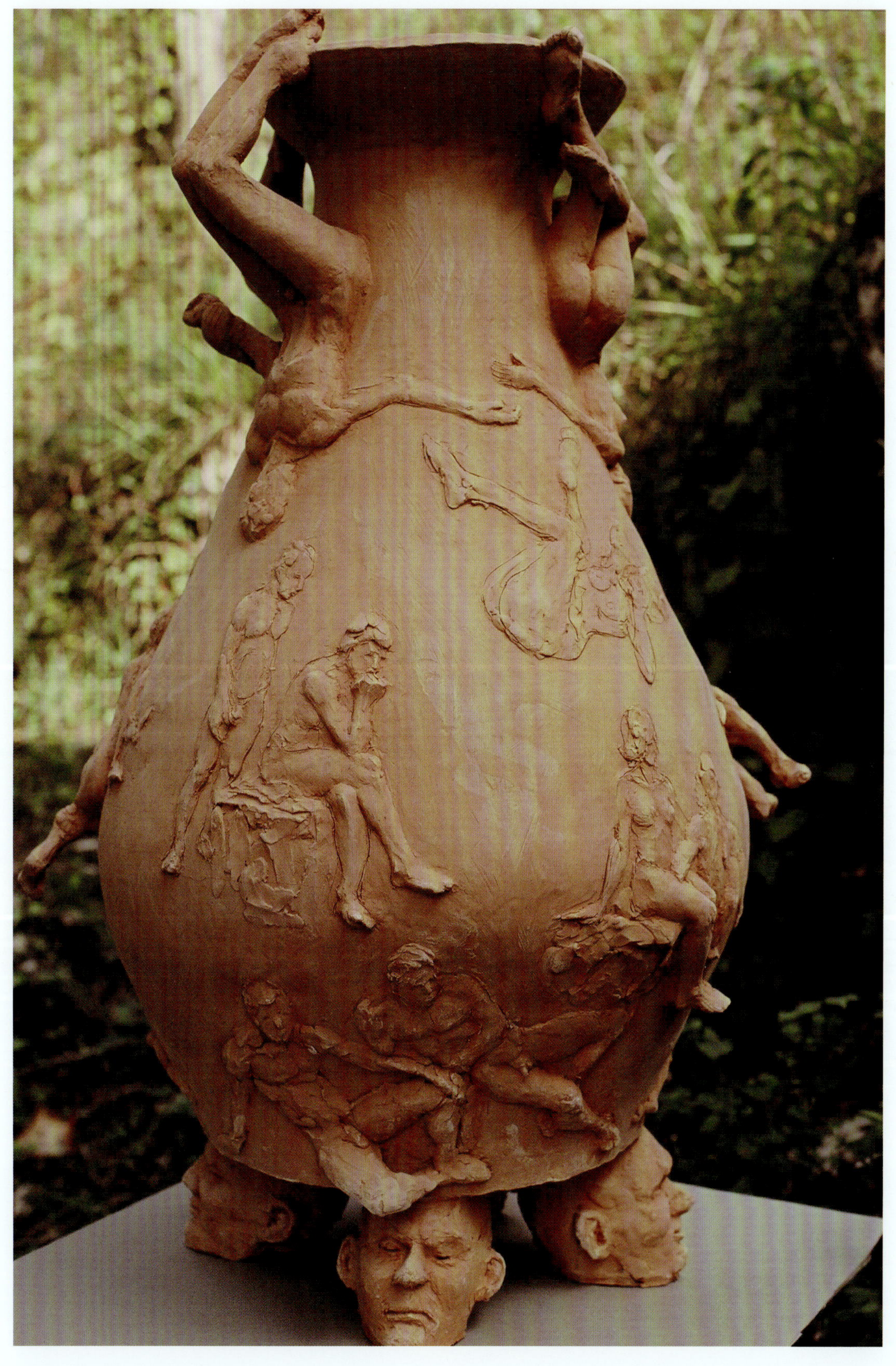

SCULPTED VASE III

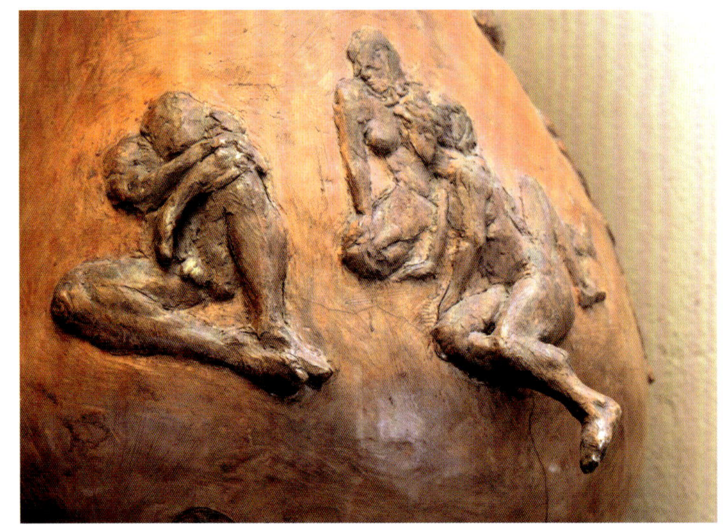

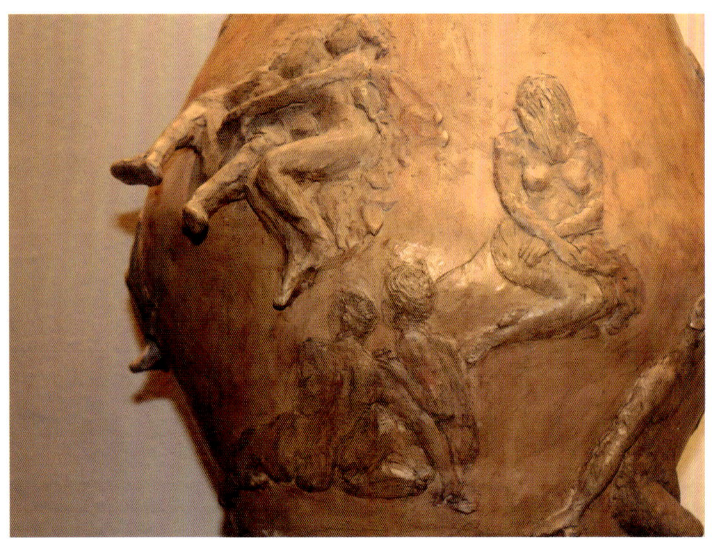

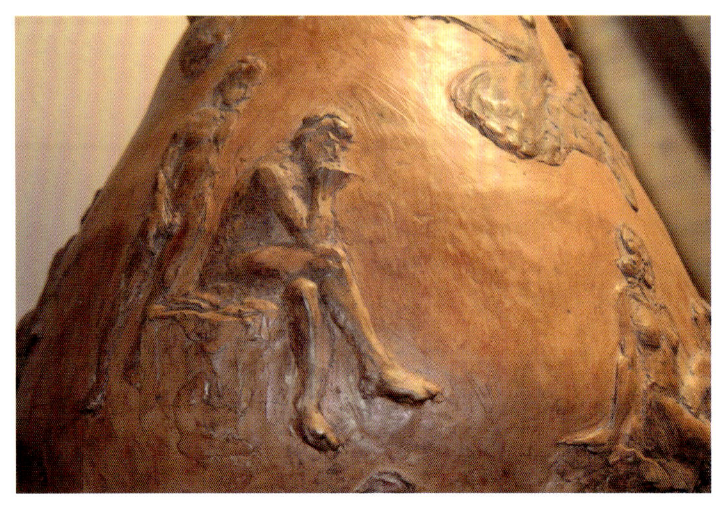

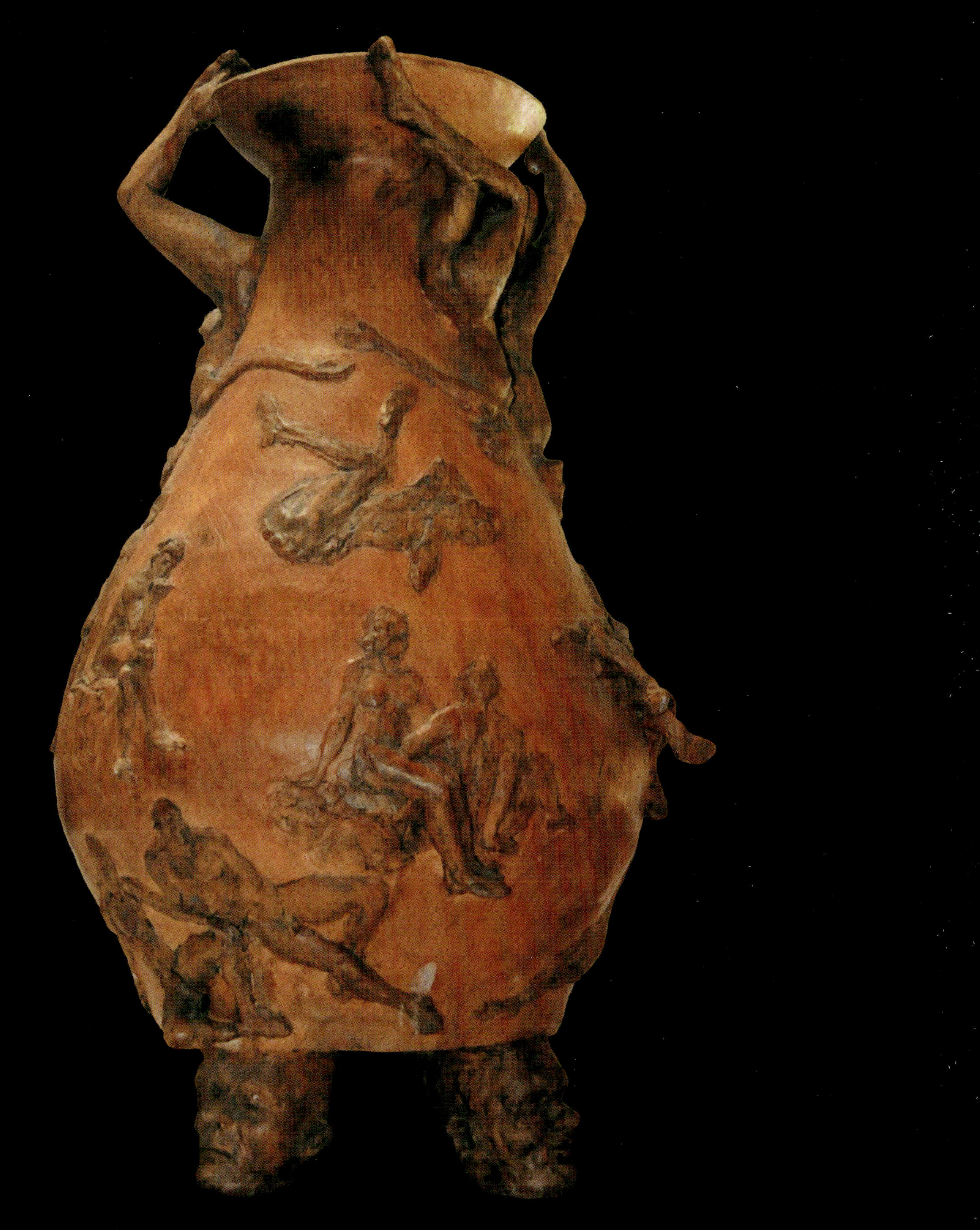

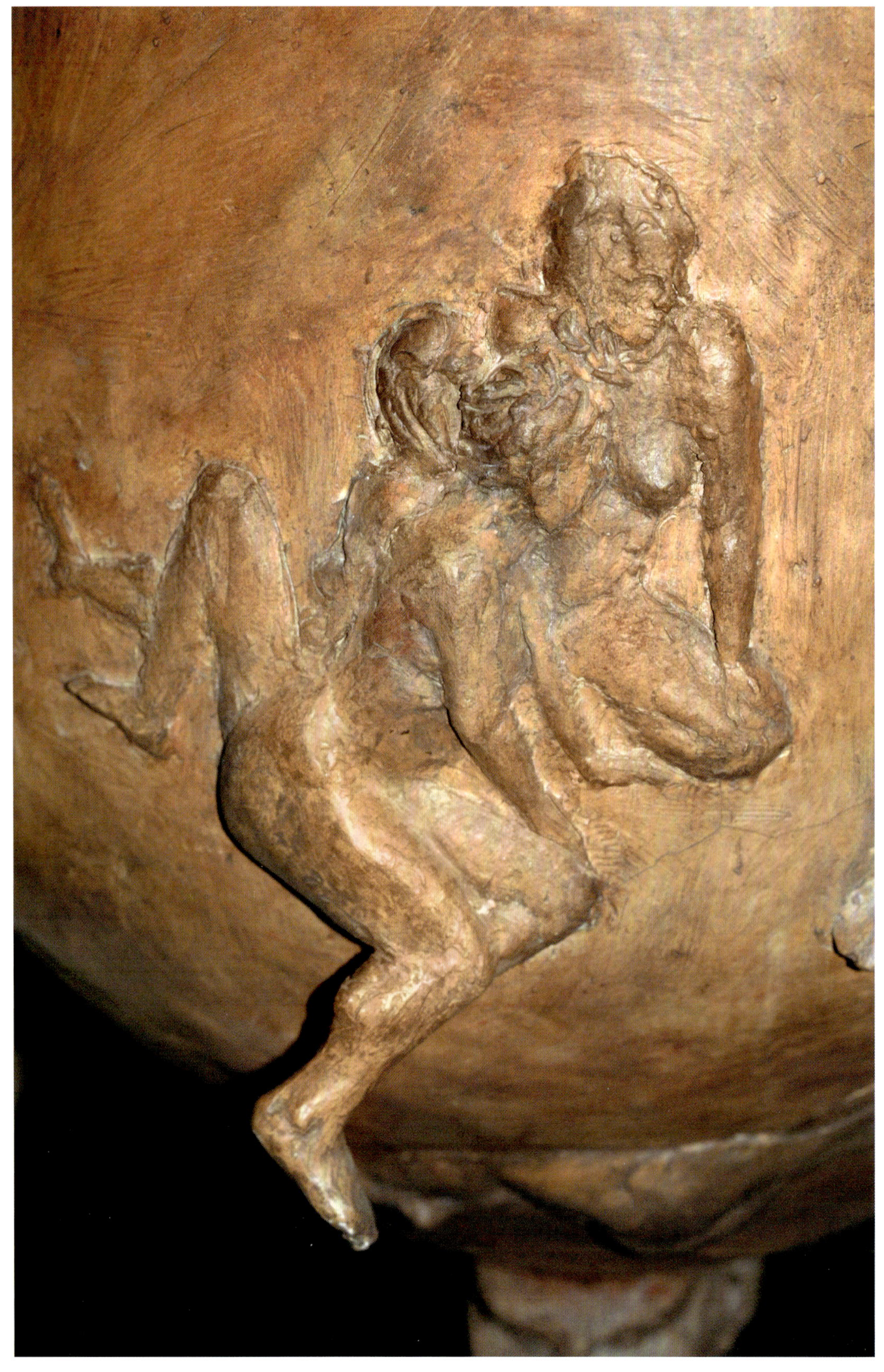

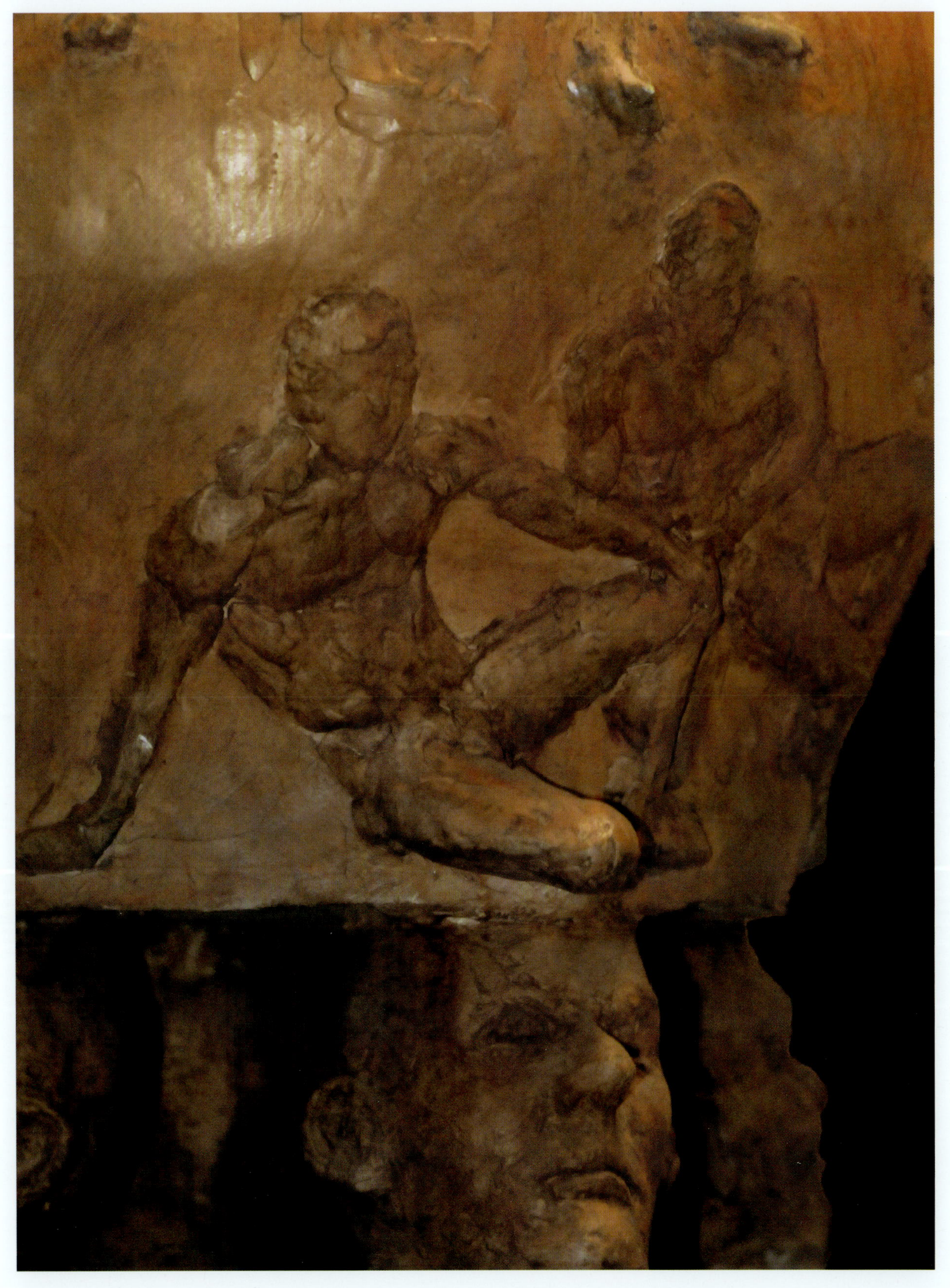

COMING TOGETHER

Born in orgasm
coming together
sperm and egg
a race of joy and love
in ecstasy–
a voyage for a new beginning—
the continuation
the culmination
the creation.
Born in orgasm
coming together
in ecstasy for a new beginning.
the instinctual drive
the personal desire–
the universal family.

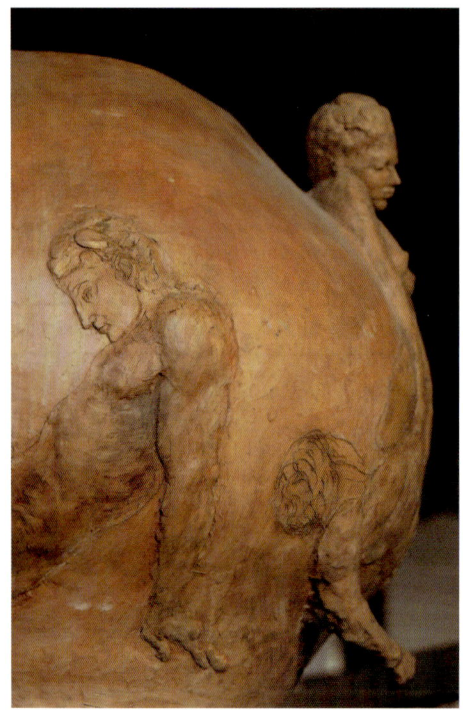

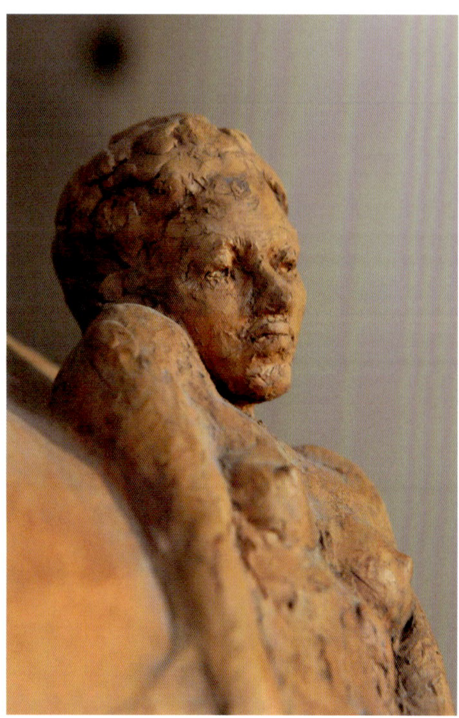

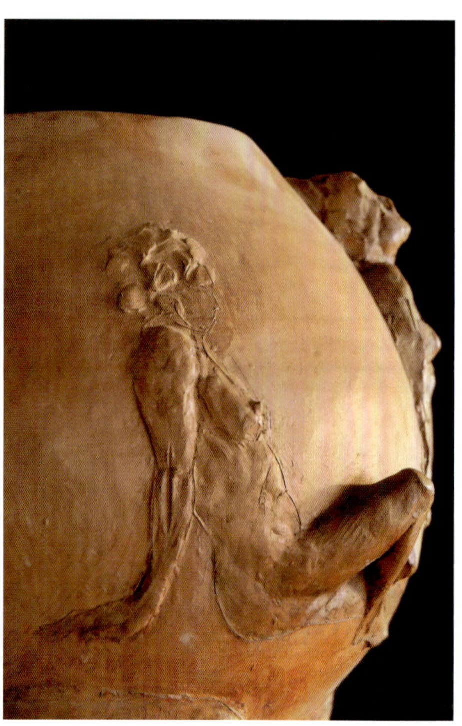

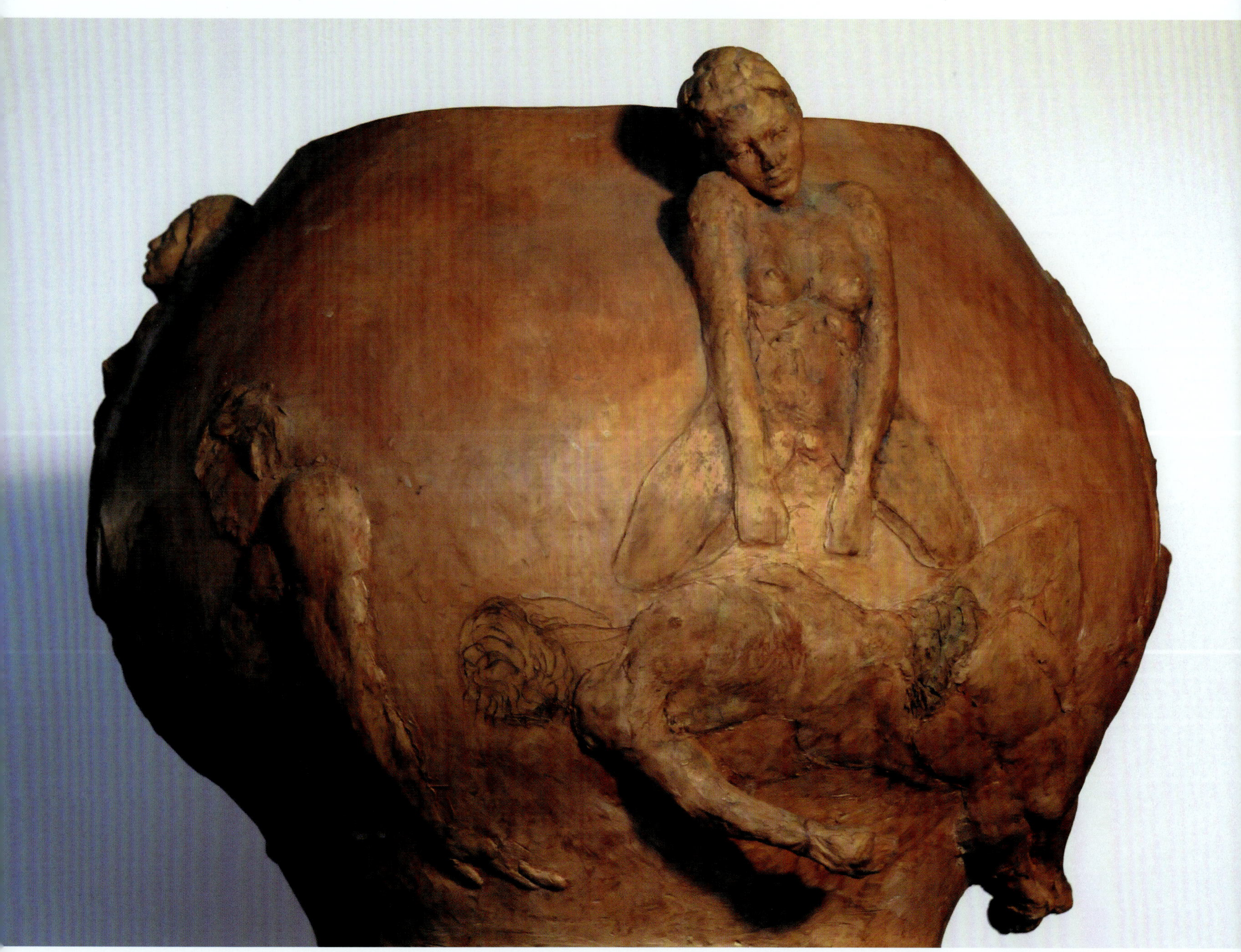

FIRST WAVES TO ROAM

From the first waves
that walked
arm in arm in the sand
and foot prints that left no trace
in the quiet still sea water …
the warmth
of an August nocturne turned
radiant on the shore.

I watched you turn gently
from summer to fall and falling
leaves a blanket,
to be kept warm in your bed.

In your eyes, your arms, your embraces,
history is written of Rome
and a thousand years
and I held you close as we walked
the cobblestone streets of a city without
an end.

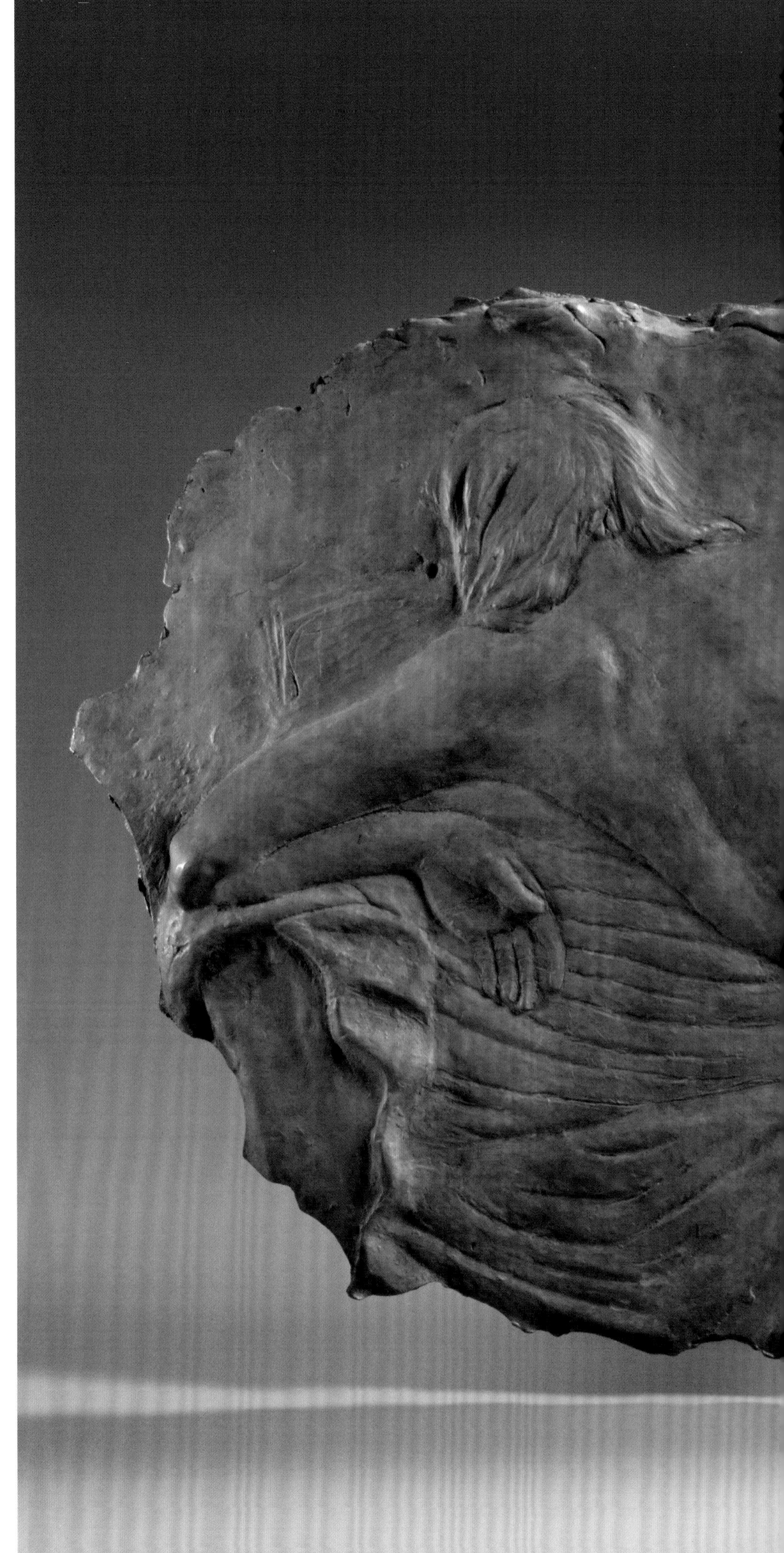

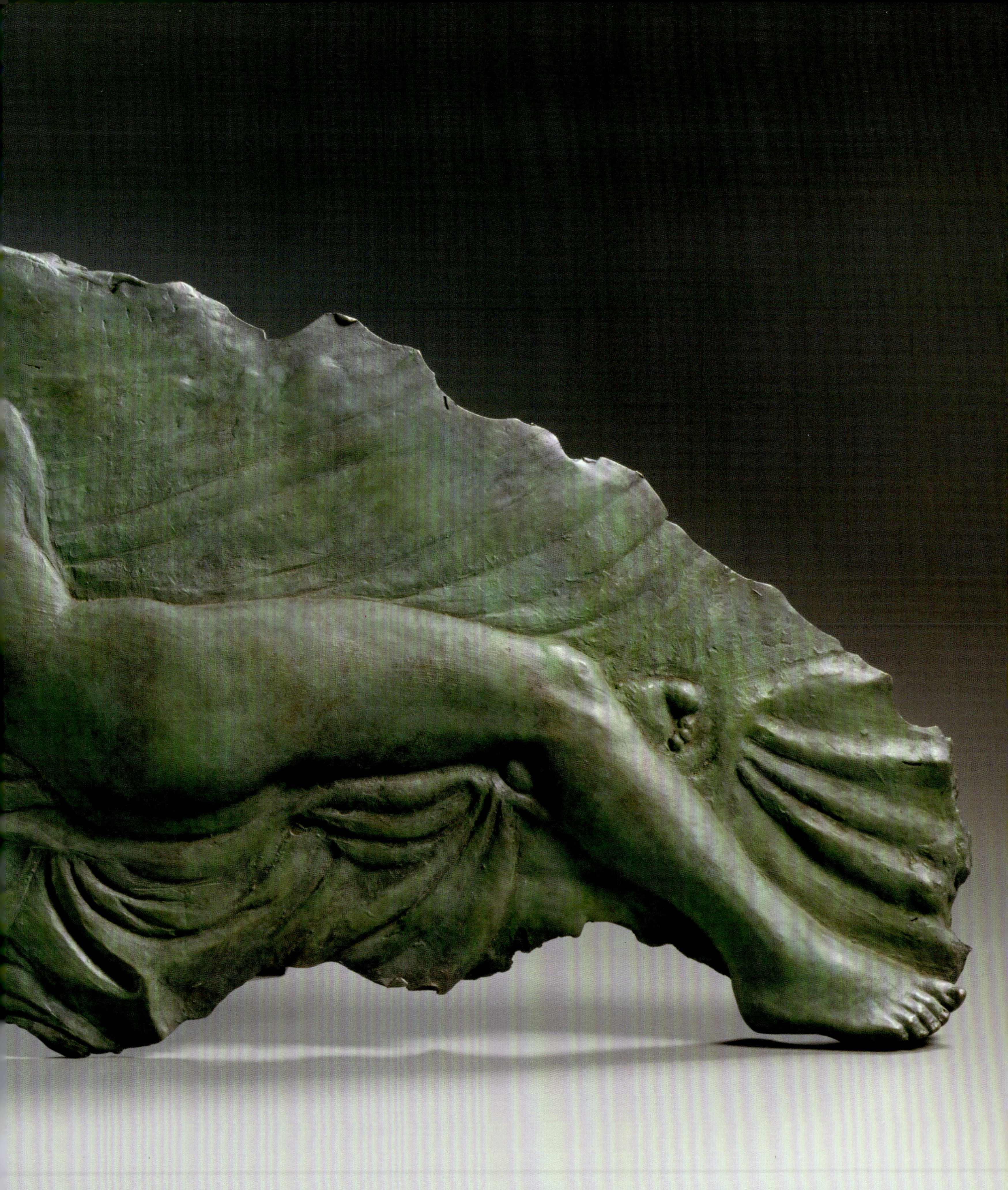

The nude is paying homage to an archetypal form. It deserves reverence, respect, love, appreciation, compassion, knowledge, wisdom. I need to educate the public. It is a mirror of our history, our potential, our contribution, our spirit. Realism can also depict our shortcomings, our downfall, our humanness.

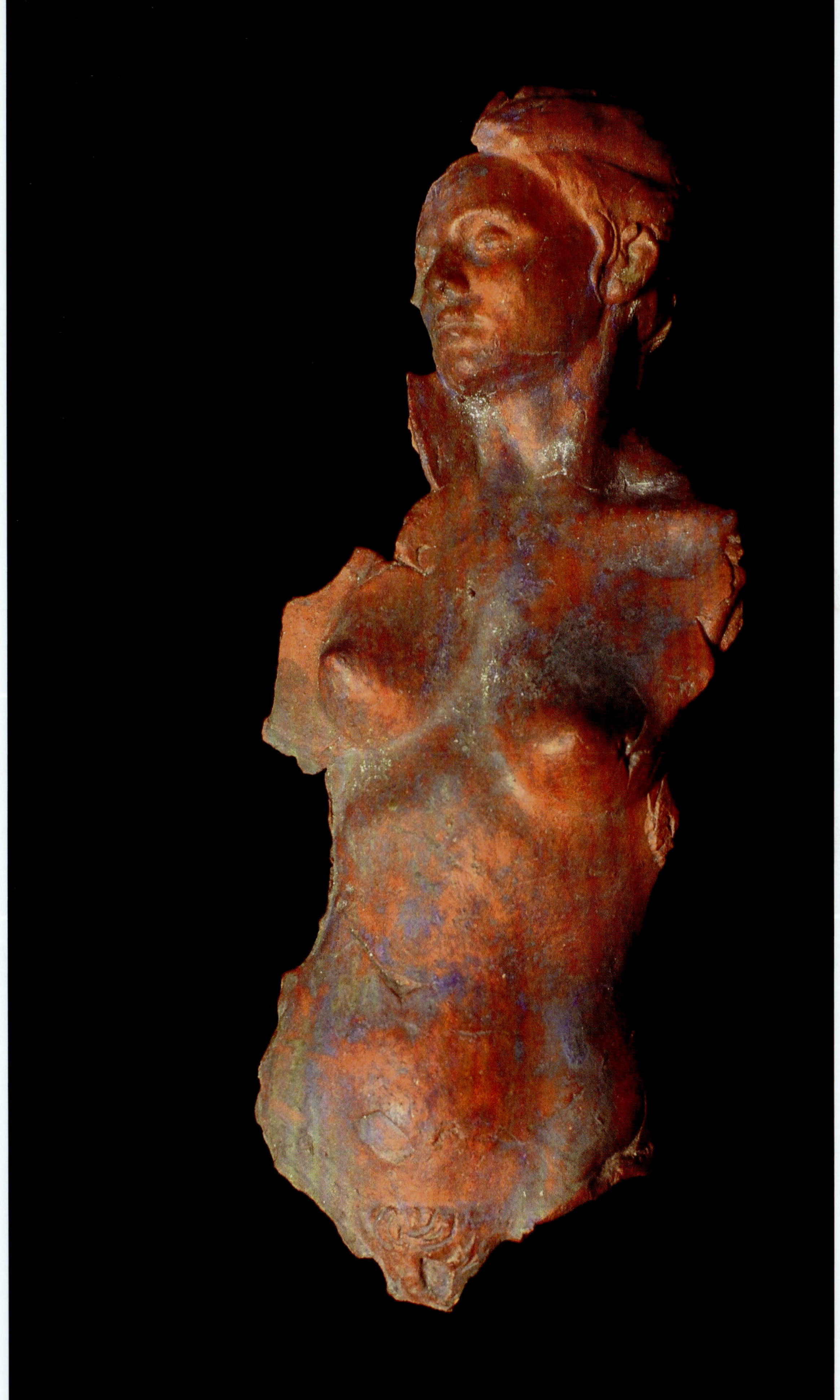

THERE IS

There is so much woman
behind your eyes.
So much wisdom and insight
and ability
to grow beyond the trap door.

Dig your peasant toes into
the noble earth
and blossom a flower
that turns with the sun.

Be strong in the light and not
the shadow of one thousand
dew drop mother tears
and mature in the harvest
of one hundred mornings
of summer.

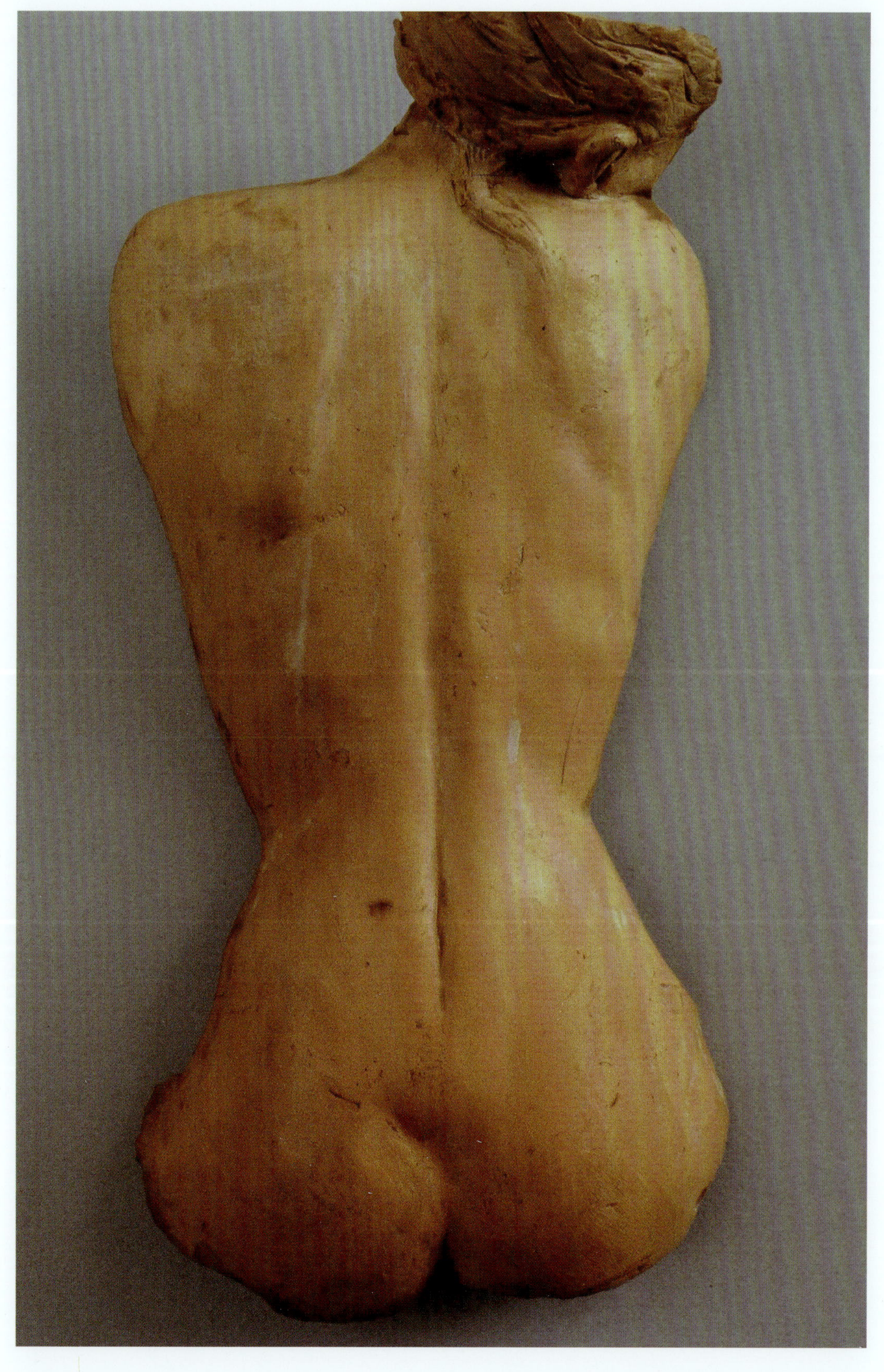

The advantage to being 'out of step' with the mainstream of contemporary art is that I bring the viewer in to have a visceral and visual dialogue with the self. This art is not meant to be exclusive, elitist, alienating or inane.... I believe the average person can identify and relate to my work because the human form brings us back to our most common element ... our own bodies.

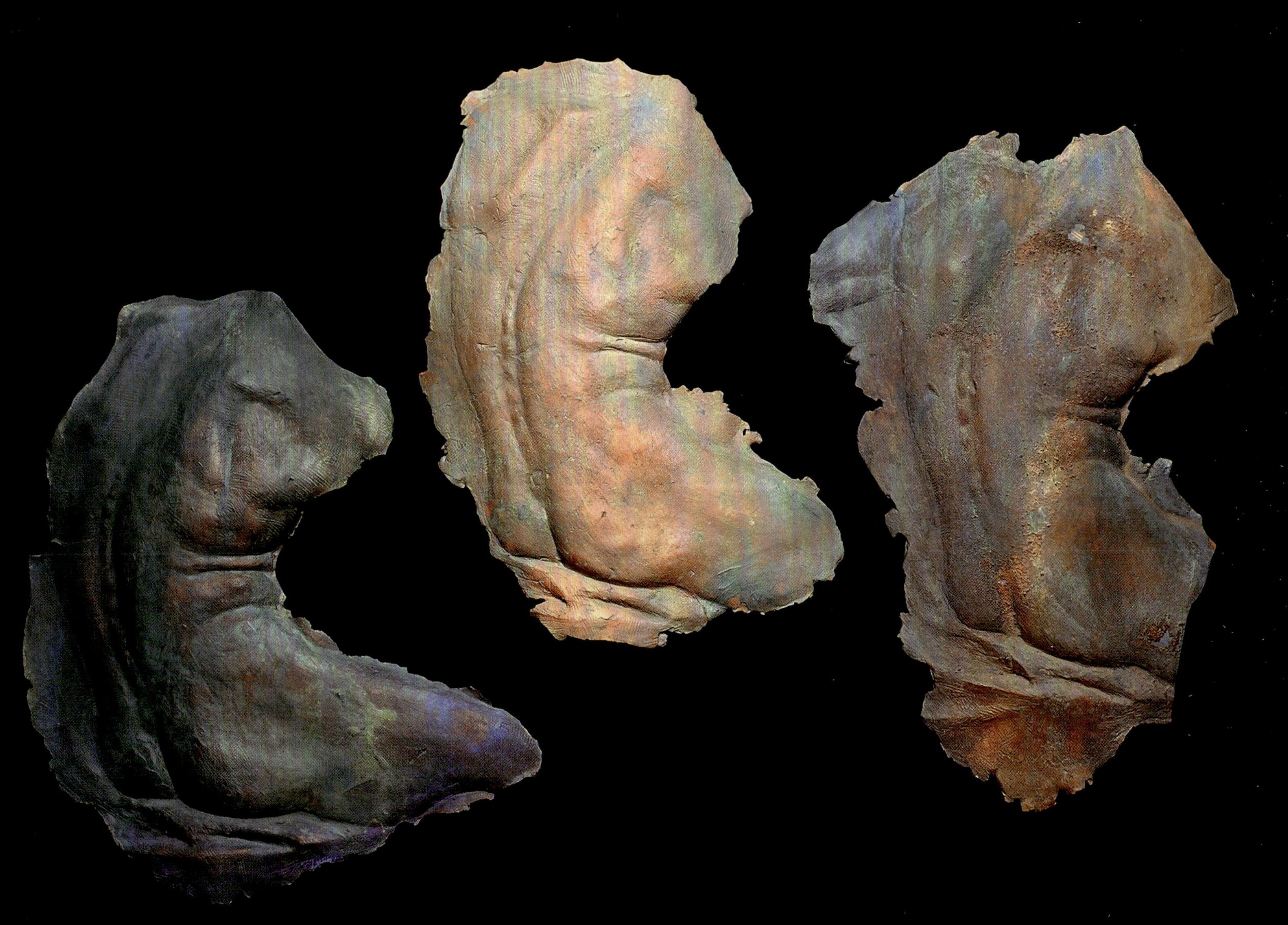

STRAIT OF MESSINA

In the midst of the sea
the sun dripped its rays of honey
on the silky clouds.
They caressed the vibrant air
with different notes played
by flutes with different lengths.
Only one ray touched the sea...
And so, it was an unforgettable sky.
And so, I wanted to move closer to it.
A woman, woman, woman–
A sky, sky, sky—came back to mind.
So beautiful it was—so beautiful she was.
It was so beautiful, so beautiful.

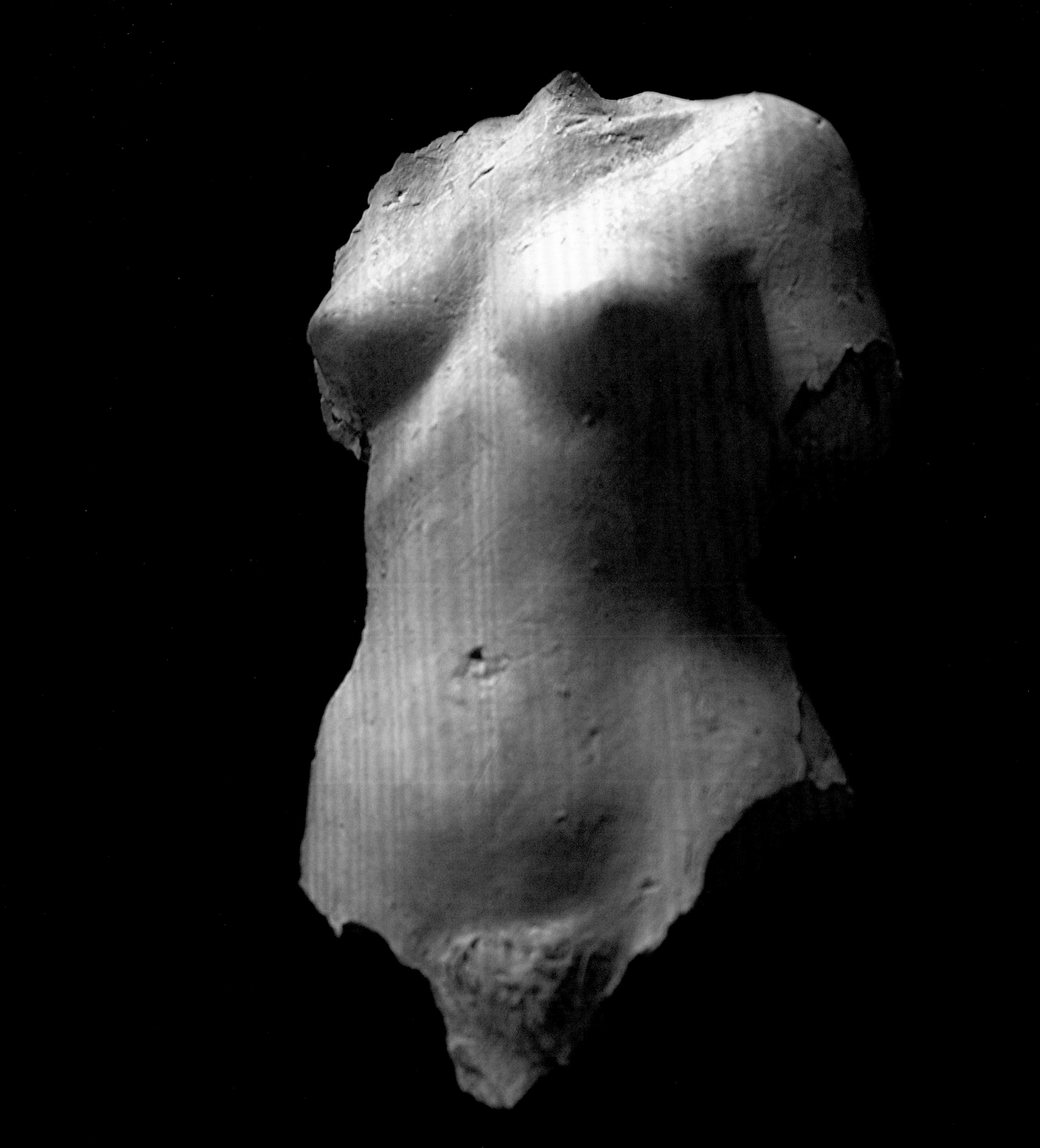

MY GOD

My God exists but I know not
in what form
My God lives inside of me
My God is a man & woman
rock & tree
My God is supportive and nurturing
powerful & loving
My God protects me yet allows me
to make my own mistakes
Yet I am not ready to meet my God
I have not yet created my God

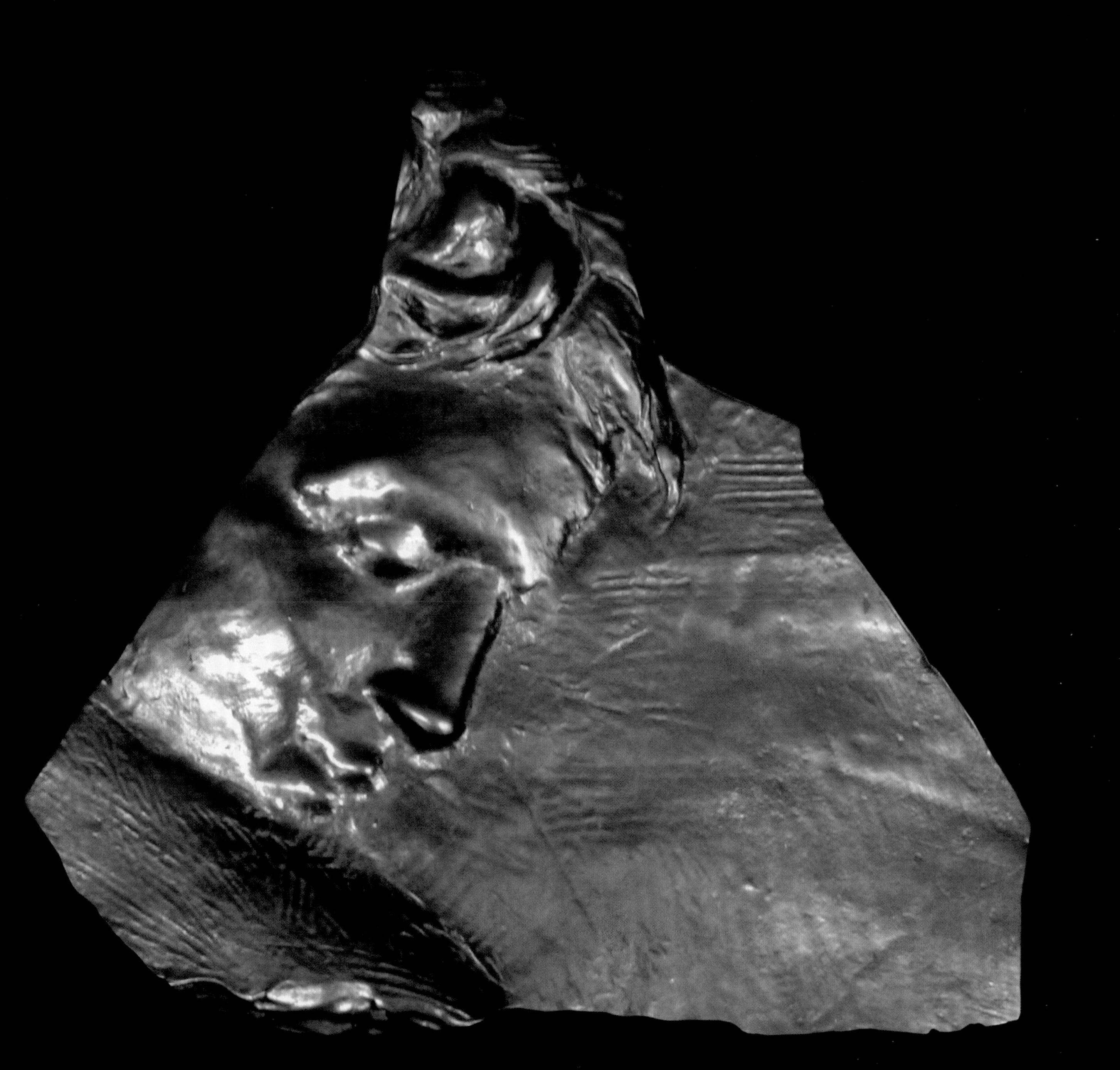

Life the great mystery, death the
great unknown. What sorrow. What fear.
How little we are prepared to meet
death. Portraiture in the ancient world
was born out of representing the dead
as recognizable as possible, so that the
soul would find its body and insure a
joyous afterlife.

Every day must be like a life,
and every evening a death.
Every morning a new life
and every evening a death.
It's what you do in between
which determines how
you wake up.

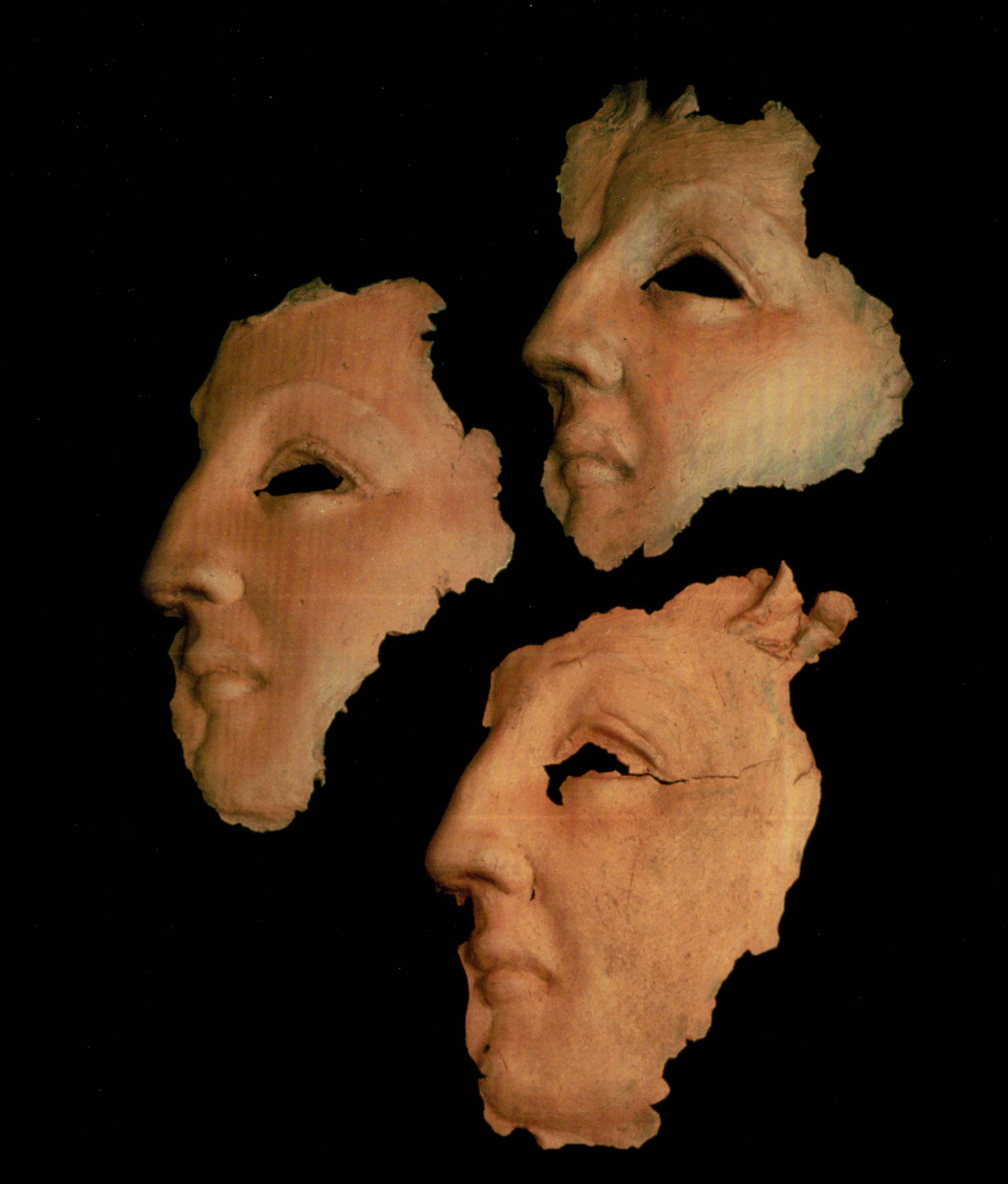

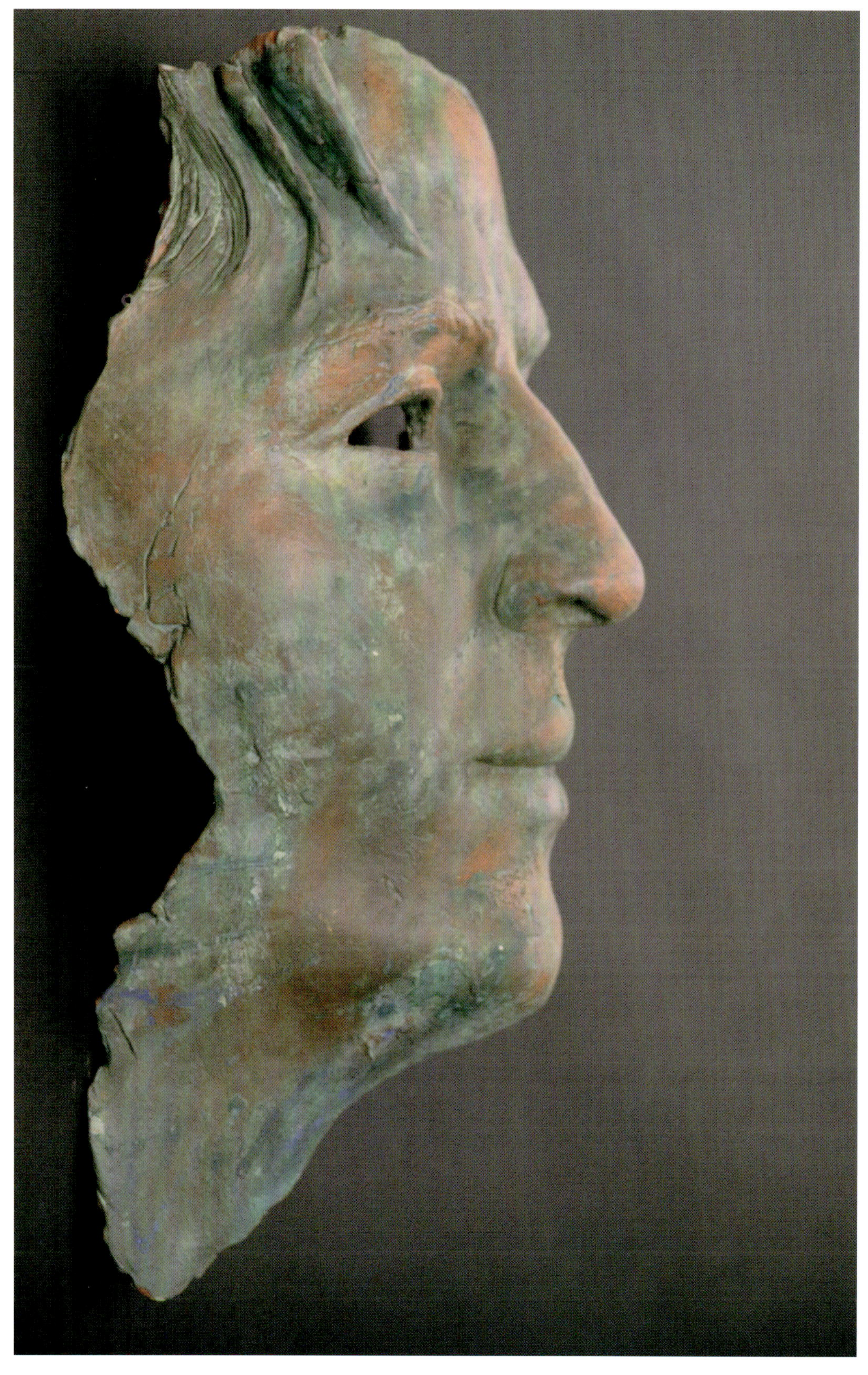

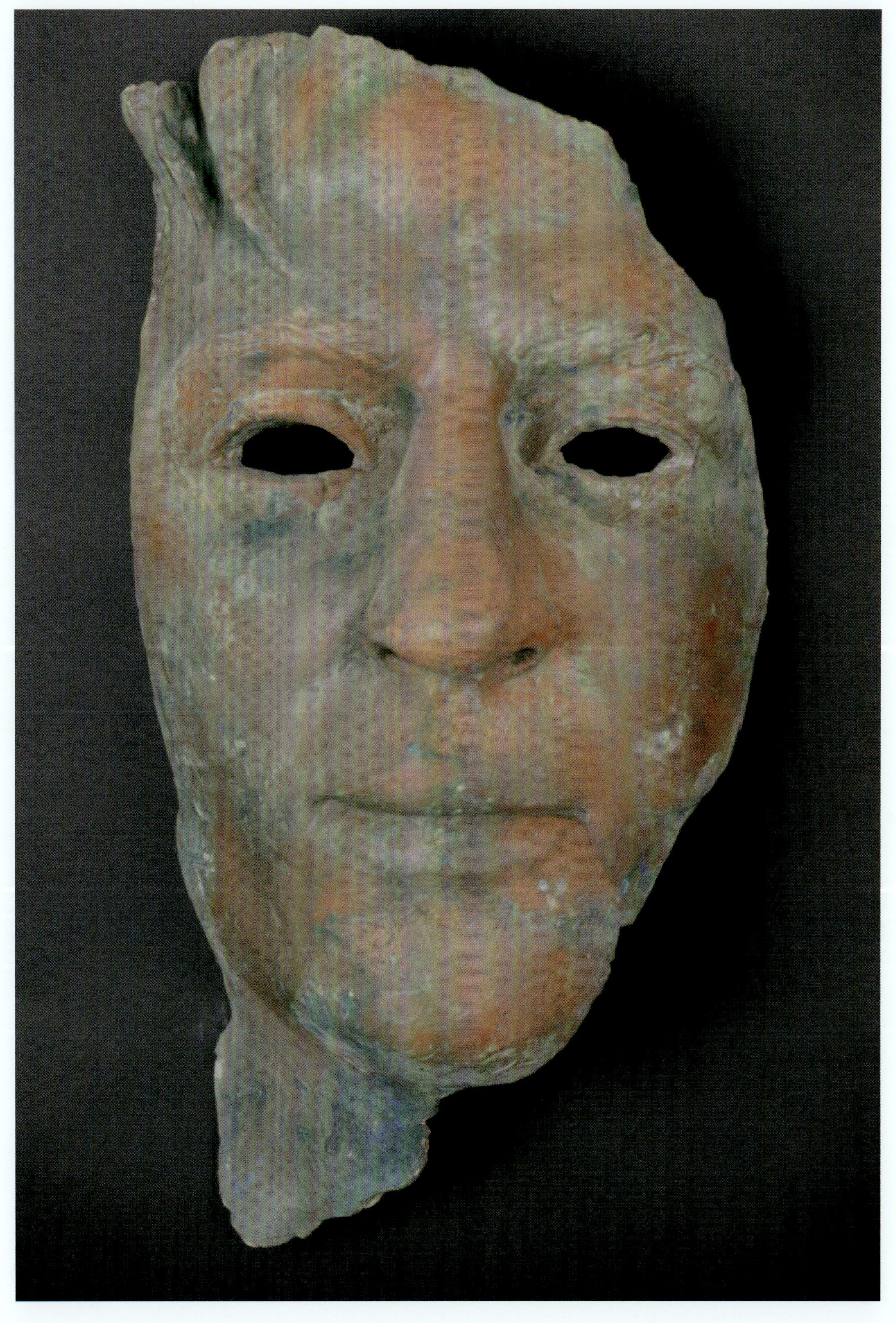

Om Santi Om

La Tomba

The terra cotta *santi*, or saints, which hang (as if gold) by brass wire from the grid ceiling represent the celestial-Spiritual. The spiral formation of the *santi* is disguised by their multiplicity. Their varying lengths and patterns allude to the chaos and order of the universe.

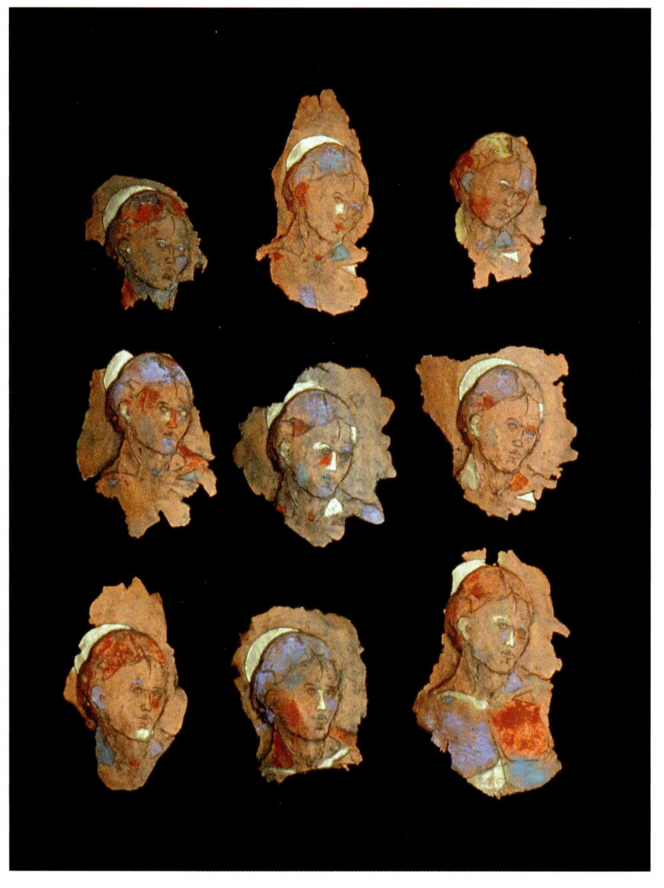

On the floor is a fractured structure made of raku fired clay, and above it hangs a cast paper form, lighted from above, which represents the cerebral Mind. The spirit longs to become form as body, therefore spirals upward toward the mind so it can enter a body. The *santi* are *spermi*. The mind is "impregnated" by the spirit to return as form to the earth.

Piled, scattered and partially buried on the floor are *frammenti*, or fragments of my life in art. These objects represent the Corporeal realm, and refer to the earthly body fragments of memories, life experiences, and temporal dreamlike existence. The body represents the manifestation of this life with its jewels and garbage, searching for order–enlightenment as a way to the spirit.

The body nears the mind.

The mind rests on the body.

The different states of consciousness created by this installation encourage reflection on the nature of life, death and afterlife.

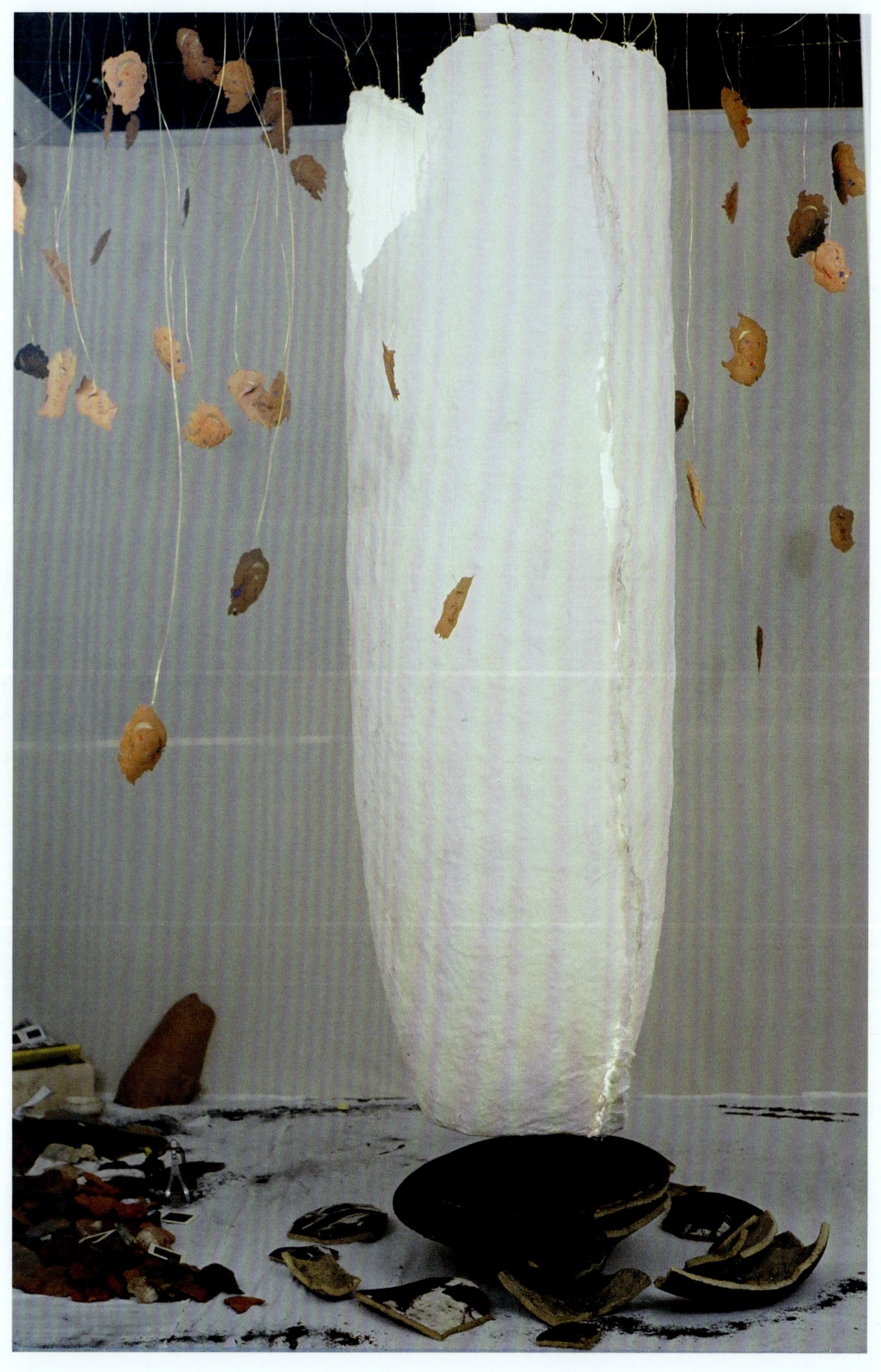

I have been accused of living in the clouds.
A dreamer … Days melt into days. Sometimes
I even confuse the seasons. It has happened
for several years now—there is a time in spring
and a time in fall, I cannot tell the difference.
My life has become a continuum.
I let go of days, months and years.
I stare at blossoms on trees and see
autumn leaves. I see colors and think of flowers.
The light and the weather are the same.
Perhaps I am too old.

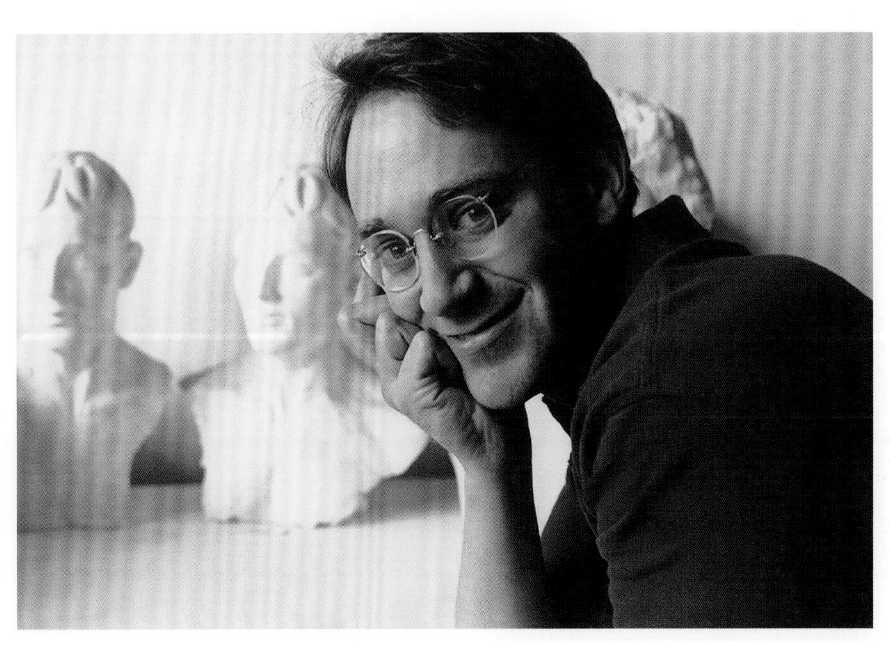

MONTE ALTISSIMO

I never should have left
your broad shoulders,
I never should have left
your marble shores.
Proudly you stand
steep with striations
of pure white marble,
uprooting rhythmical
random design.
A symbol, an inspiration,
a motivation
of your power divine.

"Cyclist of the world's hills, lover of its people, *Italiano* his soul language, the classic humanist tradition his devotion, impractical jokester, nature's poet laureate, surveyor of the human spirit, reverent sculptor for antiquity's gods, rebel warrior, born creator unwilling to let institutional orthodoxy silence his muse, activist for antiquity, worshipper of the human form, friend of many, inspiration to us all. Beloved son, brother, lover, cherished uncle, brother-in-law, hummingbird, dynamo, winged gift, *maestro*."

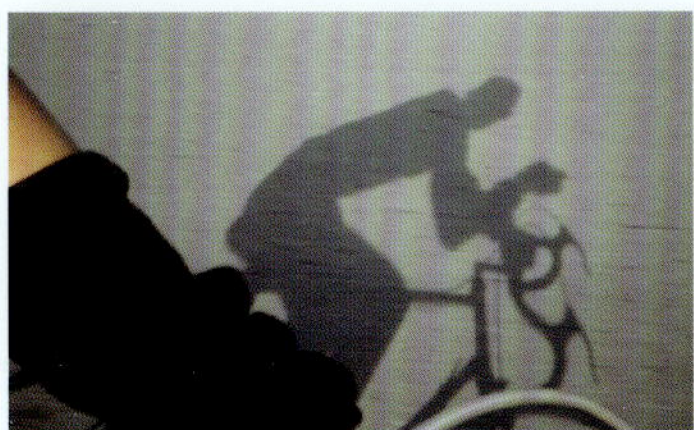

So read the newspaper obituary of Jefferson D. Rubin following his tragic mountain accident on August 27, 1995, at the age of 36.

His proclaimed "true love" ... "mostly Italian, a little Japanese ..." his *bicicletta*, carried his visions and accompanied him on his solo wandering and wonderings through France, Austria, Germany, Switzerland, Greece, Israel, Egypt, and Italy, (often covering 120-140 kilometers daily) to arrive back in Rome on Christmas Eve, 1989, after his own 167 day epic hero's journey, spent journalling, photographing, drawing and painting. "The bicycle truly is my saving grace, my relief, my drug ... my meditation. I am glad it is feminine in the Italian language. I am writing to you now flanked by two beauties."

Jefferson had added up a lifetime 67,640 miles of cycling from high school summer voyages with intimate friends, and onward.

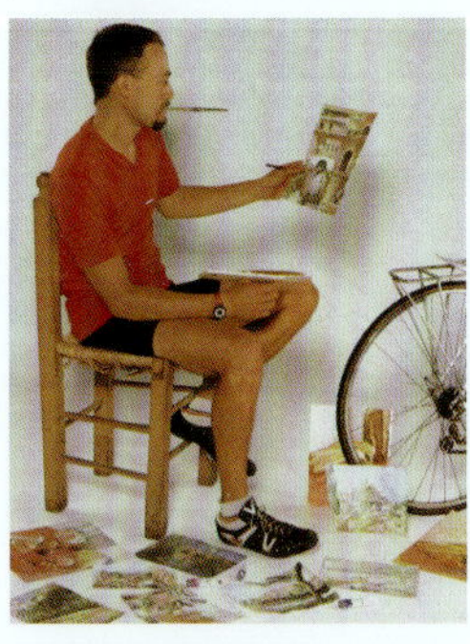

His engaging illustrated article, "*Il Ciclo-Artista Americano*," written in Italian and published in the Italian journal, *La Bicicletta*, told cyclists how they could pragmatically enrich their experiences with "the very special relationships that are born on the road." His own plan for cycling the entire globe, "painting portraits of people, painting landscapes, and with days of good riding," found no significant sponsors despite his serious efforts. His best industrialist donor prospect gave him, instead, a bicycle and cycling gear. "Corporate businessmen are no Medicis."

Jefferson, during an earlier stay in Rome as an undergraduate art student, had worked as a restoration apprentice at the Museo Nazionale Romano. There his Italian fluency was fostered as "*la gente parlano solo Italiano*."

> "... Restoration is a good mix of art, archaeology-anthropology, geology, applied sciences, as well as a good moral commitment." But "namely with potential carcinogens (acetone, *epoxia*). And altho' I have a commitment to the ancient, I don't really want the god-damned chemical industry to claim my body."

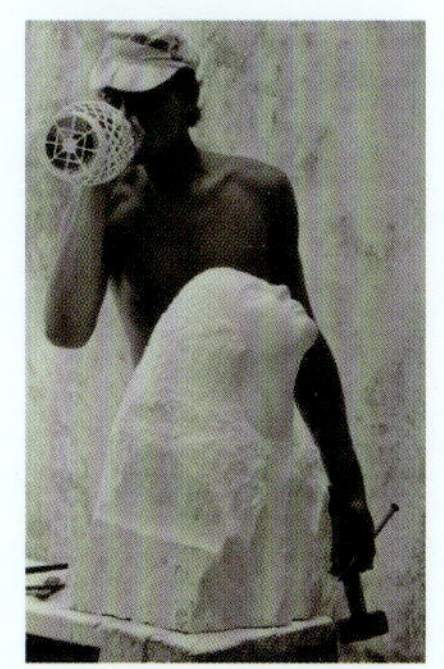

It was at the museum that he had met Carla Angeletti who was to become the subject for his first marble sculpture, *Il Bacio*, which he carved at age 21. *La Madonna* was the name given this work by those who passed by the sculpture garden site. Jefferson was to discover on visiting the site several years later that this portrait had been stolen.

While studying Italian in college, his Italian language and civilization professors referred to him as the "Giovane Michelangelo," so moved were they by his study of the ancients and his humanistic devotion reflected in his early figurative sculptures and portraits. In contrast, his art major department and graduate school, both driven by a post-modern mentality, pressured against his resistance and his insistence on affirming his own destiny, one devoted to beauty and spirit as exemplified by the figure.

With the encouragement of a friend, Cinzia, of Italian descent, Jefferson taught Italian on his returns from Italy to the US, and named many of his works in this language in response to his muses' callings. He wrote:

> ITALIAN
>
> Italian builds to a passionate pitch
> like a wave breaks the shore,
> like an earthquake shakes,
> like a volcano roars,
> reverberating the air,
> higher it rises and drops.
> And I, a log—adrift
> within the wave,

Jefferson Photographing Jefferson Cycling. *Il Ciclo-Artista*. A Pause with *Il Bacio*.

rumble within the molten crust,
bob, breathe air and swallow water
on the edge of comprehension.
Hands like branches blow in the wind
sway towards the listener
whose voice
returns to sea—an undertow
rebounding the sound
ebb and flow.

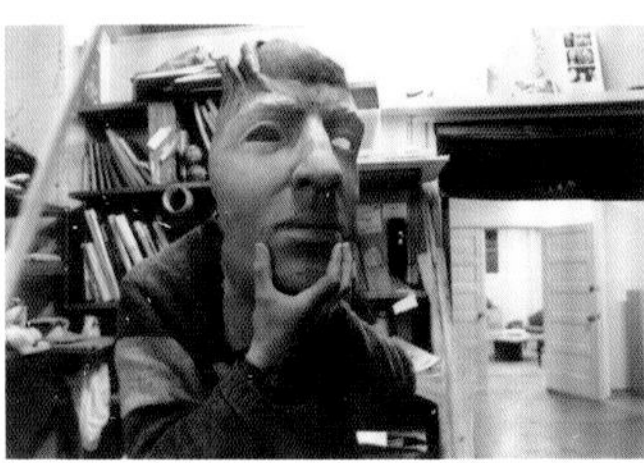

Jefferson was a bard by nature and delighted in sharing his poetry, memorized or spontaneous, as well as storytelling adventures. His several hundred poems reached from deep philosophical introspection and depth of love and pathos to light hearted humor and parody. Poetry, as the longing of his heart and a source of liberation, was written and spoken through his adopted pen name Ruscello.

"He is the poet and the true Buddha inside of me, the great lover that needs to be nurtured. He is *corso d'aqua*, a small brook that leads to a stream that leads to a river, which finds its way to the sea. A raindrop to an ocean ... the seer, the visionary, the messenger of the gods. Was Hermes a poet? Apollo was. I am the banks of Ruscello, in which the water flows—the creativity.

"Ruscello is the creative, intuitive flowing brook of consciousness ... the heartfelt, emotional, perhaps at times, melancholy for the sake of creative space to write. However, once a poem is complete, he is very happy and satisfied with himself. Many times he has memorized his poems after he has completed them. Of course the struggle to bring forth words set to meter, rhyme, but always rhythm is his great play.... Ruscello can enter into my art as well. He is the inner artist which my goal is to release and bring to the surface....

"I'm not a work-aholic, I'm a sculpt-aholic and I am prolific, pro-life & pro-choice, and [a] pro-artistic child."

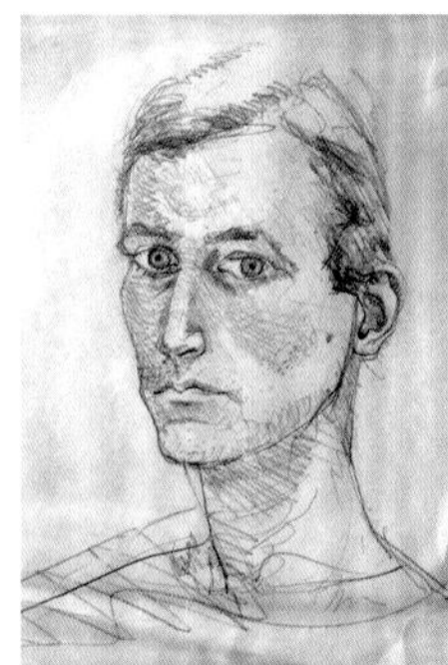

Jefferson would affirm that he was a monk.

"... a social monk, not a hermit. I love people. I worship their form and dignify their spirit. I draw from interaction. I'm an image gatherer. When I am *colpito*, or struck, I take an image to verse through paper, stone or clay. Sometimes I feel the presence of my masters. When I'm lucky, I feel a loving, guiding creative force. Some call it God. I know it is my true nature, my Buddha nature."

He always turned to nature as his nurturer.

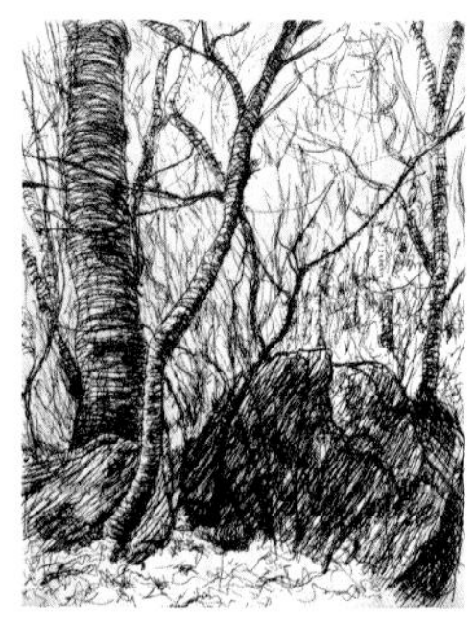

"I watched the water at three different streams falling into the pool ... a fast drip (infancy), a clear wall at a steady speed to maintain it (youth) & whitewater cascading (mid-age). So I felt about life & our concept of its passing, its ever increasing speed. In infancy time drips; in youth we are strong, proud and beautiful; in mid-age we can't believe we have left youth behind and old age is nearing at a frightening, roaring pace, but we must go along with it. I thought about the force of water, the greatest sculptor, and how it moves rocks downstream, packing them between each other, building a wall, filling every space with its torrent."

His own passion in shaping the clay or marble was to "call forth life" while proclaiming his responsibility to foster the awakening of a new renaissance of idealism.

This third-born child, self-named as "the oldest," was naturally imaginative, and with his spontaneity of spirit easily awakened his own creativity. Beginning with his childhood, he shared how, when encountering beauty whether in nature or art or archaeology, his "racing heartbeat" would identify his feeling.

A 250-mile family bicycle trek through English country sides continued afterwards with exploring Italy where Jefferson became "stone captive" to Michelangelo, whom he called "The Great One." He had wanted to remain there to apprentice at eleven years of age, believing that apprenticing began at nine years of age. He, of course, found his own way back to Italy ten years later, apprenticing to himself.

Two summers, while in junior high school, Jefferson spent digging at archaeological sites in New Mexico and Illinois. That became a logical progression of his personal search for discovery and the meaning of existence.

Hearing Martin Luther King, Jr. speak in Denver, and his affection for civil rights activist, Dick Gregory, had enlightened his inherent sense of social justice and compassion.

A photographic darkroom was built in the basement of the family home. There, Jefferson and his brother Steven spent long nights and weekends developing and printing their film, enlarging and

 Behind *Maschera*. Self Portrait in Pencil. At Central Park.

experimenting with their images. Steven went on to a career as a photojournalist around the world and to his present position as a professor of photography at Pennsylvania State University. Sister Marjorie joined them at times and became a textile artist and print maker. Jefferson went on to photo-document his journeys and his art works.

Jefferson's auditory-photographic memory captured myriad moments and carried recollections and detailed stories of events, loves and longings. With his death his brother Steven cried out, "Who will be the family archivist?"

Jefferson would "perform" all nine Beethoven symphonies with his unique hummingbird whistle while shaping clay, chiseling marble, or cycling kilometers through the terrain. Bob Dylan "taught him" the mournful blues harmonica, and he owned one in each key, which he played to the mountains and forests, or to companions. Drumming, banjo plucking, guitar strumming, and dancing were part of his personal and social being. And from his flute, he danced and improvised—an enchanting Pan.

"I began sculpting in the ceramics room in high school. I was dropping classes, staying after school to work, and sculpting during my lunch period. I had the bug. I felt an affinity. I wanted to sculpt humanity ... to blend anthropology with art. My art was never dead."

A few days following his graduation from the University of Colorado, he mounted his bicycle and rode it all the way to New York City to enroll in the New York Studio School of Drawing, Painting and Sculpture, to pursue working with the figure. He rested his bicycle in Chicago to revisit the Field Museum of Natural History to again experience *Tribes of Man,* the Malvina Hoffman sculptures of indigenous family groupings that had so awed him at age nine. Anthropology and archaeology had become embedded in his psyche.

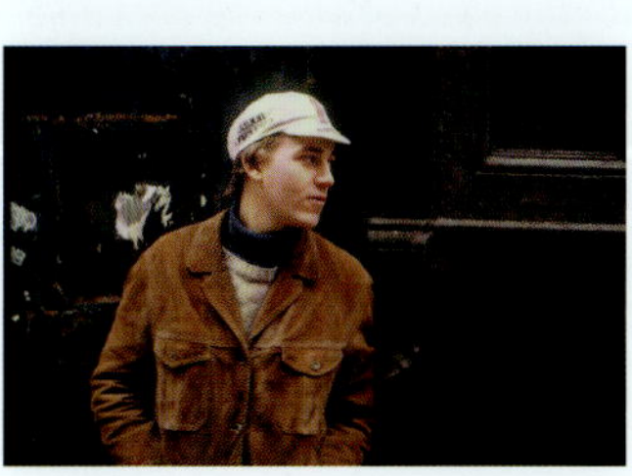

A year later he found a job at the Metropolitan Museum of Art, exchanging more formal education for use of the Met as his university. His concern had been that the Studio School's shift to an MFA program lacked its prior vitality and "would have an effect on my work, and I'd become slick and polished and driven towards a finished accomplishment, not the struggle in the mud ... a living artist, not a manufactured one."

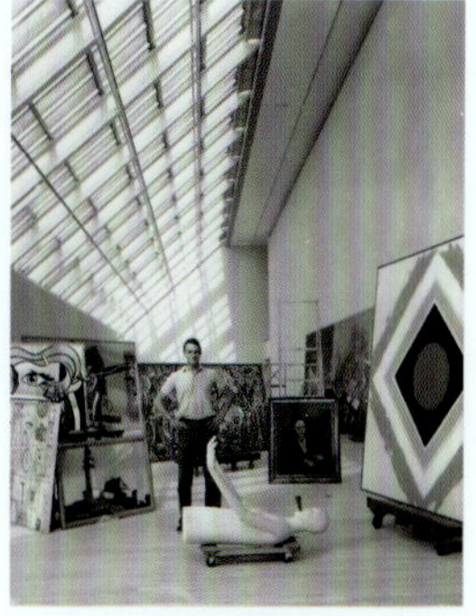

For five years he worked at the Met as an assistant installer in the Objects Conservation Department (helping to ready the new Egyptian wing), as a craftsman in the Reproduction Studio, and as a technician in the Department of 20th Century Art.

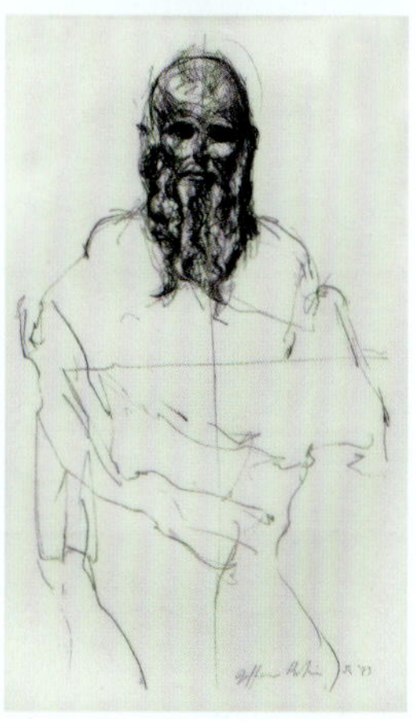

Drawing from sculptures on his lunch hours, thirsting for the knowledge and comprehension that the Met so fully offered, he met the great masters. He wrote, "but all my mentors are dead."

The landscape of Central Park was another site for drawing and painting. He felt that drawing, a discipline of his practice, was a form of meditation and a tool for understanding one's conceptualizations. To a young friend he wrote, "Draw, draw, draw—remember it is what happens while drawing, not what you produce. Never say I don't know how ... it is the foolishness of youth. It is a discipline, do not avoid it."

During this period he carved his portrait of museum co-worker George Bethen and created the *La Donna Striata* marble. "When I raise a hammer and chisel I feel the surge of strong energy, perhaps an illusion, *uno scherzo*. Toying with my mind that says, *sei bravo, bravo.*"

He was commissioned to restore six ancient marble figures at the J. P. Morgan Library as a result of the restoration experience he had gained at the Museo Nazionale Romano.

He and a love, who also worked at the Met, developed an aerobic class for employees. It met three times each week when the museum closed at 5 pm. The setting: the Impressionist Gallery! (The participants donned T-shirts designed by Jefferson.)

He had a "love-hate relationship" with New York City. Italy continuously beckoned and he responded to its call. The prelude of this stay

Age 22 in New York City. At the Met. Lunch Hour Drawing.

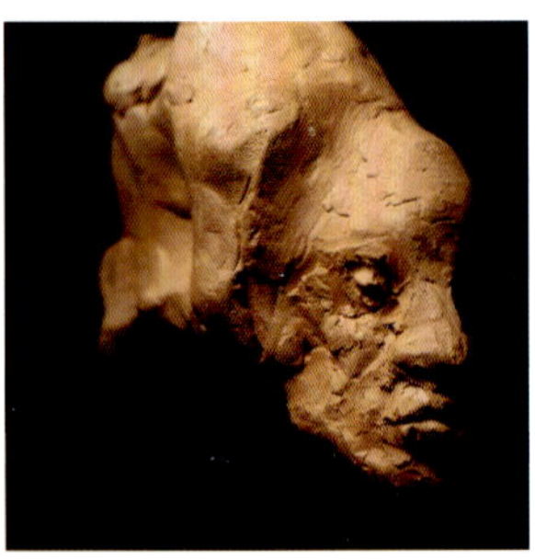

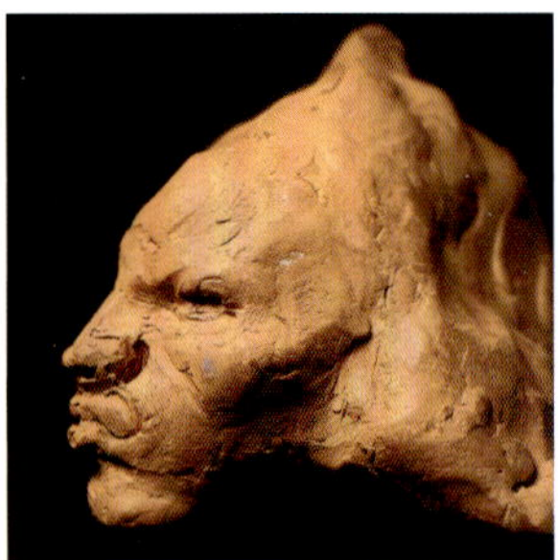

was his seven-month, eight-country bicycling tour. He then found his way to the Italian sculpture community of Pietrasanta and to meet his soul brother Marcello. He wrote, "Pietrasanta, Holy Stone, my *Cittá del Marmo*, surrounded by artists and craftsmen specialized in the field of my interest, an international studio for sculptors. There is a comfort and energy in this international language—diminished in winter months, leaving only the spirit to work."

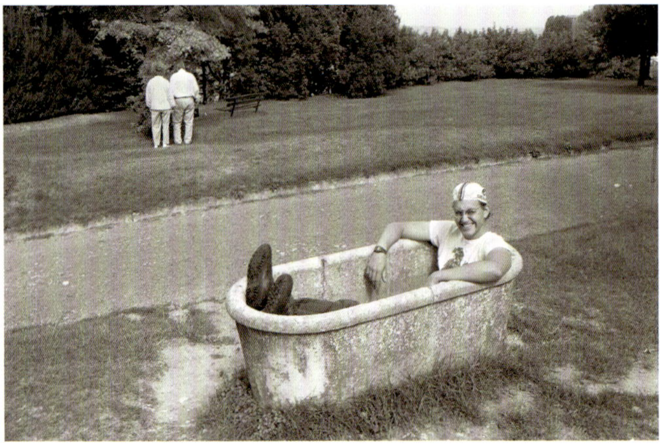

He was drawing, painting, and especially sculpting as he was forming friendships over espresso and conversation at the Michelangelo Café. He took on jobs as a *raspatore*, rendering the marble into "flesh," and as a *lucidatore*, polishing other sculptors' works, for his survival and sustenance. Growing in skill and imagination, he began creating his vase series as well as the *Regal Portrait* and *La Donna sulla Spiaggia*, while always listening to his muses.

The vases were constructed with the ancient coil method. These shapes were more organic for him than throwing them on the wheel. They were his "canvases." On these he sculpted bas-reliefs, and because of their sensuality he referred to them as his "vaserotics" or "sex pots."

When frustrated with his vase-making or marble-carving he would cycle to Florence ... "to be with Michelangelo. I felt a stronger sense of form in my work today, because of it." Many of his sculptures from this period were exhibited in Pisa, Carrara, Florence, and Pietrasanta. Going to Pietrasanta's open market was a daily delight for Jefferson, and it was there he came to know:

PAOLA THE POLLIVENDOLA
She has a complexion
Of a freshly plucked chicken,
ed ogni volta che passo, dice
[and every time I go by, I say]
un pezzetto delpetto di pollo
[a small piece of chicken for my pot, please]
per la padella per piacere
[or a small piece of chicken breast for the frying pan, please]
and she laughs ...
And I look into her beautiful blue eyes
and wonder what sounds surround
those large circular earrings?
What does she think of life
working daily amidst ...
dead animals? ...
pluck pluck
and she laughs ...
She seems out of place
so pretty and delicate with grace.
A long swan
with a
big sharp knife ...
pluck pluck.
["pl" pronounced as "bluck bluck" in high falsetto]

Poetry was the longing of his heart and a source of liberation. His words echoed with depth, humor or pathos.

On returning to Colorado he was to teach sculpture at several Denver art centers and adult education programs and to conduct several summer seminars at Western State College in Gunnison, Colorado.

Jefferson founded La Scuola, a classical sculpture school in Denver, adjacent to his own studio, out of concern for the limited foundation provided aspiring sculptors in other settings. La Scuola invited its students to "study the masters in a one-room schoolhouse" and to search for one's own individual vision through courses aimed at nourishing and energizing self-expression. The school's purpose was to offer disciplined core study and skill enhancement, all in the

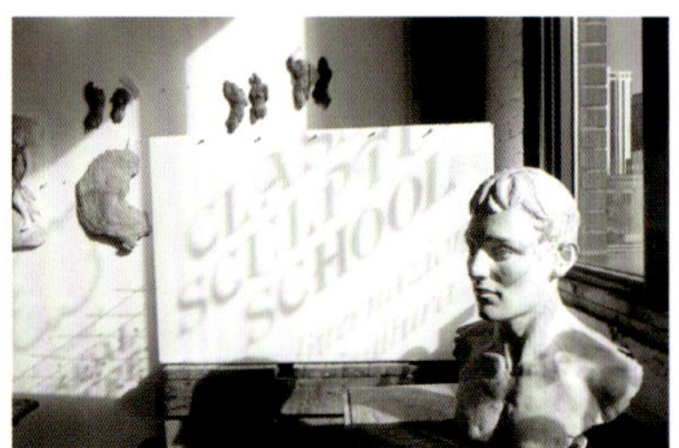

 Angry Man on the Subway, 1986 Terra cotta with wax $3 \times 4 \times 2\frac{1}{2}$" In Roman Bathtub. La Scuola.

spirit of spontaneity, hard work, collaborative interchange, focused attention, and mindfulness, and thereby to find greater clarity of purpose. Jefferson and his small faculty accentuated the qualities of beauty, harmony, balance, and integrity. They emphasized the ever-essential historic sources. And they stressed the indispensable necessity of anatomy and drawing ("the basis of all art").

"*Pazienza, pazienza*," always reminding himself and others that art is not separate from life. "Learn to build form quickly and express the freshness of the pose."

His encircling manner, charm, and infectious laughter extended also to his style of teaching. As one student wrote, "Setting aside his awesome power as a master sculptor, he would, with gentle humility, guide an insecure ego. He'd tease, cajole, but never humiliate. Push, pull, cut, scrape. Together we'd laugh, and then we'd try again. Add, take off—seems a pity, but how's a body to grow?"

His dream to create an extension of La Scuola in Pietrasanta, Italy, as well as to bring Italian students to La Scuola was not to be fulfilled.

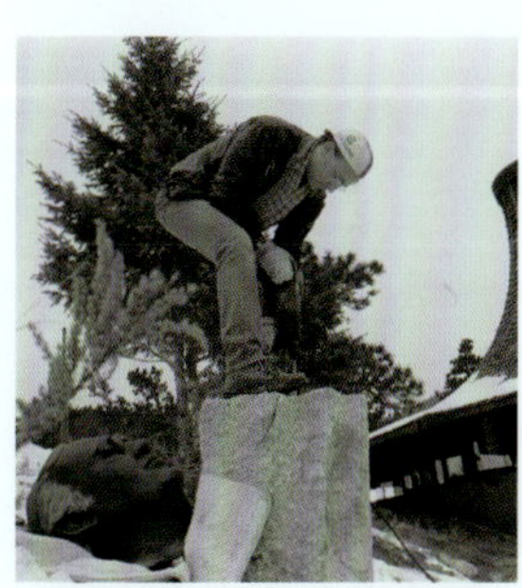

He was to create *Adam*, *Colossus*, and numerous other works and fragments, and have his sculptures exhibited in galleries in New York, Santa Fe, Taos, Telluride, and Denver.

It was no surprise, except to the administration of Vermont College of Norwich University, that his graduate school colleagues chose him as class spokesman to deliver its commencement address. He had chosen this program that allowed him to be in residence only 9 days per semester, so that he might continue with La Scuola and his own work. He completed his *La Tomba* thesis installation, *Om Santi Om*, an expansive and somber parody of the School's repeated disapprovals of his keeping alive the idealism of the human form ("the living artist presented dead").

On his final flight to Vermont he wrote,

> "Life is beautiful in the air. My Buddha nature is above me and the clouds of earth below me. I feel a difference between life on earth and life in the air. My bird nature. It is good to see life from the air ... time and space are relative ... I could have died in the future ... and as we are alive we must create."

Ironically the future was 38 days. He had met his maker on a Sunday.

At a gathering at his parent's home one Sunday later, many spoke tenderly of his extraordinary qualities, one comparing him to Mozart who, too, had died so young. A memorial service was held later that week at La Scuola where over 200 persons both mourned and celebrated his life, reciting his poetry and teachings while his sculptures watched on. Spontaneously, a procession formed, with lighted candles and arm-in-arm, and circled through the neighborhood chanting "This Little Light of Mine." This was reminiscent of the procession that had followed the death of Michelangelo 400 years earlier.

Jefferson's ashes have been placed in sacred sights in five continents—continuing their way to encircle the globe he had wished to travel.

The board of La Scuola and his students tried to continue this unique educational program following Jefferson's death, but the school could not be sustained long in the absence of the *maestro*.

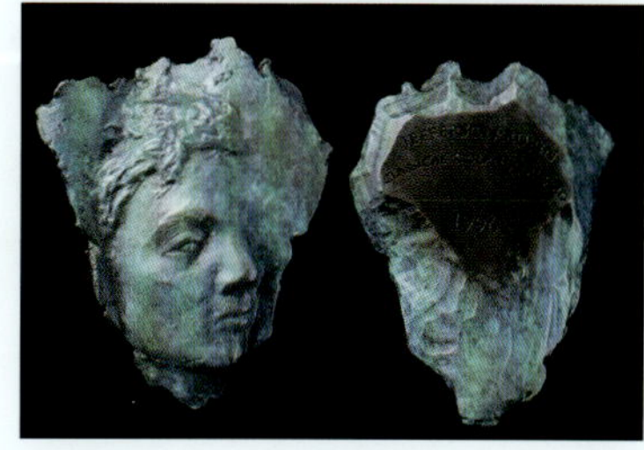

Jefferson had persuaded the Denver School of the Arts to allow a promising art student to apprentice with him each semester. The Jefferson D. Rubin Memorial Fund now awards an annual monetary grant together with a medallion of a bronze casting of a *frammento* to a graduating senior whose work best reflects the humanistic devotion that Jefferson embodied in his art.

"What has been my contribution in this life? I have worked and lived and loved and followed my heart, and grown and fallen, and risen again. I am but one wave in a great ocean of minds, souls and bodies. Yet my wave has affected many waves. I have made waves! I have carried life and past lives in the primordial soup. I have reached for the sky and crashed on the floor. I have returned by undertow, carried by the winds and pulled by the moon. I have lived and relived..."

Jefferson D. Rubin

1959-1995

Installing *Colossus*. Annual Award Medal.

REFERENCES TO IMAGES

APPRECIATIONS

It has been the committed devotion of the Board of Scuola Internazionale della Scultura that stimulated and enabled *Frammenti della Vita* to be realized.

It is to the so many that knew, loved, and were a part of the *Vita* of Jefferson that this book is dedicated.

Acknowledgment is made of the photographic contributions of Jefferson D. Rubin and of Thomas Howard, Andy Katz, Matt Kinslow, Patrick McMullen, Chris Perez, Bunny Rosenthal Rubin, Steven D. Rubin, Mark Sink, and Randy Zahn.

Library of Congress Control Number
2009927984

ISBN 978-1-934491-14-0

First Edition

Editor: Marian Granfield

Publisher
Fresco Fine Art Publications, llc
Albuquerque, New Mexico
www.frescobooks.com

Design and Production
Fresco Fine Art Publications, llc

Printed in Italy